TESTS THAT WORK

TESTS THAT WORK

Designing and Delivering Fair and Practical Measurement Tools in the Workplace

Odin Westgaard

JOSSEY-BASS/PFEIFFER
A Wiley Company
www.pfeiffer.com

Published by

PFEIFFER
A Wiley Company
989 Market Street
San Francisco, CA 94103-1741
415.433.1740; Fax 415.433.0499
800.274.4434; Fax 800.569.0443

| **www.pfeiffer.com** |

Jossey-Bass/Pfeiffer is a registered trademark of John Wiley & Sons, Inc.

ISBN: 0-7879-4596-X
Library of Congress Catalog Card Number 99-6073

Library of Congress Cataloging-in-Publication Data

Westgaard, Odin.
     Tests that work : designing and delivering fair and practical
measurement tools in the workplace / Odin Westgaard.
         p.   cm.
     Includes bibliographical references and index.
     ISBN 0-7879-4596-X (alk. paper)
     1. Employment tests—Design and construction.
2. Business—Examinations—Design and construction.   3. Psychological
tests—Design and construction.   I. Title.
HF5549.5.E5 W473   1999
658.3'1125—dc21   99-6073
                                                                                    CIP

Acquiring Editor: *Matthew Holt*

Director of Development: *Kathleen Dolan Davies*

Developmental Editor: *Susan Rachmeler*

Senior Production Editor: *Pamela Berkman*

Manufacturing Supervisor: *Becky Carreño*

Cover Design: *Laurie Anderson*

Printing   10 9 8 7 6 5 4 3

TABLE OF CONTENTS

PREFACE

I've spent a lifetime working with, taking, and building tests of every type and description. It's been something of a love affair partly because tests provide a needed service and partly because good fair tests are a satisfying experience. Mostly, though, I like tests because they're fun. What? Fun? Tests? Well of course they are. Understand that I said good fair tests.

Two adjectives, good and fair, are the keys to testing. Without them tests become one of the most hated elements of modern living. With them tests can be uplifting—even fun.

I know what a good test is and how to produce one. Of course, not every test I ever made was a good one. On the contrary, I have produced some tests I don't care to recall. But I learned from those. I learned that no one benefits from a bad test. And I learned how to make good ones. I'd like to share those skills with you. With these skills, you can avoid problems and produce good fair tests.

Odin Westgaard, 1993

As I prepare this edition for my friends at Jossey-Bass/Pfeiffer, I'm reminded of an old saying, "The more things change, the more they stay the same." The world has changed dramatically since the first edition of this book just six years ago. But testing hasn't. Sure, we can now put tests on the World Wide Web, we can score them with sophisticated electronic scanners, and we can use complex software packages to develop and produce them. Still, no matter how we present them, tests are tests. The skills test makers required six years ago are the skills they must have today. This book is still, in my opinion, a required reference for anyone who seeks to improve human performance.

We still have to evaluate—pass judgment on the efforts of others. We can do it by the seat of our pants. We can observe and try to assess through our experience and knowledge of the situation. Or we can measure the results of those efforts and base our judgments on valid reliable data. Which would you rather see happen? A good test doesn't have to be a work of art. It can be designed, developed, produced, administered, and evaluated by anyone who has the tools and knows how to use them. The tools are in this book. You can learn to use them well through studying this book. And when you do, I can safely say you will enjoy the experience.

Odin Westgaard, 1999

ACKNOWLEDGMENTS

I'd like to say a heartfelt thank you to Dorothy Woods. I sincerely hope she feels this is a worthy continuation of the fine work she did so many years ago.

Just as important is my thanks to Jossey-Bass/Pfeiffer. When *Good Fair Tests* went out of print I was confused, embarrassed, and left with a difficult problem. Many people who had ordered the book couldn't get it. They called, they wrote, they fumed, and I wished I could hide somewhere. Then out of the west rode a new publisher, a new champion, a new opportunity to get this important information to the people who can use it well and to their advantage.

Finally, I must say a grateful thank you to all the people who have supported this effort. To Judith Hale for her many contributions of advice, expertise, and moral support. To Roger Kaufman for his continuous belief in the worth of the effort and unselfish contributions to the book's integrity and comprehensiveness. To Rick Rose, who badgered, encouraged, and showed great faith in what I was doing and why. To countless others who have critiqued and encouraged, praised and panned—and especially to all of you who have used this book to provide good fair tests for your respondents. Thank you very much.

Odin Westgaard, 1999

INTRODUCTION

In a sense, we are faced with tests continually. Simply getting up in the morning, for example, can test a person in several ways. It's a test of how well you slept, of whether you are prepared for the coming day, of how well your body adapts to abrupt change, and of several other factors about you. Pursued to absurdity, you could come to the conclusion that every step, thought, or feeling is somehow a test (or is being tested).

It's not my intention to be absurd. Testing is far too important for that. It is appropriate, therefore, to begin this discussion with a definition of what a test is (or should be). Here is the working definition I've adopted for this book: "a test is a deliberate attempt by people to acquire information about themselves or others."

Four words in this definition are important: *deliberate, people, acquire,* and *information.*

test
A deliberate attempt by people to acquire information about themselves or others.

A test is a *deliberate* attempt to acquire information. Unplanned or serendipitous discoveries are not the results from testing. People who have such experiences may feel that they were tested, but if it was not deliberate, it was not a test. For example, suppose you approach a wide puddle in the street. You eye it and decide you might be able to jump over it. You take a couple of steps back, run, and leap. Whether you clear the puddle or not, you have just conducted a test. It was planned. But if you happen to jump over a puddle without thinking, it is not a test.

Now consider a boy being chased by a dog. He runs to a tree and quickly climbs it. He has just demonstrated that he can climb that particular tree. But it wasn't a test. It wasn't deliberate. Without the dog chasing him, he wouldn't have needed to know whether he could climb that tree.

"But," you might say, "the action certainly tested his ability to climb trees."

You are correct, of course; however, he wasn't being tested. He was seeking safety. You can be tested without taking a test.

Tests are conducted by *people*. A horse may buck to try to dislodge a rider. The horse is not conducting a test of the rider's ability to stick to the saddle. The horse is trying to rid itself of a burden. It's true that animals sometimes seem to be testing. A cat meows when hungry. Whether the owner feeds it or not, it gains knowledge. It discovers whether it can secure food by meowing. Still, it has not conducted a test but has made a request.

There is an argument that the tendency to test one another is a strictly human trait. Whether this is true or not is immaterial to the discussion. But it is important to understand that the definition of a test used in this book requires people as initiators.

Of course, people can test anything. They can test atomic bombs, computer software, or the acid content of soil. The concern of this book, though, is testing other people.

We test one another to *acquire information*. As with the other parts of the definition, this seems obvious. Often, though, tests are used for other purposes, such as to punish, to coerce, or to mislead.

The information acquired depends on the reason for testing. A diagnostic test reveals the location and nature of a problem. A double-blind test (in medicine) provides evidence about the worth of a drug or treatment. An achievement test tells whether learners have learned what they were supposed to learn. A certification exam reveals the skill levels of respondents. A performance test samples the respondents' possession of targeted skills. Whatever the primary purpose, a test yields information. Sometimes it is new information. Sometimes it is a verification of old information (information about information).

The results of a test are information about someone or something. That is all. Many of us expect more from a test. The most common of these expectations are discipline and learning. The people who respond to a test are "supposed to" (according to some) become more disciplined in their thinking and/or learn something. Such an idea subverts the real purpose of a test, which is to acquire information.

Now that we've looked at the key words in the definition, let's look at it again: "a test is a deliberate attempt by people to acquire information about themselves or others." Keep the definition in mind as you use this book. Let it guide you as you work.

The book has three primary uses. First, it is a reference book. It contains the basic considerations and requirements for good fair tests. Second, it provides guidance in the selection and design of test scenarios, format, items, and evaluation schemes. Third, it gives specific step-by-step instructions for the development and construction of tests using essay, short-answer, multiple-choice, and matching items. It also provides advice on the effective use of other types of items such as fill-in and true/false.

It has two primary audiences. One is composed of people who have to use tests but do not want to be experts. For example, managers of all kinds use tests in their work. Some of the tests are purchased or leased, some are constructed for a specific purpose by an outside agency, and some are developed internally. However they come by them, managers use tests. They will continue to do so. And most of them will use even more tests in the future. If you are a manager, you can use this book to select tests, to oversee their development, or to review tests already in use.

The second primary audience is people who produce tests for business and industry. These folks are faced with problems not well known in schools. They must produce mastery tests, performance-based tests, and tests to certify competence. They are instructors, trainers, instructional designers, personnel directors, and others who develop employees.

A secondary audience includes teachers, professors, and others who wish to write and use good fair tests. The advice, techniques, and information in this book apply to any testing situation.

HOW THIS BOOK IS ORGANIZED

This book is organized with two ideas in mind. First, I want to present a cogent discussion of what tests are and how you can use them. Second, I want to help you develop good fair tests without having to consult another source.

Part One, Chapters One through Five, presents the basics: what tests are, how questions affect human beings, the different kinds of tests and test items, the difference between norm-referenced and performance tests, mastery, results, what measurement is and implies, elegance, transparency, and (among other things) test formatting. It is a discussion of practical applications and the reasons a particular process usually works better than others.

Part Two presents the fifteen steps of the testing process. Each step is examined and specific advice is offered for accomplishing each one. It is, in a way, a recipe for developing tests. If you write test items or develop tests, you will be able to use this how-to section as a step-by-step presentation of a useful test-development procedure. The emphasis is on your success as a test maker and administrator.

PART ONE

FUNDAMENTALS OF TESTING

Many who read this book will be looking for specific advice about testing. Others will only want a way to design and develop good tests. What you want is here. Part One explores the ideas and procedures that provide the best foundation for a performance test. Part Two is the "how-to" section. It's devoted to the fifteen steps required to produce a good fair test.

If you are new to testing or are in doubt about your skills, please study Part One. If you understand these ideas, you *will* produce good fair tests. Of course, Part Two will speed your work and provide the basis for quality. Without the ideas in Part One, though, your tests won't have the firm foundation they need.

I will go one step further. These concepts are foundations for performance improvement in general. You can apply them to needs assessment, job or task analysis, and most other aspects of the profession that tries to improve human performance in the workplace.

Here's a statement that might sound strange: the concepts in Part One will be valuable for you even if you never design or develop a single test. Study Part One for an understanding of what performance testing is and how to do it well.

CHAPTER ONE

TESTS

You and I build *contrived psychological tests*. Psychological? You bet. Our tests require respondents to display skills, attitudes, and abilities, the three elements that are the bases for psychology. We also *intend* to test people. These two factors (that tests are contrived and that test makers intend to test) are critical to our thinking about testing.

> **psychological tests**
> Tests that require respondents to display skills, attitudes, and abilities.

First, tests are contrived. We create them. They aren't found in nature (like potatoes) so that we can simply adapt them to our purpose (mash or fry). They are invented. We hope our inventions are useful, but whatever their nature, it's inescapable that they are contrived. Second, we intend to test people. It's our primary purpose and in the best of all worlds it's our only purpose. A test is a test. It shouldn't pretend to be anything else. More to the point, we're concerned with people. We aren't interested in testing dogs or horses or the mechanical performance of automobiles. We test people, and we do it on purpose. You and I are interested in sampling the knowledge and skills of human beings. We want a reliable estimate of what individuals or groups know, think, or are able to do. In addition, we want to test in a way that's acceptable, even pleasurable, for the respondents.

A good fair test is elegant. It's almost poetic. I have enjoyed responding to good tests and so have you. Do you remember what it feels like? It feels good. You read an item, understand it, and respond to it with confidence and enthusiasm.

But, normally, you're at least a bit reluctant to take a test. I'm reminded of Dr. Seuss's book, *Green Eggs and Ham*. In the story a character, Sam-I-Am, tries to persuade the hero to eat green eggs and ham. The hero is so repulsed by the green eggs that he refuses to try them. Like the character in the story, we approach tests with trepidation. In fact, given a choice, you and I will usually avoid a test. We might even fight against responding to it. But (if it's a good fair test) when we do take it, we truly enjoy the experience. It's exhilarating. It's fun.

Think about tests as Kurt Lewin, the field psychologist, might (Lewin, 1951). Nothing is perceived by humans without involvement of the total person. We're psychological beings. Therefore we attach value to anything we perceive or do. Tests have the reputation of being "not good." Unless we have consistently experienced good fair tests, our first reaction to any test is likely to be repugnance. We have learned not to like them. And, to return to *Green Eggs and Ham*, we don't care how they're fixed. They can be in large or small type. They can contain jokes or funny pictures. They can be presented as an inventory, a sampling device, and so forth. They can be recommended by movie stars. No matter how they are presented, our first reaction is one of distaste.

So it will be with your tests for most of your respondents. Their first reaction will be negative, but as soon as they find your tests to be good and fair, that distaste can turn to enjoyment. At the end of the book Dr. Seuss's character says:

> "I do so like
> green eggs and ham!
> Thank you!
> Thank you,
> Sam-I-Am!"*

Sam-I-Am had a good product, and he knew it. His confidence in his product never failed even though it was rejected time after time. He persisted and persisted and persisted until, finally, the product was given a fair trial. Then the product proved its own worth.

The analogy works for testing. Your respondents will tend to reject your test. You must have confidence in its quality, and you must persist until they have given it a fair trial.

Now some of you are shaking your heads. After all, you have captive audiences. Your respondents usually don't really have a choice. They have to take a test, but they don't have to *like* it. If they're convinced your test is a bad thing, they

---

* Reprinted with permission from Random House.

won't respond to it as you might wish. The results won't be a true sampling of their knowledge and skills.

Tests are psychological measures. Most authorities talk about people as being physical-, mental-, and emotion/value–driven. We have physical properties such as appearance, speed, and dexterity. We think, store information, and figure things out. We have emotions such as love, gratitude, and longing. We value our perceptions of life such as God, family, nation, good habits, and so forth.

Kurt Lewin tells us that the physical, mental, and emotional components of "humanness" are inseparable (Lewin, 1951). We can't be described as one or the other. We're always all of them. We are psychological beings. Testing the physical without considering the other elements omits valuable information and provides incomplete results. Of course, the same is true with testing either the mental or emotional alone.

This book is dedicated to helping you develop your process for building good fair tests. Most tests will measure skills and knowledge and, for most of us, they will be expressed in print. The respondents will answer with pen or pencil. Some tests will measure performance that can be seen and evaluated. Some will not. Some opinionnaires and attitude or value inventories are also tests. The names have been changed to reflect the intent so folks won't balk at using them.

I have developed a multiple-choice test in which all of the answers are correct and no alternative is preferred over the others. It's called a *value inventory*. It isn't scored in a traditional way, but it's still a test, and respondents still think of it that way. Despite the fact that they aren't in competition with other respondents, they still feel they are being assessed.

assess
To estimate or determine the significance, importance, or value of; to evaluate.

Guess what? They are correct. They are being assessed. That's what a test is for. A test is a measurement tool. A psychological test measures whether a person possesses something. Blood tests, crash tests for cars, and metal fatigue tests are different, although they have many of the characteristics of psychological tests.

Our job is to develop and write good fair tests. To do that requires fifteen distinct steps:

1. Identify and qualify potential respondents.
2. Justify the test.
3. Identify performances to be tested.
4. Establish criteria for each performance.
5. Select the type of test that best fits the desires of respondents and provides a valid assessment of the criteria.
6. Design test presentation and administration.
7. Design and select the evaluation process.

8. Write the items.
9. Review and qualify the items.
10. Pilot the test; revise and rewrite.
11. Set respondent and qualification scores (cut-scores) or other parameters.
12. Produce the test.
13. Administer the test.
14. Evaluate the results.
15. Use the results.

These steps should take place no matter what kind of test is being developed. A pop quiz for high school students and a major certification exam for professionals require the same steps. There will, of course, be time and quality differences, but all the steps should be there.

The first decision point in the process occurs after Step 2. The choice is to continue or not. The next decision point is after Step 4, when you will want to examine the criteria and accept them as they are or generate new ones. Once the test is designed (Step 7) you, and perhaps others, will okay it. After Step 11, check the results to see if they fulfill the criteria from Step 4. When respondents have finished Step 13, you can discover whether the test was both good and fair. When the final step is complete, review the whole process and document it.

It's important to keep in mind that the fifteen steps are accepted by most authorities. They may be grouped differently, but one way or another all fifteen are used in the development of any test.

Consider a quiz for an algebra class in high school. The teacher (let's call her Mrs. Carey) wants to use a quiz. It may have been planned at the beginning of the term or it may be a "pop" quiz whose appropriateness was only determined the day before. Whatever the reason for its existence, it has to be justified in some way.

Justification is optional for some activities, but for a test it's essential. It comes from the respondents' desire to respond, which is often overlooked, to the chagrin of the test maker. (More about this later.)

Back to Mrs. Carey. Once the quiz has been justified, she will select the algebraic principles to be included. In addition, she will decide how well respondents should do on the quiz to qualify themselves. In other words, she will set criteria for judging the adequacy of responses.

Mrs. Carey will decide what kind of quiz to give. She will decide how many problems to use, how to present them (on a handout, the chalkboard, a transparency, and so forth), and how the respondents will indicate their responses. Mrs. Carey will write the quiz and mentally review it to be sure it does what she intends. She will also provide the correct answers.

The quiz will be presented some way, the respondents will respond, and it will be scored. Finally, the respondents will be told how well they did on the quiz.

All of this can take place in a relatively short time. Suppose a group of algebra students has come to Mrs. Carey's class. They were supposed to turn in an assignment, but because of the basketball game the night before, most of them haven't done so. Mrs. Carey wants to know how well prepared the students are to continue to the next topic. She decides to give them a quiz.

She opens the textbook and selects six problems that represent the skill areas she's concerned about. She asks the students to work on those problems as a quiz. They respond. She then has them trade papers to check the answers. The quizzes are scored and returned to their owners. Mrs. Carey requests a report on how well the students performed. When she has that information, she can decide whether to begin a new topic or work on areas of weakness.

Mrs. Carey's little test was conceived, developed, taken, and evaluated in less than ten minutes. It measured what it was supposed to measure and fulfilled its role. All fifteen steps were used.

To reexamine the process, consider another example. You will find that whenever a test is built, all fifteen steps are actively considered. Even if a step is ignored, it will have been considered. Let's try it out on an everyday experience not usually thought of as a test.

Suppose two young men are playing basketball on a playground. One of them (let's call him George) tries to make a jump shot. He misses. The second, Tom, says, "I can do better than that."

George throws him the ball and says, "OK, smart stuff, show me." George has just developed and presented Tom with a test. Tom takes the ball, carefully places himself at the same position on the court that George used, and launches the shot. He, too, misses. George catches the ball, laughs, and they go on with their game. The test is complete.

All fifteen steps were used by George to build, administer, and evaluate the test. He identified the area to be tested and justified the test in response to Tom's laugh. He specified the performance and set criteria for success. The design and presentation were considered when Tom placed himself in the same spot and used his version of the same shot.

The idea that all fifteen steps must be used makes sense as long as we think of people as psychological beings. Remember, Lewin (1951) told us people are three things at once: thinkers, feelers, and doers. Isolating an aspect such as the physical ability to shoot a basketball reduces the scope and, perhaps, the requirement to use all the steps. The mandate is dedicated to dealing with people as human beings. The emphasis is on the respondents. Good fair tests are developed for the respondents.

The pop quiz used by Mrs. Carey is an example of a performance test featuring open-ended, short-answer items. Don't let the jargon throw you at this point. I'll define those terms as we go along. The jump-shot test was a performance test featuring a demonstration of physical skill.

What Is a Test?

According to Webster (1987), a *test* is "(1): a critical examination, observation, or evaluation: trial . . . : the procedure of submitting a statement to such conditions or operations as will lead to its proof or disproof or to its acceptance or rejection; (2): a basis for evaluation."

Webster's definition comes as something of a surprise to many people. What is "the procedure of submitting a statement"? Let's explore that.

Most tests for people use questions, not statements, so, on the surface, it seems the definition is a bit wrongheaded. Think about it. Suppose a manager wishes to discover if workers can operate a computer. What does she do? She sets up a safe situation and requires them to demonstrate their skill with the equipment.

The manager is, indeed, evaluating a statement. The statement in some way asserts her workers can use a computer effectively and efficiently. Perhaps an easier way to think about it is embodied in the following conversation:

"Joe and the boys can build that house in less than a month."
"Oh?"
"Sure they can. Let's give them a chance to show their stuff."
"OK. Go ahead."

Joe and the boys are going to be tested. The test is described by the statement that they can build the house. The fact that it could have been couched as a question is immaterial, even though questions are critical elements of most tests. They are so important that a major part of this chapter is devoted to good questions and how to use them.

The point is, Webster's definition is correct. A test is an investigation of the truth of a statement. I personally like to use the word *assertion* rather than *statement*. Normally statements aren't evaluated. They are simply accepted. If you say my hair is getting grey and thin, the truth of your statement is self-evident. If, on the other hand, you say my hair is ugly, I may want to challenge you. The new comment about my hair is not self-evident and therefore becomes an assertion. I will want proof that what you say is correct.

This is not new thinking. In fact academia has a long and honored tradition based on it. Professors investigating a problem use a device called the *null hypothesis*, a statement about a matter under consideration. An example might be, "The ability of adult men to lift heavy objects is no different than that of women." The way it's stated makes the intent of the suggested investigation apparent. In other words, there is going to be a test of whether men can lift heavy objects better than women can.

Null hypotheses are derived from assertions. The assertion for the null hypothesis above would be, "Men can lift heavier objects than women can." Such an assertion could be called a *hypothesis*.

I don't wish to become bogged down in semantics or political correctness, but the concept is important. When we evaluate the truth of a statement, we're conducting a test. Usually, the statement being considered is an assertion.

Half of the basic tasks of professors are tied to this concept. They are responsible for testing how adequately their students are prepared. A person who is trying to earn a degree at a university is called a candidate. A candidate asserts that he or she is qualified for something. In academia, the something is a degree. Professors must determine if the assertion is true.

Managers have a similar responsibility. Workers cannot do their work if management doesn't believe they are capable of it. By applying for a job, workers are asserting they can do the work. By one way or another, the manager must test that assertion during the hiring process. Often the test is an acceptance of the assertion based on evidence supplied by the applicant. Still, the test does take place. (And, by the way, all fifteen steps will be used.)

So what? So maybe we should think about tests, not as a series of questions about something, but, rather, as a deliberate attempt to find the truth of an assertion. Perhaps that's the proper point of view for anyone who would prepare or use a test.

Two things must be foremost in our minds when we adopt this definition. First, *the thing to be tested must be as carefully described as it can be.* The assertion must be clearly stated. Second, *the people to be tested must drive the test.* Our tests are opportunities for respondents.

Respondents Must Respond

Until a book is read, it simply occupies space. A musician's skill is relatively useless until he or she plays or sings and is heard. Until musicians show their skills, the rest of the world is unaware of them.

When you think about it, a respondent's desire to respond seems obvious, although maybe not in the ways you have believed. In a formula Western movie the hero pleads with the sheriff for a chance to demonstrate his skill. The sheriff is unwilling. Then the bad guys attack and the hero is given his chance. Until he proves his worth, he has little credibility in the town. After the fight, he is accepted as a good person. So it goes in the movies—and so it often goes in real life.

Most people want very much to show what they can do. They want others to know and accept them for their attributes. But if those attributes aren't displayed in some way, they don't have much of a chance. Most of us would classify the chances we receive as opportunities.

Funny thing about opportunities: they can often be very testing. Webster (1987) says an *opportunity* is "(2): a good chance for advancement or progress." Advancement and progress can't exist unless a person wants something.

If a person wants to be a doctor, the chance to go to a university is an opportunity. If the same person would like to be a truck driver, the chance to go to a university might still be an opportunity, but probably not. This point is important to test developers. We must be in the habit of thinking first and foremost about the people who will take our tests. Can they profit from the test? Does a particular test provide an opportunity, or is it just another hurdle to jump?

Good fair tests provide useful opportunities for the respondents, who desire them. The respondents define the mandate for a test. They make it appropriate.

Too often teachers and trainers think of tests as ways to validate the learning process. They give their learners tests to show the appropriateness of the program. Their attitude is, "I have a good program; the learners did well on the test."

Although it's important for trainers to feel good about themselves, it is *not* good for them to develop such a feeling at the expense of their learners. How many professors give tests to show the virtues of their lectures or courses? How many teachers give tests to "put students in their place"? How many trainers give tests because their bosses expect them to? The answer to all these questions is, "Too many." One such use is too many. Sadly, respondents are subjected to this sort of torture every day.

The key question to be answered is, "Are there people who could use a test as an opportunity to demonstrate their knowledge or skill?" The question embodies the first step in the testing process. Step 1 says, "Identify and qualify potential respondents." Find someone who wants a test. Unless you do so, any test you build is a waste of your time and an imposition on the respondents.

Fortunately, Step 1 is usually easy. People want opportunities. They yearn for them. Good fair tests are opportunities. The missing element is usually a failure on the part of the test maker to justify the test (Step 2) in the minds of the respondents. Often we forget to tell the respondents why they are taking the test.

I was once involved in an experiment to show the effect of such a failure. A group of people were selected to take an aptitude test. They were divided into two groups. The first group was told the test could help them determine what career choice would be best for them. The second group was simply given the test and told to answer the questions. You can guess the results. The first group did a much better job on the test than the second did.

Chapter Two covers several different kinds of tests and criteria for deciding which kind to use for what purpose. It discusses what the respondents desire and how to identify that for the respondents and others. For now, remember that *the desires of the respondents must drive the development of a test*. Good fair tests are opportunities for the respondents.

About Questions

What is your name? Did you answer that question in your mind without really thinking about it? You probably did. It's interesting that most people would answer any question almost automatically. The reasons are important for test makers.

Asking questions of others is something most people take for granted. They shouldn't. Tests are almost always sets of questions of one sort or another. Knowing how to ask questions well is an important skill.

If I ask a question, your mind immediately goes into a special mode of thinking. It's somewhat similar to querying a computer database. The computer stops whatever it's doing and sets itself to search and find the answer. So it is with people. Asking a question raises expectations. Dialogues are put aside for a moment. Contemplation and meditation are interrupted. The person being questioned prepares to answer. This happens no matter what kind of question is asked.

Let's use you as an example. When you started reading this, you were thinking about something else, perhaps what was in the preceding material. Then you saw the title of the section. Because you expected to see it there, you may or may not have consciously noted it, but you did see it. Thoughts about it or about other things continued. Let's assume you were wondering why there is a section in this book about questions—a whole section. Perhaps you were intrigued and interested in some way.

Then you read the question, "What is your name?" Immediately you stopped everything else and thought of the answer. Had you been warned ahead of time, you would have done the same thing. Read the question again. Your mind still finds the answer. Most people's minds work that way. One of the most maddening things for parents is when a child asks the same question over and over. Each time their minds fetch the answer. This is true even when one deliberately gives a different answer. Intelligence agents have known this for centuries. When they know a subject is lying, they keep asking. They know that sooner or later the subject will let the real answer out.

The tendency is even stronger when you know you'll be asked a question. When Perry Mason says to a witness, "I have a question," you can almost sense the witness getting ready to answer. When I write, "Please consider this question," your mind puts itself in the search-and-deliver mode.

One of the important reasons for having instructions for taking a test is to allow respondents to get ready. When that's done, respondents find little trouble understanding what is required. I recall a test I examined for a student years ago. The instructions said, "For these questions, circle the answer you believe is best" (or something like that). Looking at the test, I didn't find a single question. All the items were open-ended statements for which the respondent supplied an appropriate ending. Yet most respondents didn't complain. They treated the items as questions because the instructions had said they were questions.

The Mind as Storage

Robert Gagné (1985) has developed a model of how the mind uses and stores information. The diagram in Figure 1.1 is an interpretation of his model. Gagné says data are perceived and stored before anything else happens. The mind then retrieves and works with the data and returns the results to storage.

This process establishes a neural path to the data, which the mind references for any subsequent use. Whether information is raw or developed, it has a path. Each use or modification requires a new storage location. The mind also has a mechanism for cross-referencing information so that relationships are available.

Once information is stored it can be accessed any time. Basically, there are two reasons for it to be accessed. First, it can be called up and used to help understand other information or to establish relationships. Second, it can simply be called up.

The second activity is prompted by a question. A question is asked, and zing, pow, there is the information.

Because the activity in the mind is a bit different, is it OK to ask a question on a test? I think so. Gagné tells us information is retrieved to the same area (short-term memory) no matter which of the two prompts is used. When it is in short-term memory, it can be acted on if the mind so chooses. This makes sense. You and I have experienced both kinds of calls many times. You may call up an answer to a question and spend quite a bit of time thinking about it before you actually write it down.

The difference in the mind's response to the two kinds of calls isn't simply a matter of speedy delivery. It also involves quality issues. Think about this question, "Why do birds fly south in the fall?" Your response is probably fairly clean,

FIGURE 1.1. HUMAN DATA STORAGE AND USE.

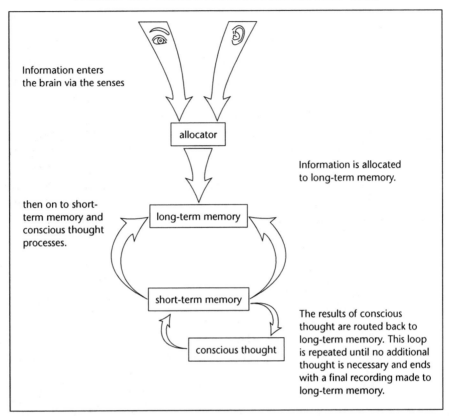

Information enters the brain via the senses

allocator

Information is allocated to long-term memory.

then on to short-term memory and conscious thought processes.

long-term memory

short-term memory

conscious thought

The results of conscious thought are routed back to long-term memory. This loop is repeated until no additional thought is necessary and ends with a final recording made to long-term memory.

without a lot of conditions or possible questions. Now what if I had said, "Discuss the reasons birds fly south in the fall." Your response would have the same basic information, but it would be couched differently. In the first instance, you would simply state the reasons without much explanation. In the second, the explanation would be the most important part of the answer.

Using the Right Question at the Right Time

What Is a Question?

Normally, a question is some words followed by a question mark. The question mark is a sort of magical symbol. It changes the meaning of a statement. To demonstrate this for yourself read these three expressions aloud:

- Come here.
- Come here!
- Come here?

The first gives direction. The listener is being told where, when he or she comes, to end up. It could be paraphrased, "You should come to this location."

The second is a command. The listener is being ordered to a specific location. It's saying, "Come to this place right now!"

The third asks the listener to supply information. The questioner wants to know where he or she should end up. It could be thought of as the opposite of either of the other expressions. "Do you want me to end up in this place?"

I've included the exclamation simply to supply comparison. Exclamation points are usually amplifiers of a statement. Question marks, on the other hand, change the meaning. To see how this happens, look at another expression and its companion question:

- Jill dug a hole.
- Did Jill dig a hole?

The first expression is a simple statement of fact. It has a noun (Jill), a verb (dug), and a direct object (a hole). It is structured in the standard order for a statement: noun, verb, object. All of the sentences in this paragraph follow the same pattern.

Now, look at the question. The only real differences are a change in the order of the words and the question mark at the end, but the sentence has completely changed its character. It now performs a different role. The real difference is communicated by the question mark.

Words like *why* help the reader understand the intent of a question. Suppose the question above read, "Why did Jill dig a hole?" In this case the respondent is being asked what caused an action. "Why" in a question usually asks for a cause. "Why did the machine break down?" "Why are cherries red?" More about that in Chapter Two.

The meaning and impact of a question are communicated by the question mark. We use the question mark to ask for the very thing we want from the respondent.

Gagné assures us that it's OK to use questions to build a test. The knowledge and skills evoked by questions will be the same as those used by respondents in other situations. But the larger consideration still remains. What kind of questions should be used? Before you can answer that question, you should know more about questions.

In the context of testing, the best question solicits the precise response sought by the test maker. What does such a question sound like? It depends on the response desired. For example, suppose you want the respondent to remember a fact. You might ask a question like, "What age group in America has the highest number of attempted suicides per capita?" The question is easy to interpret and contains enough information to avoid ambiguity. It's the easiest kind of question to write because it tests Level One cognitive learning. Generally speaking, the more complex the performance being tested is, the more difficult it is to write good questions to access it.

However, people such as Benjamin Bloom (1976) assert that tests of complex performances are better measures of human capability. He and others have spent their careers examining how people learn and what that means, not only to trainers and teachers but also to test makers.

Learning Levels and Domains

Some things are easy to learn; some aren't. The difference in difficulty is dependent on two factors. First, learning tasks range on a continuum from simple to complex. The whole area has been studied and reported by many researchers. Bloom has developed a taxonomy that's widely known and accepted. Second, learning doesn't take place in the mind alone. The emotional and physical aspects of the learner are also involved. Lewin (Bigge & Hunt, 1963) tells us that human beings are psychological in nature. We can't deal with one domain without referencing the others. We must deal with the whole person.

Learning Levels. There are many levels of learning. Bloom named at least six. Others have identified more. Because the test maker's requirement is general, for this discussion, I am content to work with three: Level One, recall; Level Two, application; and Level Three, development.

Level One learning is easily understood by most people. It implies that respondents can remember something or are able to respond because of what they can recall. Usually, it does not require much conscious thought. A Level One response is almost automatic. At times the respondent remembers more than one response and must compare or contrast among them to choose the best one. Sometimes the response requires a series of recollections—a chain. An example of a Level One question is, "What tool should be used to drive a nail?"

Level Two is primarily concerned with application. In this situation the respondent is asked to apply knowledge or skill to a known or anticipated problem. Most tests in mathematics are Level Two.

> *recall*
> Extract from memory without modification.
>
> *application*
> Use of stored information to accomplish a task.
>
> *development*
> Use of stored information to synthesize or innovate.

Respondents are asked to select and use a formula or equation to solve problems they have not solved before. The problems don't have any substantive differences, though, from the ones they have already seen: "Select a tool from the tool kit and use it to drive a nail into a board."

Level Three is sometimes called problem solving or creativity. Basically, the respondent is asked to move outside his or her experience to produce a useful response. In a math test one could ask respondents to solve problems with complicating factors they hadn't seen before. (Remember, no surprises. The respondents should expect complicating factors to be added from time to time.) In the carpentry example you could hand the respondent a screw instead of a nail and ask him or her to drive it into the board with an appropriate tool. The performance to be measured in this case is the respondents' ability to discern and carry out appropriate techniques for fastening wooden components together.

Learning Domains. Most psychologists agree on three domains for learning. The *cognitive* domain deals with thinking or cognition. The *affective* domain deals with values and attitudes. The *psychomotor* domain deals with physical aspects that involve perceptions, such as seeing, hearing, and smelling (Bigge & Hunt, 1963; Bloom, 1976; Markle & Tiemann, 1979).

We think, we feel, we do. In most cases these three are directly linked and our responses include all three. This is true even when the test itself is totally in one domain. In our carpentry examples above it's easy to see that the domains are all involved. In a math test it's not so easy. This is because our minds place information in one domain or another. We code information as being in a single domain although all three are almost certainly involved.

> **domain**
> Field or sphere of activity or influence.

Consider a math test. We automatically classify it as cognitive. It involves thought processes and that's that. But, think about this question: "Given $5x + 2y = 114$, what is the value of x if y is 11?" The respondents will have to think the problem through. They may be pleased with the process or they may not, but they will attach a value to it. That's an automatic human response, like the ability to do well. There are also physical aspects of the process such as working out the answer with a pencil. Although the emphasis is on the thought process, the whole person is involved in answering the question. Despite this fact, it's convenient to separate responses into domains. Separation allows us to select the best media for presenting questions and the right environments for their execution.

Tiemann and Markle's matrix (Figure 1.2) makes it easier to visualize the three levels and their relationships with the three domains. The matrix is useful for modeling psychological phenomena of many types. Our purpose is to talk about testing. More specifically we're interested in what happens when a person reads a question and prepares to answer. With this in mind I have taken the liberty of filling in the cells of the matrix with descriptions of my interpretation of the response patterns (see Figure 1.3, p. 22). The patterns aren't precisely defined. Nor are they derived from an authority. They are simply presented as an idea of the nature of the patterns and how they differ from cell to cell.

Basically, these descriptions conform to Tiemann and Markle's model with some modification to accommodate Lewin's thoughts about the psychological nature of human beings. We will use the matrix later to categorize performances and item types by level and domain.

As you think about these levels and domains you can see they are interconnected. However, normally a test is developed for specific knowledge or skills that impact a single domain at a particular level. To get a better idea of how that impact can affect questions, take another look at the matrix. This time the cells (see Figure 1.4, p. 23) contain questions that might be asked for the domain or level of the cell.

FIGURE 1.2. THE TIEMANN-MARKLE MATRIX.

DOMAIN / LEVEL	Cognitive	Affective	Psychomotor
I or A Recall			
II or B Application			
III or C Developmental			

Source: Markle & Tiemann, 1979.

FIGURE 1.3. THE TIEMANN-MARKLE MATRIX: CELL DESCRIPTIONS.

DOMAIN / LEVEL	Cognitive — Thinking, ideas, opinions	Affective — Emotions, values, attitudes	Psychomotor — Physical acts & conditions
I or A — Recall	A person remembers information. The information is not changed or processed.	An emotion, value, or attitude is recalled without change.	A physical movement is repeated. A sight or sound is recognized.
II or B — Application	A person uses information in a process. Thinking conforms to previous patterns.	An emotion is directed toward a person or thing. A value is used to justify an action.	A physical skill is used to achieve an end. A sound or other stimulus is produced.
III or C — Developmental	A person uses information to solve a problem or develop new ideas/applications.	An emotion is used to achieve a new goal. Values are modified to accommodate new data.	A new skill area is begun. An old skill is used in a new arena. Higher levels are gained.

Source: Markle & Tiemann, 1979.

You may have noticed that the cells under "Psychomotor" don't contain questions. Formal questions don't work well in this domain, so we use instructions. There are other instances in which questions don't work well. For example, requiring respondents to match two columns of related information is not a question as we have defined it. Yet, it *is* a part of the test that requires a response. These exceptions require us to use another term to describe what stimulates respondents' answers. We call them *items*. An item is usually a question on a test, but sometimes it is a simple statement requesting some action or a question followed by a series of answers. The term *item* is used to indicate a single opportunity to respond.

It's important to remember that level and domain don't dictate the *difficulty* of a test item. The question in the matrix above for Level One Cognitive may be more difficult for most people than the request for Level Three Psychomotor. Generally, the higher the level the more complex the reasoning involved and, therefore, the more difficult the item, but it doesn't apply in all cases. Level of difficulty is a concept that has yet to be examined. The levels in the matrix simply refer to complexity of process.

> **item**
> A single opportunity to respond.

FIGURE 1.4. TIEMANN-MARKLE MATRIX: SAMPLE QUESTIONS.

DOMAIN / LEVEL	Cognitive — Thinking, ideas, opinions	Affective — Emotions, values, attitudes	Psychomotor — Physical acts & conditions
I Recall	What are the titles of the people in the president's cabinet?	What is your feeling about increased real estate taxes?	Grip and swing the hammer correctly.
II Application	What is the net price of a $75.00 jacket if the discount is 15 percent?	Is it fair for a college athlete to receive money or a car in addition to a scholarship?	Step on the treadmill and walk in your normal way.
III Developmental	How has the reunification of Germany affected the average American citizen?	How can you use fear of ostracism in the teen years to combat enticements to use drugs?	Play softball while riding a donkey.

Source: Markle & Tiemann, 1979.

Let's return to the point of how to get at the levels and domains of learning to be tested. It's assumed that this learning has already taken place. The matrix also applies to anticipated learning, but that's another book. We're only concerned here with tests and test items.

Given the caveat above, take a moment to copy a blank matrix like the one in Figure 1.2 (p. 21). Then look at each of the questions below and decide which cell best describes its psychological impact. Write the number of the question in the cell you have selected.

A. What is the capital of Mexico?

This is obviously Level One Cognitive. (Unless, of course, you had to look it up on a map.) This illustrates another caveat: a question may be in different cells for different people, depending on their repertoires. To illustrate it further, look at the next example.

B. What f-stop on a camera is most appropriate for bright sun at a medium distance?

For a camera buff this is Level One Cognitive. A person familiar with the camera could look it up in a manual, Level Two Cognitive. Someone with a camera but without a manual might have to experiment with different settings to see what happens, which is Level Three.

Now take a look at these questions. What cell is most appropriate for each of them?

1. What three colors are used in the flag of the United States of America?
2. What sort of reaction do people have while observing the butchering of a hog?
3. Take a water pistol and shoot at a basketball from a distance of fifteen feet. How many times can you hit the ball if you are given twenty tries?

The answers are (1) Level One Cognitive; (2) Level Two Affective (although students of biology may remember information about this, making it Level Two Cognitive for them); and (3) Level Three Psychomotor for most people.

Now try another group of questions. This time select a primary and a secondary cell for each one. For example the question, "When did General McArthur return?" is Level One Cognitive, but (secondarily) it's also Level Two Affective.

4. Mary has a bloody nose. What would you want to know to decide what caused her problem?
5. How does the texture of a snake's skin differ from that of a toad?
6. John Dewey was influenced substantially by the thinking of Hegel. What kind of logic would, therefore, be appropriate for Dewey to use in the resolution of disputes?
7. How do you feel about the death penalty?
8. What is the first thing you should do in the event of a life-threatening incident, such as a fire or serious accident?

The answers are (4) primarily Level Two Cognitive and secondarily Level Two Psychomotor; (5) primarily Level Three Psychomotor and secondarily Level Three Affective; (6) Level Three Cognitive and Level Two Cognitive (just because both cells are in the same domain doesn't eliminate one of them from consideration); (7) Level One Affective and Level Two Affective; and (8) Level Two Cognitive and Level Three Affective.

You may have come up with different answers to more than one of these. That's OK. It's a matter of interpretation, and we don't have to agree totally. It's important, however, to agree that all nine cells are viable and that all contribute.

The following question illustrates why it's important to keep the matrix in mind while writing questions. It helps the test maker predict types and levels (and, therefore, the range) of responses.

9. What is the best way to approach the arbitration of a labor dispute?

The author of this question intended it to be Level Two Cognitive. Is it? Maybe, but it could easily be Level One Cognitive (there is a standard process for both litigants and arbitrators) or it could be Level Two Affective (the parties to arbitration deliberately use emotions and attitudes during arbitration). Any of these might be the object of the question from the test maker's standpoint. The argument begs the issue. To be fair to respondents, the question writer is obliged to write the question so that there isn't so much confusion. Perhaps one or more items are required to assess the area fully, one for recall of the standard (textbook) process (Level One Cognitive) and one for Level Two Affective. For example:

10. What is the standard process for arbitration of a labor dispute?
11. What attitude has proven itself most productive for labor during arbitration of important contract disputes?

Now each question calls for a specific and different kind of response. This is probably a better treatment of the subject because it affords respondents the greatest opportunity to display the depth and breadth of their knowledge and potential ability.

Before I leave this topic, I must bring up a slightly controversial subject. Some people seem to believe testing can't be done in some areas. It is true that tests can invade the privacy of individuals and that ethics and morals provide important limitations for the test maker and should always be taken into account when a test is being developed. A nice rule of thumb is, "If you can be sued for it, don't do it." Invasion of privacy is a no-no in America and anywhere else in the world. But, bear in mind, it can be done. It is possible. We can test anything or anyone. The basic purpose of tests is to measure human understanding and skills. There are, of course, rhetorical questions. However, our purpose is more direct. We wish to measure—to test. And we can. We can measure anything.

Questioning the Unquestionable

It is true, you know. Many people would like to quarrel with such a presumptuous statement, but it qualifies itself. The problem isn't what we can measure but why we measure and how well we can measure. You could develop a test to discover whether a person believes in God. You could build a test to find out whether a person uses drugs or is a pedophile. You can do these things. Whether you *should* or not is another question—a question so important that Chapter Thirteen of this book is devoted to it.

However, most instances of an invasion of privacy are unintended. We sometimes ask questions we believe to be straightforward and innocent. But, ultimately, you and I don't judge that. The respondents do. How important is a sigh? I ask. You answer. The invasiveness of the question can only be determined by you. The nature of the answer has to be judged against *your* interpretation of the question, unless there is some precondition you and I have agreed to that I can use to judge the adequacy of your answer.

That's the crucial dimension. "Only fools ask questions they haven't prepared ahead of time." The quote is taken from an episode of a television show called *The Paper Chase*. The instructor was criticizing the protagonist about a question that would be disallowed by a judge during a trial. The statement has a broader application. We could be just as foolish or perhaps more so, as the object of our questions seldom has an opportunity to complain or correct our injustices. Strange as it may seem on the surface, we're ethically obligated to ask only questions respondents will agree are appropriate.

This makes sense. It also tends to make the process of writing test items more difficult. How in the world can the test maker anticipate every complaint or objection a potential respondent might have? The secret is to be continually proactive—to provide the rationale for judging answers long before the respondent encounters the question.

Traditionally, there are two ways to do this. First, you must set criteria for judgment of answers before writing the question. Second, you must be clear and comprehensive in your instructions for taking the test. How to develop instructions for test administration will be covered in detail in Chapter Eight. Now, let's look at criteria.

Developing Criteria

Any arena of inquiry should be avoided if the questioner lacks credentials or is poorly prepared. Psychiatrists can ask questions the rest of us should avoid, simply because they are trained to do so and we aren't. They are uniquely qualified in their field. This is easy to see when we talk about professionals such as doctors or lawyers, but it's equally important for any area of expertise. Consider a sanitation technician (garbage collector). Should you or I feel qualified to ask about the nature of the work? Sure, if we're simply seeking information. But we shouldn't prepare a test for a garbage collector unless we know what should be tested and how to ask about it. Understanding the content and knowing how it's used by a practitioner are indispensable requirements for a test maker.

Other areas in this book address this in more detail, but for now, remember that we have no business testing people unless we can ensure that our questions are valid.

Testing also requires some sort of mechanism. How can a test be presented? What form should it take? These questions are addressed in Chapter Two.

CATEGORIES OF TESTS AND ITEMS

There are many types of psychological tests: quizzes, surveys, achievement tests, performance checklists, opinion polls, and so forth. It is valuable to explore some of them so, when the time comes, you will be able to make an informed decision about what type is best for your testing purpose. A categorization scheme should help in the future when you want to find a test for a specific application quickly.

With that in mind, let's group types of tests according to expected use. Psychological tests are used to:

- Discover opinions.
- Evaluate learning processes as they are being developed.
- Discover how well materials, software, or equipment work.
- Discover attitudes and values.
- Discover preferred thinking or work styles or as inventories.
- Diagnose knowledge or gaps in skills hierarchies.
- Certify, license, or qualify people.
- Discover the presence of illness or deviation from psychological norms.
- Sample skill levels.
- Compare respondents with established norms.
- Entertain.

Tests have been developed to sample almost any human activity in any of the three domains: cognitive, affective, and psychomotor. Basically, I believe they fall into one of four categories:

1. Diagnostic tests.
2. Tests of values or opinions.
3. Tests of attitudes or preferences.
4. Tests of skill levels.

Let's look at each category in detail.

Diagnostic Tests

Diagnostic tests are often called pretests, placement tests, or qualifying tests. In clinical situations they can be called lab tests. Remember that we are talking about *psychological* tests, not clinical tests to discover the sugar content in urine or whatever.

Diagnostic tests measure the presence of a trait or skill. Psychiatrists and psychologists use special tests to discover whether their patients perceive and are likely to behave normally. Depending on their use, some IQ tests fall into this category. If you want to use such a test, use the services of an expert to develop and administer it, as these tests can be dangerous in the hands of beginners. Untold harm can be done to respondents if they are used or interpreted poorly.

> **diagnosis**
> A careful examination and analysis of the facts in an attempt to understand or explain something.

The diagnostic tests you are most likely to use are the first ones mentioned above: pretests, placement tests, and qualifying exams. These are an important aspect of normal operations in almost any large organization.

Pretests

Pretests are used to clarify and set the goals and objectives for a learning experience. They give the learners an opportunity to discover what will be required for them to be successful.

> **pretest**
> Test used before an event to qualify participants.

I often teach a course called Introduction to Instructional Technology. It's my custom to give the students the final exam for the course on the first day of class. I tell them they can take it at that time without penalty and, if they pass it, they don't have to attend class or do anything else to receive a B in the course. The test samples skill in everything covered during instruction. Therefore, if students can pass it, they already have the skills and don't require the training.

Pretests are also used in training situations to discover which knowledge or skills are most needed by the learners. Then the instructor or trainer can modify the learning experience to concentrate on the needed areas.

Placement Tests

A placement test is used to place people within a hierarchy of increasingly complex skill performance levels. This type of test can be used in formal learning environments and in almost any work-related arena. The idea is to discover an individual's standing with respect to job requirements or a skill set and to place him or her in a situation consistent with it. For example, suppose a university accepts a new freshman who wants to major in mathematics. The freshman's transcript indicates she has taken differential and integral calculus in high school. The university knows that such high school courses qualify some freshmen for higher math, but not all. Rather than take a chance, the university asks the student to take a placement test in math to determine more precisely where she stands in the field.

> **placement test**
> Test used to ascertain eligibility.

Placement tests are very good when they are acceptable to the people concerned. They can create problems, however, even for people who have agreed, in principle, to their use. Private corporations have tried to use placement tests to place new hires in their organizations. The tests can predict the job type and level of responsibility the new worker is probably capable of handling. Unfortunately, other workers may object to this practice, especially if the new hire is placed in a position above them. When unions are involved, the use of placement tests can lead to real trouble.

Qualifying Examinations

Many kinds of qualifying exams are used. Many are similar to placement tests. The bar exams for lawyers, medical licensing exams for M.D.'s, and flight tests for pilots and flight instructors are examples of qualifying exams.

> **qualifying exam**
> Test used to certify competence, usually in a professional arena.

Generally, qualifying exams are connected with a license or permission to perform a job or function. I have taken qualifying exams to become a wrestling official, a psychometrician, and a marksman. Perhaps the most important for me was the Graduate Record Exam (GRE) for entrance into graduate school.

Qualifying exams can be critical. For example, the law school graduate who doesn't pass the bar exam is not allowed to practice law. Graduate students who don't pass their "comps" are not granted the degrees they seek. Architects, psychologists, public accountants, and many others must pass tests to become licensed to practice their professions. Today many more people than ever before depend on qualifying exams to establish their ability to do the kind of work they want to do. Automobile manufacturers require mechanics to take and pass exams. Would-be secretaries are asked to take tests of typing accuracy and speed.

Unfortunately, some qualifying exams are not good fair tests. They can have the same shortcomings as other kinds of tests. The effects on individuals can be disastrous.

Tests of Values or Opinions

Tests of values or opinions sample the affective domain. They have two primary purposes: (1) Discovery of individuals' opinions. (2) Clinical exploration.

Most of you are interested in what is sometimes, laughingly, called a *smiles test,* an inventory given to participants at the end of a session asking them how they liked the session. These tests can be checklists, multiple-choice items, or rating scales. They can be quite valuable because they give the test maker an opportunity to evaluate how well the session worked and to find areas in which improvements can be made. They will be discussed in some detail later in this chapter.

Other value inventories are used to discover people's favorite management styles, political preferences, learning environments, television shows, and so forth. Many times such tests are used purely for entertainment. At other times these tests have very serious purposes. Many value inventories are used by clinical psychologists to discover tendencies toward antisocial behavior or other disorders. I have used a value inventory to identify people with tendencies toward paranoia or schizophrenia.

So-called *opinionnaires* are used by marketing specialists to discover and qualify markets. They provide information valuable in directing marketing and sales campaigns. Such instruments are often used for direct mail sales. Sophisticated statistical interpretation of the results allows the sponsoring organizations to focus advertising on people who are most likely to buy. Many people have been victimized by unscrupulous sales organizations that have used an opinionnaire to locate them. On the other hand, organizations with new products and limited financial backing often are able to start through such efforts. When a direct mail campaign is effective, it can bring large financial gains almost overnight. Effectiveness is predicated on the quality of the test used to define the market and the way results are analyzed.

Tests of Attitudes or Preferences

Tests of attitudes or preferences are similar in a lot of ways to tests of values or opinions, but there are three important differences. (1) They are almost always prepared and used by professionals or technicians. (2) The respondents know why they are responding. (3) The results are used to make decisions about groups based on the preferences of individual respondents.

Many high school students have taken a test called the Kuder Preference Test. They are asked to select one of two activities from each of a long list of pairs. The test items look something like this:

1. Would you rather be a doctor or a lawyer?
2. Would you rather be a lawyer or an accountant?
3. Would you rather be a secretary or a retail clerk?

The respondent is given hundreds of such choices. Many jobs are repeated (paired with different choices). When the students have finished, the test maker, using sophisticated scoring strategies, is able to report fairly accurately what the person's current preferences are.

Marketing organizations use these tests to discover consumer preferences and trends. The blind tests in which consumers taste different kinds of soft drinks and state their preferences have a serious purpose, even though they look like fun and games on television. Some companies (for example, Coca-Cola) have changed the basic nature of their products because of the results of such tests.

Several preference inventories are used by hiring officials to make decisions about job applicants. A retail chain that specializes in music and recordings of all kinds uses two preference inventories. The first discovers what kinds of music an applicant prefers. The second develops a profile showing how an applicant prefers to receive information and what kinds of presentations they heed most. Consider two young people applying for a job with this firm. Albert likes hard rock music and is auditory (most likely to understand information he hears). Janice likes country music and is visual (she understands information she sees). Assuming they have the same qualifications, which one would you hire as a clerk in your record store?

Tests of Skill Levels

Most tests developed by individuals are of this type. These tests measure knowledge and skills. For the most part, this book is about this type of test. It tests performance, achievement, and other attributes related to learning. How these tests of learning differ is discussed in Chapter Three. For now, consider the forms they can take. They have many uses and descriptions, but basically there are two kinds.

Many years ago I was told there are two types of tests: subjective and objective. *Subjective* tests are those that require the respondents to supply the answer. *Objective* tests are the ones with answers available from which the respondent chooses. The two terms refer to the effort required by someone trying to evaluate the results. Subjective tests require the scorer to use judgment and make decisions. Objective tests are scored simply by recording the respondents' choices as right or wrong. The labels seem inappropriate to me because they focus on the test scorer instead of the respondent.

Later I learned there are two kinds of tests, *supply* and *choice*. These terms refer to respondent activity. They either have to supply an answer or choose one. The two kinds of tests are also called open-ended and closed. Closed is further broken into forced choice and freedom of choice (or something like that).

Now we're being told tests are either *juried* or *machine scored*. It seems we are back to the original kind of thinking, which concentrates on the task of arriving at scores, rather than on the impact of the test on respondents.

However tests are categorized, it seems there are two kinds of tests. There are tests where the respondent has to come up with a response and those where he or she can choose a response from those provided. Either the response is provided or it isn't.

This chapter provides a fairly comprehensive description of items for which the respondent supplies the answer. Later chapters examine characteristics of items that provide the respondents with choices.

Types of Items

Responses Not Provided

Basically, there are three types of items that require the respondent to supply a response. They are, for lack of better terms, essay, short-answer, and fill-in items.

Essay Items. An essay item requires respondents to supply an answer, complete with explanation and rationale. Most of us think of an essay test as a situation in which the respondent sits and writes an explanation of something. Indeed, that is usually what happens. But it doesn't have to. An oral exam is usually an essay type test. Even physical skills can be tested through the essay test idea. For example, dressage is a test of a rider's ability to negotiate a series of obstacles with a horse in a minimum amount of time without knocking anything down or missing something. A slalom race by skiers requires the same kind of demonstration. Both of these can be considered types of essay tests.

> There was a young man from Berlin
>
> Who was so excessively thin
>
> That when he essayed
>
> To drink lemonade
>
> He slipped through the straw and fell in.

The use of the word *essayed* in this classic limerick is appropriate. The term, used as a verb, means to try. The point is that an essay test can take many forms.

Essay items tend to be Level Two or Level Three. They usually emphasize the cognitive domain. They fit easily into the cells indicated in the matrix used earlier. The matrix in Figure 2.1 gives an example in each cell of a skill that could be assessed through an essay test. These are *not* recommendations. I, personally, would prefer to use another kind of test in most of the cells. However, an essay test could be used in each case. In cells 7, 8, and 9 (Level Three) essay tests are usually the best choice.

A good fair essay test is seen as appropriate by respondents. It fits their expectations. It provides them with an opportunity to show their stuff. These are the same criteria I spoke of for any test, and so it should be. But the essay test is often the principal reason many people are afraid of tests. The reasons for their fear are real. I can think of three good ones. The questions below illustrate each of the three.

1. When did you stop beating your wife? (Inappropriate assumptions about the respondent.)
2. Why did the Bull Moose Party wither and die in the 1930s? (Trivia test.)
3. Can you contrast the efficiency of COBOL with the effectiveness of Fortran II? (Mixed references.)

FIGURE 2.1. TIEMANN-MARKLE MATRIX: ESSAY TEST APPLICATIONS.

DOMAIN / LEVEL	Cognitive Thinking, ideas, opinions	Affective Emotions, values, attitudes	Psychomotor Physical acts & conditions
I Recall	1 Repeat a telephone sales pitch verbatim.	2 Demonstrate a range of emotions required for a role in a play.	3 Demonstrate your ability to play a symphony.
II Application	4 Modify a sales pitch to fit the customer's mood and wants.	5 Explain how a statement fits with currently held values.	6 Use a schematic to find electrical problems.
III Developmental	7 Create a strategy for developing a new market niche.	8 Provide emotional support for a stranger.	9 Design space for a manufacturing process.

Inappropriate Assumptions. The beat-your-wife question is, in effect, the definition of a *double bind* or a *catch-22*. There are two obvious ways to answer, although neither is desirable to most people. Even a wife beater will be reluctant to respond. Other examples of this abuse can be seen in questions such as, "Why don't you like school?" or "How old were you when you started abusing alcohol?" or "What policy should our organization adopt for people like you?"

The dilemma is obvious. The respondent doesn't have a viable avenue for his or her response. If you say you never beat your wife, you have deliberately avoided answering the question. It doesn't ask if you ever did it; it asks when you quit. Read the question again. Chances are you've been asked to answer one like it.

The Trivia Test. The question quoted earlier was taken from a test in a college history course. Here's one taken from a ninth-grade math test. "What culture first recognized the significance of the concept zero?" This might be a good question for an anthropologist, but it usually shows up on math tests. There are literally millions of examples, such as, "Why does Barbara Bush prefer blue?" The answers to the questions are useless to the respondent except as trivia. So the respondent's first response is usually a muttered, "Who cares?"

Essay questions of this type have a tendency to give respondents a false set of values. When a person responds to an essay question, it is usually a complex process and the person uses a great deal of energy in the attempt. Such a concentration of energy tends to impress the respondent with the importance of the question, whether it is important or not. For example, there were world-shaking events taking place in the 1930s, but because I spent energy on a question about the Bull Moose Party, I have mentally equated it with such things as the fall of the stock market and the rise of Nazi Germany. How absurd.

mixed references
Two or more opposed major premises in a single item.

Mixed References. Remember the old adage about not mixing apples and oranges? The mixed references in the third question are the words *efficiency* and *effectiveness*. The two terms are used together often because they are both descriptive of human endeavors, but they refer to two very different properties. The question writer is saying that COBOL is efficient and Fortran II is effective. Contrasting such value statements is difficult at best. What the writer probably wanted was a discussion of the kinds of applications for which COBOL is preferred and applications for which Fortran II might be a better choice. If so, the writer should say so.

Let's look at another example: "Construct a matrix showing the relative effect of different cultural emphases on learning styles." Here the respondent is asked to use a fairly specific and limited device (a matrix) to explain a very complex notion. Once again the test maker has requested an inappropriate response to what is probably an important question requiring in-depth thinking and explanation.

An essay question must be phrased very carefully so respondents can exhibit the *flexibility* and *comprehensiveness* the item type is supposed to elicit. Flexibility and comprehensiveness are the reasons essay tests are important tools in the test maker's kit.

Flexibility. An essay item allows flexibility in two important arenas. First, it allows the test maker to ask for information or skills he or she may not be able to define well or completely. Second, it gives respondents a platform from which they can say virtually anything they want. The test maker can ask for things he or she may not completely understand. Of course, you must not ask questions out of the blue. You must know the content well enough to justify the question.

The essay format gives you an opportunity to provide respondents with an opportunity to be innovative, to create, to pursue original thinking. If you choose to use essay items, remember that you must evaluate the responses. You must pass judgment on the answers and score them. This demands a good grounding on your part; you must know the content well enough to provide a credible assessment of the respondents' efforts. If you can't, you do respondents a disservice by asking the question.

Probably the most representative example of an essay test is the comprehensive examination given in most graduate programs. Students in such programs refer to it as an opportunity to "spill their guts," and so it is. Consider this question:

1. Given the current state of economic difficulties between the United States and Japan, suggest a diplomatic strategy that could lead to a comprehensive policy acceptable to both without compromise of basic social or political values by either.

The professors have asked a question for which they probably don't have a good answer themselves. Still, it is a good question. It addresses the area of expertise being sampled. It provides direction so respondents know exactly what is required. Yet it gives the respondents an opportunity to express opinions and ideas they might not otherwise air. It's tough, but it is good and fair. Of course, we must assume the professors will score the answers well.

Many sporting events are analogous to an essay test. Golf is very appropriate. The rules are clear and easy to use. All players are restricted to the same number of clubs and those clubs must conform to established criteria, but the golfers can hit with any of those clubs in any way they want. The result for each is an individual expression and execution of the game. There are literally millions of golfers, all of whom play the game differently. Part of the elegance of the game is that uniform rules and scoring make it possible to compare all those millions and come to conclusions about their relative ability to play.

Responding to an essay test is something like playing a round of golf. Suppose a golfer scores well. The results are as much internal as external. The golfer's satisfaction is usually more important than the specific score he or she posts. In golf it's great to win, but it's more important to play well.

Essay tests are like that if they're well written and presented and if the rules are clear and easy to follow. The onus falls on the test maker. A good essay test is not something you can dream up on the spot. The questions must be carefully crafted.

Comprehensiveness. Many tests are called *essay* simply because respondents are forced to write long answers. I must digress with a horror story. When I was in graduate school, I took a class from an English professor who had recently received her degree. I complained about what I thought was the archaic and inappropriate requirement for students to memorize things they could easily look up in a thesaurus or dictionary. She became very indignant and informed me that, for her comprehensive exam, she had memorized 2,000-word distillations from the works of twelve different authors (24,000 words). When I asked if she then used them for references on the exam, she said no, she had repeated them verbatim in response to the appropriate questions.

That wasn't an essay test. It failed in the exact arena it was trying to assess: comprehensiveness. The idea the examining committee had was that students should have a broad grounding in the works of those twelve authors. They were looking for a thoughtful discussion. They received a recitation. Where did they go wrong? In the ways they asked their questions.

Let's suppose the examination committee wrote this question:

1. Explain the relevance of the writing of the following expository authorities:

   Milton.

   Clemens.

   Thoreau.

Any well-thought-out answer would be appropriate. Students could write a well-developed response months in advance of the test, memorize it, and do well. They could have someone else write it for them—someone who had been successful in the same situation before. Now look at a fanciful example of what the professors could have asked:

1. Mark Twain (Samuel Clemens) wrote a critique of James Fenimore Cooper's style in his *Letters from the Earth*. Select three of his points and discuss their qualifications as advice to aspiring authors. (Twain's critique is reprinted as part of the question.)

How is this question more comprehensive than the other? It assesses respondents' knowledge of Twain's time and literary context. It asks for an exploration of style in general and commentary on Twain's interpretation of what he thinks is appropriate. It allows respondents to interpret and report their own thoughts about a somewhat controversial passage.

I believe that comprehensiveness in this context doesn't connote total license. To be comprehensive, an essay question must be worded in such a way as to elicit scope *and* depth. In other words, it should help to develop insights as well as descriptions. I suspect it is quite valuable for professors of literature to be able to recall a considerable volume of information about important people in the field. It is probably even more important for them to be able to discuss who those people were, their motives, and their ambitions in a way that makes a contribution to contemporary situations.

Be careful about being comprehensive. Many of us believe comprehensive means all there is about everything in a context. And so it does, but that meaning includes interpretative thinking and logical projections. A good essay question will generate responses that do a great deal more than simply parrot what the teacher or another authority has said.

Often an essay test is a distasteful ending to what was a beautiful experience. Learning is rewarding. It's hard work and often painful, but the pain is forgotten in having accomplished it. Then comes the test. In the best of all worlds the test will reinforce the wonderful feeling of having learned. It will provide the learner with a fine opportunity to show off. If that opportunity is to be offered through an essay test, you can be better assured of success if you can keep the test flexible and comprehensive.

Examples. The following questions are offered as several different ways to sample learning and opinion. My comments are offered as food for thought only. Precise criticism is difficult.

1. Tiemann and Markle have provided a matrix with three domains. They feel that restricting the domains to cognitive, affective, and psychomotor provides the matrix with enough flexibility to make it more useful. Assume you disagree with this conclusion. How could the domains be modified to enhance the usefulness of the matrix for test developers?

If we assume such modification has *not* been discussed prior to the test, the respondents are presented with a difficult and, perhaps, an interesting task. The question is cognitive, probably Level 3. It doesn't require respondents to remember the domains, but it does assume they know how to use the matrix.

This item could be used in a spring training camp of a professional baseball team.

2. Assume Ted Williams is the batter. Our pitcher is going to throw a fast ball at or below his knees on the inside portion of the plate. The count is two balls and two strikes. Take a position on the field to defend against Ted's swing.

Even though the response will be completed in moments, this is still an essay question, which brings us to an important point. Most test makers are prone to combine psychomotor items or include three or four in one set. Nevertheless it's best to present a test one item at a time quickly. This allows the respondent to consider and act on each one independently. When the player has adjusted his position to demonstrate his ability to play a hitter like Ted Williams, the coach can easily repeat the item using a different hitter, a different count for the same hitter, or a different pitch. It can be done quickly and cleanly. And (assuming it's a good fair test) when it's completed, both the respondent and the test maker know how well the test worked.

The tendency among test makers is to rely on verbal responses to essay opportunities. The item above demonstrates that this isn't always the best approach. However, verbalizations will be appropriate for most of our needs.

3. Many of the major issues that caused the Cold War have eroded or disappeared. Assume that the current state of world politics and the tendencies of European governments are as they have been discussed in class. Devise a strategy for entering and expanding a market opportunity in Europe that is consistent with our company's mission and fiscal capabilities. Predicate its success on economic considerations.

Tough question. Maybe too tough. Not everyone who is in a position to respond to such items is equipped to respond well. This is a major problem with essay tests. Too often the respondent is extended beyond what should be expected of him or her. Even a seasoned diplomatic veteran with years of experience as an executive of the company would be hard-pressed by this question. It isn't fair for most folks to have to address such things.

More examples of this sort of item are given below.

4. Use the materials and tools provided to build a machine that will. . . . Innovative approaches will be given bonus points.

You have just asked the respondent to develop an invention. Even if he or she could do it, you may be out of line. What if it's patentable? Just kidding. There is another problem here. Bonuses are usually inappropriate. Anyone who has trouble with this item is at a double disadvantage. Such schemes put some respondents in a no-win situation. If they cannot come up with a reasonable solution, they lose both the credit for an acceptable answer and the bonus points. Not fair.

5. Assume you usually respond with anger to someone who coughs during a music recital. You feel like yelling at them to stop. Suggest two ways you can counter this emotion with another. Demonstrate how you would use those alternatives.

I suppose this has been part of a learning experience. Still, it doesn't seem fair to put it to a test. It may be important, but it's better to use it in a practice exercise. I stand by my injunction that anything can be measured, but I'm not sure everything ought to be. Judgment should be used. A test is a situation in which those who can do something are rewarded and those who can't are not. Ask yourself if you are looking for an opportunity *not* to reward folks who can't do something.

An acquaintance who is a psychological therapist does not test people who attend her seminars for these kinds of reasons. The skills are extremely valuable to be sure, but she can't justify putting people who don't master them at a disadvantage.

Drawbacks. Three problems plague essay items. These problems are sufficient to make essay the poorest item to choose for most applications. The problems are:

1. Essay items take a lot of respondent time.
2. They usually don't sample the content very thoroughly.
3. They are very difficult to score consistently and fairly.

Essay tests force people to work hard for a long time. I once took a test that had one question. I spent four hours working on that one question. I should add that it was time well spent, but that is often not the case. I would guess that 90 percent of the time used for essay-type exams could be better used some other way.

Because they take so long, essay tests contain few questions. Five questions is about the maximum. People simply don't have the time or energy to answer more. Those five questions have to cover the content, but usually they don't. The test maker must consider this very carefully. What will be the consequences of covering bits and pieces of the content very well and ignoring the rest? This is an important question. The answer usually precludes the use of essay questions on the test.

The final objection, scoring difficulties, is the most important. It takes an astute impartial judge to score essay tests well. Most of us simply aren't skillful enough to do it. Because of this, we risk making unfair judgments about the respondents. This makes the test unfair, by nature, and consequently abuses the respondents.

> **scoring guide**
> A verbal template used as a guide during scoring of essay or short-answer tests; it is usually a list of points to be covered or logic to be used.

Unfair scoring of essay tests has done a lot to give tests in general a bad reputation. Two basic reasons for scoring difficulties are *lack of consistency* and the *inability to judge the worth of innovation and creativity.* Being consistent is difficult because wording, syntax, and presentation vary from one respondent to the next. Two answers that have essentially the same content can earn radically different scores. This is magnified by what the scorer learns in the process of scoring. The scorer is affected by what he or she has seen earlier. Respondents whose work is seen last can receive much different results than those who were evaluated first. Many test makers try to counter this problem by setting up scoring guides. This makes sense until you consider the difficulty of judging innovation and creativity.

A scoring guide works fairly well as long as the respondents try to respond in the ways the test maker has anticipated. As soon as a respondent goes on a different tack, however, the guide becomes a hammer rather than a crutch. This is unfortunate because the basic reason for an essay test in the first place is to allow respondents flexibility and freedom in their responses. If a respondent is criticized or punished for being innovative, the value of the test is lost.

Short-Answer Items. Short-answer items are one of my favorite types. They have many of the attributes of an essay test but are much easier to score and it is easier to provide comprehensive coverage of the material. A short-answer item asks respondents to provide a quick but well-thought-out response. Each item is restricted to a single topic or function. An essay question might ask about a complete manufacturing process. The short-answer item specifies a single step or phase.

Test makers must be careful not to let respondents view short-answer items as if they were essay items. It is usually appropriate to specify time and space constraints for the answers, for example, a single written paragraph of not more than fifty words.

Short-answer items must be carefully constructed or they can become something else. Suppose a supervisor wants to test employees on the basic tasks they perform: maintaining a large office building. The supervisor writes a short-answer test leaving ten lines of space under each question:

1. What is the procedure for finding and correcting an electrical problem?
2. What is the procedure for finding and correcting a problem with furniture, fixtures, or equipment?
3. What is the procedure for finding and correcting a problem with one of the elevators?
4. What is the procedure for finding and correcting a problem in the heating system?

5. What is the procedure for finding and correcting a problem in the cooling system?
6. How would you report the nature of a problem?
7. How do you document your work?

One of the building engineers (trusted to do good work) answers the questions this way:

1. Troubleshoot.
2. Troubleshoot.
3. Troubleshoot.
4. Troubleshoot it.
5. Troubleshoot.
6. Call the supervisor.
7. Fill out the form.

Those are short answers. At any rate the supervisor didn't get the kind of answers he was looking for. Why not? First, he failed to provide instructions for the test—to explain what he wanted. Second, he was probably testing in the wrong domain. When asked about it, the supervisor who actually wrote the questions said he wanted the people to show two things: (1) he wanted them to demonstrate that they knew how to do the work and (2) he wanted them to show how much they liked the work as they did it.

The supervisor did two things to help the test work better. Instead of asking the workers to write their answers, he asked them to tell him what they would do and show him how they would do it. As they worked, he asked them how they felt about the people who used the building, their superiors, and the other people in building maintenance. Their answers were recorded on a simple checklist. The new version of the test worked well. He was able to make major improvements in the quality of work his people produced as a result.

Both tests the supervisor produced were examples of short-answer tests. One worked very well; one did not work at all. Now let's return to the first test above. Suppose the supervisor didn't have time to administer the second test and had to use a written test. What could he have done to make it better?

First, he should supply good instructions. Essay tests require few instructions, if any, because the requirements of each item are embedded in it. This is not true for short-answer items. They require instructions that contain three elements:

1. A brief explanation of what is expected by the test maker.
2. A description of the constraints that will be enforced when scoring each item.
3. How points will be awarded and what will be considered a good score.

The supervisor could have said something like, "Use the space provided to write a brief outline of how to do each of these things. Your answers should indicate how you know there is a problem, what you do to find it, and, briefly, what you do to solve it. Each question is worth 3 points. A total of 17 or better is required to pass."

There are other problems with the test, for example, the workers may have trouble with writing skills. But at least by adding instructions the supervisor has a chance to achieve one of his goals.

Short-answer items are good choices for many test situations. Perhaps the most obvious is when respondents must demonstrate their ability to remember and use processes and procedures (Level Two Cognitive). Quick demonstrations of skill or knowledge are almost always best tested through short answer. For example, a coach may want to know if a basketball player can shoot a jump shot. A teacher may want to know if a student can use an algebraic equation. A supervisor may want to know if a worker can fill out a form. A director may want to know if an actor can show an emotion. All of these situations can justify a short-answer item. If the skill can be sampled simply by asking for a demonstration, the short-answer item is probably the appropriate choice.

I believe the short-answer item is the best choice for most Level Two situations. It's clean, convenient, and comprehensive enough for most applications at that level. But although the essay item can be used to test in almost any cell of the matrix, short-answer items are not as flexible. Figure 2.2 demonstrates the problems, particularly in cells 7, 8, and 9.

The situations in cells 1, 2, and 3 demonstrate that short-answer items work well at Level One. However, as you shall see, there are better ways to test at that level.

The activities in cells 7, 8, and 9 indicate that these cells might not be appropriate areas for short-answer items. It's difficult for respondents to work at Level Three in a short-answer environment. Developmental tasks normally take more time and effort. Cell 8 is especially difficult to test with short answer, yet it is often attempted.

A test maker might ask a question such as

1. How do you feel about current world conflicts?

Many people would be able to answer quickly and concisely, but those who have complex feelings about the situation would be at a severe disadvantage. It's not a fair question simply because there is not enough space or time for some of the respondents to reply.

FIGURE 2.2. TIEMANN-MARKLE MATRIX: SHORT-ANSWER APPLICATIONS.

DOMAIN / LEVEL	Cognitive — Thinking, ideas, opinions	Affective — Emotions, values, attitudes	Psychomotor — Physical acts & conditions
I Recall	1 Recite steps in a short process.	2 Demonstrate an emotional reaction. Cry on cue.	3 Play a major chord on the piano.
II Application	4 Name an alternative step for a given circumstance.	5 Report how you feel about a topic or question.	6 Modify a movement as suggested. Correct a golf swing.
III Developmental	7 Ad lib.	8 ?	9 Improvise as circumstances change.

Examples. As you peruse these examples, notice that many of the attributes and drawbacks of the essay test are present. However, the short-answer test can provide more opportunities for respondents (more items per test) and better coverage for the test maker.

Again, good instructions for taking the test are very important. Without clear instructions, respondents are forced to read the test maker's mind, a task that (for most test takers) is practically impossible. These instructions are typical: "Read each item carefully. Be sure you understand what is required before you start to write. Make your answers short and to the point. (Use only the space provided.) If you feel you should have more space and/or time, do the best you can and note the difficulty in your answer."

Here are some sample short-answer questions, followed by my comments.

1. Interior designers must develop a plan for any design before they begin actual modification of an existing facility. What is one critical consideration for this phase of the work? Please explain why your choice is critical to the success of the design.

Respondents may want to provide a long detailed explanation of their choices. If space will not allow it, they are forced to avoid such journeys. Although it is appropriate here to restrict answers to Level Two, it may *not* be on other items. You must think through the kinds of answers respondents may wish to supply for any item. This is particularly important for short-answer items.

2. A designer has chosen mauve drapery to complement a maple parquet floor and forest green upholstery in a cocktail lounge. Specify one problem this choice may generate. Why is it a problem?

This is a classic short-answer item. It contains elements that cause respondents to think at Level Two, yet the responses should be short and pointed. Note that the test maker has told respondents to specify a single problem. There may be several. If the test maker wished, the item could be moved to Level One as follows.

2. A designer has chosen mauve drapery to complement a maple parquet floor and forest green upholstery in a cocktail lounge. What is the most costly problem this choice will generate?

Now the basic nature of the item has been changed. Respondents simply state the answer and move on to the next question. Little, if any, deliberation will be needed. Note that the use of absolutes forces respondents to work at Level One.

3. What is one of the interior designer's responsibilities as far as building codes are concerned? How is it best accomplished in most designs?

Here the test maker has used the word *best* to justify scoring, saying, in effect, that the test maker will not accept frivolous or arcane reasons. Some respondents will grasp for an excuse when they discover they haven't responded well. Many times they will say, "It's a reason. You didn't say it had to be the most important reason." It's wise to guard against such nonsense simply by addressing the issue in the question.

4. Third parties flourish in other countries. What is one dependable reason they have difficulty in the United States?

Here the item writer has made good use of the word *dependable*. Of course the respondents must know what is being asked. Now look at an example at Level Two Affective.

5. An interior designer deliberately bid lower than her own costs to secure a contract, knowing the client would tolerate a moderate cost overrun. In fact the client could justify a small cost overrun more easily than he could a contract for the total cost. Therefore, the designer has done the client a favor. What is your reaction to this situation?

Ah, ethics. In cases like this, the short-answer item can be a lifesaver. The test maker can construct several items testing the same objective in different ways. The essay test would be hard-pressed to do as well.

Now an example of the best application of all, Level Two Psychomotor. If you are a coach, you use this kind of item almost exclusively.

6. Show me how you would adjust your stance if you were starting to feel fatigue.
7. What should you eat to get ready for the game tomorrow?

The same approach can be used with almost any process- or task-oriented activity.

8. Demonstrate how you start up the computer and move through the menus to the Carstairs software.
9. Many of the people you call on will be preoccupied with other matters. How will you get them focused on what you have to say?

Drawbacks. Most of the problems we discussed with essay items also apply to short-answer items, although they may not be as critical. Respondents still have to think out their answers and write them down (or demonstrate them), so they do take time and energy. They cover more content than essay items, but compared with multiple-choice items, they are very limited. They are also hard to score. Different respondents use different words in different ways. The evaluator must use good judgment in determining if those words respond to what the question asked.

Be prepared for responses to your short-answer items that don't make sense or are flippant. As is often the case, a major attribute spawns a drawback. The respondents don't perceive the items in the spirit the test maker intends. Therefore, they don't value it in the same way. The consequences can be hilarious. Remember the responses to the questions for building engineers? The respondent made a mockery of the test. This can happen even when the instructions are well written. What can the test maker do? Not much. Make sure it is really happening before you mark them all wrong. The problem could be caused by test maker error, but if it isn't, you have no choice but to allow the respondent to fail.

Fill-In Items. Often called "fill-in-the-blank," these items ask respondents to supply a single word or phrase. They are of little value for any use other than direct recall of specific facts. They work well for Level One Cognitive testing but practically nowhere else in the matrix.

Fill-in items are valuable, however. They serve to establish the presence of enabling knowledge as well as or better than any other type of test. Before we look at some examples and an explanation, it's appropriate to examine what this kind of item looks like.

Normally a fill-in item is a statement with a blank in it somewhere, an incomplete sentence. "Jack and Jill went up the . . ." By filling in the blank with the correct response, the respondents demonstrate their repertoire. They show they know the answer.

What is a *repertoire?* Earlier I said fill-in items are good for discovering enabling knowledge. Usually, the skills and knowledge that enable someone to do something are contained in an internal repertoire. Webster (1987) tells us a repertoire is "the complete list or supply of skills, devices, or ingredients used in a particular field, occupation, or practice." Perhaps no one has a *complete* list of this sort, but we all have a list of things we know and can do. The basic purpose of a fill-in test is to discover the extent of each respondent's list. The term *list* may be a bit misleading because it is common to think of a wrestler as having a repertoire of wrestling holds or a truck driver a repertoire of defensive driving tactics. In highly technical occupations, specific repertoires are essential. Medical doctors, for example, must have an extensive repertoire of knowledge about medicines and treatments.

It's important to think of repertoires as being internal. They are part of our thinking. They are the knowledge, experiences, and behaviors that provide the basic set of tools people use in every part of their lives at work or play. Mathematicians cannot do simple problems if they don't know what integers are. Golfers can't play the game correctly if they don't know what par is.

Format. In effect, the purpose of fill-in items is good, but the form is troublesome. Most fill-in items are created by replacing simple questions with incomplete statements. The statement above could be rewritten, "Where did Jack and Jill go?" or, if you want to reduce the answer to a single idea, "What did Jack and Jill climb?"

The fill-in item is a natural choice for poorly informed test makers. Suppose you want to find out if a soldier knows the major parts of a rifle. It seems natural to write, "The three major parts of an M-1 rifle are the ___ , the ___ , and the ___ ." Of course a question asking for the same information would be easy to construct. "What are the three major parts of an M-1 rifle?"

Study the two examples in the preceding paragraph for a moment. Which would you have the least trouble answering?

Aha! You're beginning to see the rub. Look at these examples. Answer them as you read them:

1. The essay type test is most effective at Level ___ .
2. At what level is the essay test most effective?

Chances are that you had less trouble understanding what was required for number 2 than you did for number 1. There are two basic reasons for this. First, number 1 is more ambiguous; and second, the nature of number 2 (it's a question) prompts your brain to go into the search-and-retrieve mode I talked about in Chapter One.

If you use fill-in items, you will be testing your respondents' ability to understand incomplete items (reading comprehension) as much as or more than you will be testing the extent of their repertoires.

Allow me to illustrate with two sample tests. One has fill-in items. The second asks for the same information using a question format.

1. There are ___ moving parts in a Wankle engine.
2. The Wankle is basically ___ efficient than engines currently used in automobiles.
3. The Wankle engine was developed in ___ .
4. The basic patents for the Wankle are held by ___ .
5. ___ , ___ , and ___ are now licensed to use Wankle engines in automobiles produced in _____ .

Compare these short-answer items asking for the same information:

1. How many moving parts does a Wankle engine have?
2. How efficient is the Wankle compared with engines currently used in automobiles?
3. In what country was the Wankle engine developed?
4. Who holds the basic patents for the Wankle?
5. What three automobile manufacturers in *the United States* are licensed to use Wankle engines in their cars?

Which test would you rather take? The second, I think. That's fairly obvious. It isn't as obvious, though, that they are pretty much the same test written two ways. Both are fill-in type tests. By changing the statements to questions, I merely reformatted the first test. It still tests for the same information in the same way. The difference is simply one of presentation. I suppose some experts would dispute this assertion. That's OK. After all, it was a fairly large change in form.

The point remains. Both types of items test for the same kind of information. Both are Level One Cognitive. The principal difference is that questions are more user-friendly than blanks. Respondents can understand and respond to them much more easily.

Most testing at Level One is done this way. A question is asked. A response is given. The response is valued (given a score) and the thing is done. My opinion is that questions are the best way to probe repertoires. The test taker is presented with a more forthright challenge; he or she does not have to guess what information is wanted or in what order.

A test that simply asks questions is a supply-item test. The respondents supply answers. There are three levels of complexity: essay, short answer, and one word or phrase. The fill-in test exemplifies the simplest (one-word-or-phrase) level. The fill-in test can be used in all three domains. Cognitive and psychomotor are easy to visualize, as in these examples:

1. What is the capital of Alaska?
2. How do you shoot a jump shot?

Affective is a bit more difficult, probably because we don't usually think of emotions, attitudes, or values existing as repertoires. Look at the examples below.

3. What idea about American democracy do you value most?
4. What assertion in this company's mission is most valuable to the local community?

In the matrix shown in Figure 2.3, fill-in items work well in three cells. Fill-in tests are simply not recommended at all for Levels Two and Three. A simple question at Level Two almost has to be a short-answer or essay item. At Level Three it's most often essay. Asking someone to actually fill in a blank at Level Two or Three is difficult to imagine.

Drawbacks. Two major drawbacks for incomplete statements are mentioned above: they tend to be ambiguous, and they are interpreted differently than questions. One other drawback is important no matter how the items are formatted: fill-ins are often used instead of the kind of test that should be used.

FIGURE 2.3. TIEMANN-MARKLE MATRIX: FILL-IN APPLICATIONS.

DOMAIN / LEVEL	Cognitive	Affective	Psychomotor
	Thinking, ideas, opinions	Emotions, values, attitudes	Physical acts & conditions
I Recall	1 A worker names the tools and equipment he must use.	2 A nurse displays emotional reactions for severe trauma victims.	3 A mechanic turns a wrench in the correct direction to loosen a bolt.
II Application	4 ?	5 ?	6 ?
III Developmental	7 ?	8 ?	9 ?

Most of the testing done in organizations today is used to qualify people in one way or another, perhaps to certify workers or to discover the managerial style of supervisors. There are literally dozens of applications.

Seldom do managers really want to test the extent of repertoires. So why do they use so many fill-in type tests? Perhaps they don't realize what they are doing. If that's your excuse, please don't do it any more!

Not many years ago the company I worked for was asked to help a major agency rebuild its certification exam. The exam is used to certify professionals in a very important field. At the time, their test consisted of many pages of fill-in type questions. Respondents had to know almost every term and the names of all the techniques used, but they weren't required to demonstrate how to do the work. They were expected to be experts in the trivia of the field. There was little evidence (from the test) that they could perform the tasks required at all.

Responses Provided

Generally there are three types of tests for which the test maker supplies the answer along with the question:

- Dichotomous, true/false.
- Multiple-choice.
- Matching.

Actually, they are all renditions of the same theme. There is a question (called a *stem*) followed by two or more responses (called *alternatives* or *distractors*). Respondents read the stem and then select the response they feel answers the question best. There are many modifications and innovations in the use of the form. The basic nature of the test, however, remains the same.

dichotomous
An item that provides two usually opposite or antithetical choices, such as true or false.

multiple choice
An item that has three or more plausible alternative responses.

matching
An item that has two columns for which the respondent selects a response from one column for each of the entries in the other column.

If the test maker decides respondents don't have to remember the answer or how to present it, these kinds of tests can, and probably should, be used. They have many advantages. They are much easier to score. Except for true/false items, they are less ambiguous. They are generally less time consuming for respondents. They provide immediate feedback to respondents about success or lack of it. They are popular and, therefore, familiar to respondents. People know how to respond.

Most important, tests in which the test maker supplies the answers are appropriate for any cell in the matrix. They can even be used successfully for Level Three.

The multiple-choice item has become the item of choice for most testing in America today. It is found in standardized tests of all kinds, from the SAT and PSAT for high school students to graduate school selection exams to certification exams for the professions. It's used informally in school and business. It will be featured in this book as well.

If you can write a good multiple-choice test, you can probably do any of the other types without having problems. This is true because the basic principles and construction are the same. What you must consider for one type of test, you must also consider for another, whether you supply answers or not.

Format. Detail about the format of multiple-choice items will not be provided at this point. You have seen thousands of them, so you know what they look like. They have a stem that presents the problem to be solved or asks a question. It's followed by (typically) three to five alternatives from which respondents choose the answer.

1. What provides the best analogy for a multiple-choice item?
    a. The menu in a fast-food restaurant.
    b. The keyboard for a typewriter.
    c. A grocery list.
    d. A congressional debate.
    e. A child's board game.

Items that provide responses can be written in many ways, but the basic pieces remain the same. They can be written or oral. They can be pages long or as brief as the one above. They can use words, phrases, paragraphs, numbers or other symbols, maps, graphs, signs, photographs, or line drawings as alternatives. The flexibility of the format is a major benefit of the item type.

The most common variation is the matching item. The example below shows how knowledge of nine facts can be sampled using one set of item directions and only four possible responses.

Directions: select the response from Column B that most accurately answers each question in Column A. Place the number of your choice in the space provided. You may use a response as many times you wish.

__ a. Who was the first general to become president of the United States?

__ b. What president signed the Emancipation Proclamation?

__ c. What president was a surveyor before becoming president?

__ d. What president was defeated when he ran for governor?

__ e. What president made the United States protector of the Western Hemisphere?

__ f. What president was in office during the Spanish-American War?

__ g. What president was in office during a worldwide depression?

__ h. What president was noted as an orator?

__ i. What president set a precedent by serving only two terms of office?

1. Washington.
2. Lincoln.
3. T. Roosevelt.
4. F. Roosevelt.

The test is Level One Cognitive, a good illustration of a matching item.

Drawbacks. The major drawback of selection items is that respondents don't have to remember the answer to respond. They select by recognizing the best answer and choosing it. Most respondents do go into the search-and-retrieve mode to answer, but not all. This is especially true if the test is poorly constructed. People can analyze the way the items are presented and respond according to the results of their analysis. People who are test-wise can pass such a test without being able to use the knowledge being tested in any other context. Most other drawbacks for this kind of item originate with test makers. Either they don't know such a test can be used for Levels Two and Three or they don't have the skills to produce one.

As I said before, there is much more to say about selection items, particularly multiple-choice. You will find references and specific guidance in the chapters that remain.

Summary

This chapter has provided an overview of the kinds of tests used today and of some of their characteristics. There are four basic categories:

1. Diagnostic tests.
2. Tests of values or opinions.
3. Tests of attitudes or preferences.
4. Tests of skill levels.

Of these, tests of skill levels are of the most concern to most test users and makers. They come in two general types: (1) supply-type tests, for which the respondents supply the answers, and (2) choice tests, for which the respondents choose the best answer from those provided by the test maker.

Supply items come in three basic styles: essay, short answer, and fill-in. *Essay* items provide opportunities to answer comprehensively and in some detail. They are flexible and test well at Level Three. Unfortunately, they are time consuming and very difficult to score consistently or fairly. *Short-answer* items provide some of the advantages of essay and can sample a broader range of content. They can be used to test almost any application, but they must have good instructions. They are difficult to score, although not as difficult as essay tests. They usually do *not* test well at Level Three. *Fill-in* items are poor measures if they take the form of incomplete statements. In the form of simple questions, though, they are excellent measures at Level One. They are much easier to score and can sample a large amount of content.

Choice tests are efficient and effective for several reasons. They will be discussed in detail later in this book. Next, it makes sense to talk about what you might intend to do with the tests you develop. In essence, tests are used to measure human psychological characteristics—usually knowledge or skills. Chapter Three is about measurement and what that concept implies for testing.

MEASUREMENT

M any people visualize a ruler or a tape measure when they think about measurement. Or perhaps they think about weighing something, using a meter to measure electric current or a cup to measure flour. Musicians think of a short interval in a piece of music. An attorney or politician may think of an ordinance or law.

Webster (1987) defines *measurement* in several ways, one of which is particularly pertinent here: "an estimate of what is to be expected." The term implies testing in some fashion. An ordinance or a law is a measure in that it sets a standard for compliance. The test of a law is the debate between lawyers in a court case.

Consider the following quote: "It was a measure of their ability to justify their preferences." The "measure" in this instance is a decision-making process—a test of some people's faith in themselves. Consider another use of the term: "Play the third measure after B in the coda." Here, when the musicians play the "measure," they will test not only their ability to interpret the measure itself, but the style, beat, and meaning of the composition. When electricians use meters to "measure" voltage, they are testing to see if the voltage is what they expect it to be. When a carpenter uses a tape "measure" to find the length of a board, he or she is testing to see if it is long enough or too long. In each case, measurement can be interpreted as a test. You might think this is stretching the point; nonetheless, it is such an important point that this chapter is devoted to it and its implications for testing.

Measured Results

measured results Results that can be reported as concrete quantitative data.

The word *measure* connotes many things. In this book it's a synonym for *test* used as a verb. A test is a measurement instrument; used as a verb, to test means to measure. It really doesn't mean anything else. Tests are measures or, if you prefer, measurement instruments.

Measuring implies discovery. You and I measure people or things to find out something. Maybe we want to know how long a board is, how deep a well is, or how much voltage an outlet delivers. Maybe we want to know if a worker can do a job or whether a colleague values his or her work. Maybe we simply want to know if a learner gained the skills he or she set out to learn. Whatever we want to know, measurement provides a means of discovery, a way to investigate, a test.

The process of discovery has been examined and explained by experts. John Dewey, for example, promoted it as the proper way to educate children. He developed the so-called *discovery method* of teaching (Dewey, 1938). He and others felt that discovery was a natural and efficient way for people to learn. Inherent to the discovery process is the idea of investigation. People discover by investigating. Arthur Conan Doyle had Sherlock Holmes tell us that investigation is the process of eliminating all the solutions to a problem until only one is left, plausible or not. Investigation is a process used to discover (or uncover) truth.

It is instructive to review Dewey's thinking about discovery. He viewed it as an example of reflective thinking: people perceive a problem, define it to the best of their abilities, select a set of plausible solutions, review the solutions to find the most promising one, and put the solution selected to the test (find out if it works). If the selected solution proves itself, the person has discovered something. If not, the process is repeated with another possible solution. Sounds familiar doesn't it? The general public was caught up in an enthusiasm for Dewey's methods during the 1930s and 1940s. Reflective thinking and the discovery method are part of that legacy.

Dewey made discovery sound a bit mechanical. Perhaps he was correct. Our goal isn't to validate his process, but to observe its nature. He, in effect, suggested a series of tests the results of which will determine the adequacy of suggested solutions to a problem.

Dewey also implied that each test is the process of measuring the effectiveness of a selected solution against predetermined criteria to determine whether the solution is adequate. Recent innovations such as the "go/no-go" decision and the "if-then" statement are consistent with Dewey's process. Again the underlying justification is a test.

Remember that the tests discussed in this book are psychological tests. They test human beings' ability to perform in any of the three domains (or all three at once). Dewey's methods can be seen in the same context. He wasn't interested in discovering whether an automobile performed as it was designed to perform. Even though his process can work for testing automobiles, his purpose was to provide insight into how human beings learn and, consequently, how that learning should be sampled. That is also my concern.

Sampling the Skills of an Individual

To sample, in this context, means to examine chunks of respondents' repertoires, instead of trying to examine the whole thing. Measuring human skills and abilities depends on sampling, because people are too complex for any test to measure accurately their total capability in even the most rudimentary skills. The best test ever made (if there were such a thing) could only provide a sample of the skills of respondents.

Suppose, for example, you want to test a group's ability to lift weights. You invite them to a place where there are machines specifically designed for the purpose. You make sure they are well rested, have eaten properly, and know the nature of the test. You ask them to lift weights until a limit is reached (they cannot lift any more). How sure will you be that they have truly demonstrated their ability to lift weights?

Try another example. An English teacher selects twenty statements of varying complexity. Students are asked to find and mark the subjects and predicates in each of the sentences. All of the students find all of the subjects and predicates in the twenty statements. Given these results, how sure can the teacher be that all of the students will be able to identify the subject and predicate for any other statement?

Here's a third example. A supervisor asks employees to fill out a time sheet. They all do it correctly. How sure will the supervisor be that all of them will do it correctly in the future?

> **dependable**
> Trustworthy; reliable.
>
> **significant**
> Of or pertaining to an observed departure from a hypothesis too large to be reasonably attributed to chance.

In every case your answer to these questions was probably something like, "Pretty sure, but not completely sure." Why wouldn't the three people be completely sure? Simply because they are testing people and because people are too complex and too variable to categorize absolutely. Every measure of human potential or skill yields an estimate. *No matter how thorough we are, our efforts always provide samples rather than totally complete results.*

Test makers must fall back on terms like *dependable* or *significant* to describe results. It's OK to do as long as you take steps to ensure that the sample you have is a good one.

The term *sampling* is also used to describe how to represent a population through a small group. I will discuss mechanisms for sampling populations in Chapter Four. At the moment, the emphasis is on sampling the abilities of an individual.

Measurement

Measurement is what happens when a test does what it is supposed to do—when it is valid. Measurement is the intent of testing. A test with any other purpose is *not* a test. It's something else. Some teachers try to get students to think a specific way by giving them a test. This is not a test. It's a teaching tactic. It just smells like a test. Managers sometimes impress their people with the importance of a process (or policy) by giving them a test on it. That's not a test. It's a threat.

Perhaps the teacher and manager would protest that they are trying to measure. That may be so, but because having other purposes blocks measurement, the tests they give are not really tests. Remember that the purpose of a test is to *measure.*

James McCampbell (1983) is an advocate of "measured results." He works to examine and refine the concept and popularize it. His motivation comes from the idea that most people who develop or use tests don't really understand that useful results are the important part. That bears repeating. *Results are the important part.* McCampbell would quickly add, "If they aren't measured, they aren't very useful."

Examples are easy to find of "tests" given for the wrong reasons. Suppose you attend a seminar purported to give you better management skills. And suppose, when it's over, the instructors ask you to fill out the customary "smiles test." They give you an instrument with about twenty items, on which you rate the seminar by how you felt about it. You respond to questions, such as, "Was the instructor cordial?" "How easy was it to see the transparencies?" and so forth. Now, how useful will the results from that test be?

Smiles tests are good for sampling opinions and establishing acceptance, but they don't tell us much about what people learned or how well they learned. If those are the results we're most interested in, and they usually are, a smiles test won't measure them.

In a moment I'll talk about how to measure results. First, though, a point about attitude. When I was in high school, the world was being introduced to the computer. Remember Univac? It was constructed from electronic hardware available at the time using all the technology of the day. There were some who said it was the epitome of what could be achieved. The computer contained thousands of vacuum tubes and miles of wire. It was cooled by hundreds of gallons of water.

It required a lot of space, a whole building. It was huge. Today, I own a little hand-held calculator that can outperform the first Univac. Why is that possible? There's no secret about it. Some people felt Univac could be improved. So they did it.

Not long ago many politicians and diplomats had resigned themselves to a world forever split, to a cold war that would last for centuries. Today the cold war is history. The problems of today will be resolved. People are already working on them.

It's easy to think about these wonderful discoveries and the progress science has made and to believe that testing can be perfected also. But, like actually building a new computer or a handheld calculator, the doing part is not always easy. Possible, yes. You can measure anything, but perfecting the test to do it can be a chore.

Some tests are fairly simple to develop. A performance test of physical skills usually is. To sample someone's ability to peel a potato, for example, you simply hand respondents a spud and a peeler and have them try it.

Even though the skill may be complex and demanding, testing it can be fairly simple. For example, each year hundreds of young men and women elect to become professional golfers. To qualify for the professional tours, they are tested by the PGA or LPGA. The tests are simple. They are asked to play golf and score within a certain range. Doing it, though, is very difficult. Only a handful make it every year.

Testing recall, Level One Cognitive, is also usually simple. The test maker simply asks respondents to remember something. Again, coming up with the response may not be so easy. When I was in the fifth grade, I was asked to repeat Lincoln's Gettysburg Address. Asking me to do it was easy. Doing it was something else.

But what about Levels Two and Three? What about the affective domain? What about love? How does one measure that? It's ridiculous. How could anyone even suggest measuring such a thing as love? It's impossible! Well, if you believe that it's impossible, it probably is. But what if you think it can be done? From the precedents above, from the evidence of all human history, the thing is possible, do-able.

Suppose we accept the definition of love as "to subsume one's personality completely in awe of another." How can you measure that? Look at it. What are the critical attributes of the statement? For the sake of this discussion, there are two: a lover must be able to subsume and a lover must have awe of another.

How can you measure someone's ability to subsume his or her personality? *Subsume* means "to include or place within something larger or more comprehensive" (Webster, 1987). You might give respondents an inventory in which they are to choose between alternatives that are either egocentric or other-oriented. Instruments can be contrived. This essay question might be an example:

Assume you and your best love are exploring the desert in the summer. Your jeep breaks down in a lonely spot seventy miles from help. Although both of you are physically OK, the prospect of hiking out is not pleasant.

You have a small tent, a half gallon of water in a half-gallon glass jug, concentrated rations for three days, a small AM/FM receiver with extra batteries, a ground cloth, two hundred feet of nylon cord, two hunting knives, an axe, extra socks and underwear, a complete change of clothing for each person, soap, razor, towels, broad-brimmed hats, sunblock lotion, matches, a powerful (five-cell) flashlight with extra batteries, a gasoline lantern, a small stove, one gallon of fuel for lantern and stove, plastic garbage bags, blankets, a small-caliber rifle with fifty rounds of ammunition, spare boots, and a six-pack of beer on ice in a cooler.

In discussing the situation, you and your love come to the conclusion that there is a 50–50 chance that the jeep will be spotted in the next three days. You decide one person should stay with the jeep and hope for rescue and the other should hike out to find help.

Make two decisions. (1) Decide who will stay with the jeep. (2) Go through the list of supplies and decide what the hiker will carry on the trek. Describe your reasoning for each decision.

There are other tests that could deal with a person's ability to subsume, but the problem presented by this scenario should serve to sample relevant awareness. The point is that such a thing *can* be sampled. How you measure something depends on how you define it.

So until someone proves differently, I will continue to believe I can measure anything. If I can, you can. So there you have it. Now all you have to do is do it.

Results

What are results? Dumb question? Not really. We assume if we ask a question, we will receive an answer, a result. There are times when it doesn't happen, but usually it does. The problem is knowing if what you receive is what you requested. What is a result? How do you know one when you see one? More specifically, what are test results?

> **result**
> A response that conforms in some way to the test maker's expectation of performance.

For the purposes of this discussion a *result is a response that conforms in some way to the test maker's expectation of performance.* The performance expectations should be specified somewhere, but they may be inferred.

However they are expressed, there must be performances. When my teacher asked me to recite Lincoln's famous speech, she had a specific performance in mind. My recitation had to conform to it.

"Because of discrimination, blacks in America have more difficulty making a living or establishing themselves as viable members of society." This statement infers that the troubles of many black Americans are a result of discrimination. Is discrimination a performance? Certainly. The lower standard of living for blacks as a group is considered a result of that performance (by the statement's author). Could the statement be tested? Yes.

I've used this example deliberately to emphasize a point. Results are neutral. I believe racism is evil, but my belief doesn't affect the results. They stay the same; they are not good or bad. They simply exist. I could make them seem to support my feelings, but that would not be right. Results exist. For the test maker, that is all that can be said. Evaluation, judging the worth of results, is not part of testing. More about evaluation will be covered in Chapter Twelve. For now, think of obtaining results as the proper function of measurement.

I repeat: *obtaining results is the proper function of measurement.* Nothing else is. You measure to get results. You should not attempt to promote discipline, provide practice, or achieve any end other than measurement through testing. Further, results should reflect respondents' skill. Some test makers go to great lengths to demonstrate their own skills as test makers (or content experts). The answers to such a test aren't results in the spirit of this discussion.

Non-Results

> **non-results**
> Responses to a test that do not conform to the performance the test maker is trying to measure.

Unusable results are non-results. These usually occur when the responses to a test don't conform to the performance the test maker is trying to measure. Suppose you wish to know how well a swimmer can swim. You position respondents at the end of a pool and prepare to time their performance. Then one of them defies you and leisurely paddles toward the end of the pool. Because the swimmer is *not* performing in the spirit of the test, his or her attempt doesn't really count. It's a non-result. It should not be classed with results from the other swimmers who tried to do their best.

Non-results can mess up the works. Considering them beside legitimate results invalidates the legitimate results. Let's look at some more examples of non-results. Ofiesch (1972) said at least 10 percent of the people who show up for a training session aren't qualified to undertake the training. They either don't have the prerequisites or are unable (because of personal problems or other reasons) to acquire the skills intended. Sometimes the percentage is larger. Sometimes administrators and instructors are able to reduce it. Such people do, however, show up. They produce non-results.

Consider a college student who celebrates heavily the night before a big test. No matter what his or her score on the test is, it's probably not as accurate as it should be. Therefore, he or she has produced a non-result. Think about it. Professors often accept such scores. They seem to feel that if students are stupid enough to befuddle their minds with alcohol before a big test they deserve whatever they get. That may be true. But the fact remains that the score is *not* a valid reflection of the student's ability to perform. It's a non-result.

Now consider another favorite of many college professors, the pop quiz. A pop quiz is used to see if students are keeping up with their studies. It's a surprise for the learners. (Not to be confused with a "spot quiz," which is announced beforehand.) Because learners were not allowed to prepare, the results will be tainted by apprehension (in some cases, panic). Strong emotions cloud performance. Some students have learning styles, such as diligence, they can't employ to prepare. Ergo, the students produce non-results.

Finally, consider the nature of the test. Most of us would not try to measure swimming skills with a multiple-choice test. To do so would be to sample the wrong skill set. Too often our tests ask for the wrong thing. When I was a wrestling official in Washington state, the qualifying exam was two hundred true/false questions. At best, it sampled our ability to apply the results of the sport. It could not reflect our ability to officiate.

Results Are Consequential

Measurement is meaningless without something consequential to measure. The word *consequential* is important. Have you seen a child with a new ruler? He or she will wander around a room measuring everything. A tablet is almost nine inches wide. The door is about three feet wide, depending on where the thumb was put to keep the mark while the ruler was moved.

The child soon tires of the game. Who cares if the door is thirty-two or thirty-six inches? The mover cares. To someone trying to take a couch through that door, its width is important, but, to the child, it's just a number. The ruler soon becomes something other than a measuring device, a bridge perhaps or a missile launcher.

Some results are consequential; some are trivial. Suppose you are asked to take a ten-item true/false quiz. It could be on any topic. The chance of your scoring five correctly is a given. You could do so by randomly selecting true or false. Your chance of doing 50 percent better or 50 percent worse is 50–50. So unless you score less than 2 or more than 8, your result is trivial, inconsequential.

Before continuing, let's look at some other terms that are often confused with results. Consider the term *outcomes*. You can visualize the difference if you ask the question, "What are the outcomes of the test?" Outcomes *include* results and a lot of other things. If learners acquire a distaste for tests, that is an outcome.

Another important term is *score*. Scores are contrived representations of results. Test makers or administrators find some way to express the results of a test with symbols. Usually scores are an expression of the ratio between the number of *right* answers and *wrong* answers. Because they have (often arbitrarily) assigned functions, scores have limited value as representatives of results. Such representations will be covered at some length in Chapter Seven.

Some people believe measurement always results in numbers. They expect so many inches of rain, so many miles per hour, so many ideas, and so forth. This is unfortunate in many cases. Sometimes a descriptive measure is more informative than numbers. Suppose the wind is blowing at twenty-seven miles per hour. Most people don't really know whether that's bad or good. However, if they hear that the wind is blowing too hard to fly a kite, they'll have a better idea of its force.

The point is that results can come in a variety of forms. A good test develops results in all three domains. Most tests emphasize results in the cognitive domain, but there are times when the affective or psychomotor domains are important too. The test maker should be conscious of this and should have a plan that is fair and makes sense to the respondents.

Let's explore an example. Suppose you have developed a workshop to teach bank tellers to encourage customers to take advantage of a variety of bank services. The overall goal of the instruction is to increase sales of CDs, specialized savings accounts, and IRAs without loss of revenue from checking. Your workshop will end with a performance test of skills in selling bank services. What should the results of that test depict? What will you measure?

The nature of the question dictates the nature of the result. If you know the result you want, it is easier to ask appropriate questions. Let's look at examples of some of the types of measuring instruments and the kinds of results you would expect them to generate.

Kinds of Results

Continua

Results can be recorded or requested from a defined continuum. Many inventories use continua. You've probably seen several yourself; you may have developed one or two. The basic idea is to define a response area that has two extremes: hot and cold, for example. You would draw a line, label one end "hot" and the other "cold," and ask respondents to pick a location along the line that represents how they feel about a temperature or a temperature range.

1. How warm is your town? Mark the line in the place you think best represents the temperature range in your city.

Hotter than Tucson, Arizona   Colder than Bangor, Maine
_____

This continuum is a pretty poor measuring device because it's not very specific. Most answers would be like, "Closer to Tucson than Bangor." It's difficult to decide very precisely what that means. What is required here is *rigor.*

Rigor, according to Webster (1987), is "the quality of being unyielding or inflexible." The key is what is meant by "unyielding or inflexible." The continuum above is *flexible.* A response along it has little literal meaning because there are only two limits with nothing in between.

> **rigor**
> Connotes an attempt to obtain as much precision or meticulousness as possible.

It's difficult for some people to think of rigor in terms of imprecise measures, but the quality of the measurement depends on the amount of rigor used. The continuum line becomes more rigorous if you label the positions between the two extremes, for example:

Tucson	Tulsa	Pittsburgh	Chicago	Bangor

Still there are problems. In effect, the labels provide the same kind of measurement as before, except there are more possibilities. Now a city might be "warmer than Pittsburgh but cooler than Tulsa." The scale is more rigorous, but still not rigorous enough to make direct comparisons. The obvious solution is to provide the scale with numbers.

Tucson	Tulsa	Pittsburgh	Chicago	Bangor
1	2	3	4	5

Now a respondent can simply mark a place on the line about a third of the way between 2 and 3, indicating $2\frac{1}{3}$. This is more rigorous because, once a decision is made, an evaluator can treat it as if it were the most profound of realities and subject it to statistical treatments and other devices for comparisons and other uses. Although for the respondent there is virtually an infinity of possible choices, once a choice has been made, it becomes set. It is unyielding, inflexible. This is true even though the intervals are not actually equal. A casual observer would immediately note that Pittsburgh and Chicago are probably much closer together in terms of temperature than Tulsa and Pittsburgh, yet the interval is the same. In this particular example that is OK (for now) because respondents are asked to characterize their towns' temperatures, rather than to define them precisely.

Rigor is the term used here instead of *precision* for a very important reason. Although I might say the new designations for temperatures have more rigor than before, I would be hard-pressed to say they are more precise. If you wanted to be precise about temperature, you would probably ask people what the mean temperature is for their city. You would expect the answer in degrees (probably Fahrenheit in the United States). Suppose the person said, "42 degrees." That may still not be precise enough. You may want an answer such as "41.673 degrees."

Then you could definitely say the person's city is colder or warmer than Tucson. Or is it? The problem is that you are still asking for a person's opinion. Comparing estimated mean temperatures won't provide the answer. Think about a man who washes windows at night in Flagstaff, Arizona. Flagstaff is near the desert and has an altitude above five thousand feet. The temperature often drops below 40 degrees Fahrenheit in August. That window washer would not call Flagstaff a warm place, but his girlfriend, who works on a highway construction gang during the day, would.

The point is, when a question requires a qualitative answer, precision often doesn't help much. Rigor does. Precision can, in fact, be misleading. Suppose, for instance, the average rainfall in your geographic area is 24.7 inches per annum. That is more than two feet of rain. For some purposes, it would make more sense to say your area receives enough rain for farmers to grow corn and soybeans without recourse to irrigation.

Test makers can apply rigor to characterizations, even when precision isn't possible. Questions such as "How much love is enough?" or "When is it safe to trust another person?" yield results, although the results can't be precise. Still, we can develop a test using those questions. We can construct it in such a way that the results will be measured. We can apply rigor—and we should.

Let's continue with the example about temperatures and how they're experienced by different people in Flagstaff. Suppose we asked a sample of about one hundred Flagstaff residents to respond to this question:

1. How would you rate the temperature in Flagstaff during the month of August?

Hot	Warm	Temperate	Cool	Cold
1	2	3	4	5

Not everyone will provide the same answer. The window washer and his friend will probably disagree. The results of the survey will not be precise, but they can have rigor.

Rigor is achieved through thorough testing and intelligent treatment of the results. Thoroughness in testing is accomplished through sampling and other techniques. Treatments such as Analysis of Variance can provide valuable insights. These ideas are explored in depth in Chapter Seven.

Likert Scale

There are two ways to present scales like the one above, with an even number of choices or an odd number. When there is an even number, the respondent is forced to take a position favoring one extreme or the other, as in this example:

1. What is your opinion of the value of wool as a fiber for use in rugs?

Very Good	Good	Poor	Very Poor
1	2	3	4

When the number of choices is odd, respondents don't have to favor one extreme or the other.

1. What is your opinion of the value of wool as a fiber for use in rugs?

Very Good	Good	No Opinion	Poor	Very Poor
1	2	3	4	5

Even though either method provides rigor, the second is much more sensitive to respondents than the first.

Likert (Westgaard, 1986a) was one of the first to note the difference for respondents and advocate using an odd number of alternatives. He pointed out three distinct advantages:

1. Respondents aren't forced to take a position when they don't want to.
2. The test items aren't dichotomous.
3. The test maker can more easily assume an objective stance.

Forced Positions. An even number of alternatives forces respondents to take a position whether they want to or not. Look at this item.

1. What is your opinion of the work of our current mayor?

Very Good	Good	No Opinion	Poor	Very Poor
1	2	3	4	5

Suppose the item writer had not included "No Opinion." Respondents would be forced either to support the mayor or to reject him or her. What if they liked some things the mayor did and disliked others? What if they didn't have an opinion? In my opinion, forcing them to take a stand would invalidate the survey. But this would be relatively innocent and aboveboard. Look at the next item.

2. The governor has recently begun to support MADD, Mothers Against Drunk Drivers. How do you feel about this action?
   a. It's a very good idea. Drunks shouldn't be allowed on the road, period.
   b. It's a good idea. People under the influence can be dangerous while driving.
   c. It's a poor idea. The governor should not support any special-interest group.
   d. It's a very poor idea. If MADD is successful, people will lose fundamental rights.

By supplying reasons within the scale the item writer has forced respondents to go one way or another and also to endorse an accompanying descriptor. The only way to avoid being labeled is to refuse to answer the question. If the item writer had simply added a response that said something like, "I don't have enough information to form an opinion," both of these difficulties would have been avoided.

There is reason to believe that test makers who use an even number of responses are trying to get people to commit to an idea or position. Tests are not the proper medium for this sort of thing.

Dichotomy. Items with an even number of choices on a scale tend to be dichotomous. Either you are or you aren't. Look at any of the examples above with an even number of alternatives. They can all be replaced with true/false items. One could even say they are true/false items disguised to look like something else. That's deceptive. In my mind it's neither good nor fair.

Now consider items that use a Likert Scale. They cannot be reduced to true/false. The minimum number of alternatives is three: yes, no opinion, and no. The basic problems of dichotomous items are avoided. These problems are discussed in greater detail in Chapter Eleven.

Objectivity. The Likert Scale allows the test maker to be objective about the results of the test. Whether respondents take a stance or not is up to them. The test writer has no direct influence over the decision process and can, therefore, maintain a healthy distance from the results. This is true even when the test maker has a well-defined and articulated bias about the content. Of course, such a person must take care not to let his or her bias creep into the stems (or alternatives), but it's much easier to prevent this with a Likert Scale.

Before we leave the discussion of Likert Scales, there is another aspect to keep in mind. When you provide a central position on a scale, respondents may choose it. They probably won't, but they may. The results will reflect choices you do not expect. Consider the following example:

3. What major political party do you tend to support most often at the polls?
   a. Democratic.
   b. Republican.
   c. Neither.

In this case, some respondents will choose alternative c, even though they were asked to choose a major political party. Perhaps a majority will. Those results could be valuable information that would be lost if alternative c were not offered. The results obtained through the Likert Scale are often more valid because they offer respondents a fuller range of choices. The decision matrix is expanded and more information can be accessed. In most cases, the results are a better reflection of the attitudes being sampled.

Now let's look at a different sort of results, the kind you might record on a checklist.

Checklists

A checklist is a way to document results. It's usually a paper-and-pencil form with steps recorded on it. One person uses a checklist to record whether or not another has completed a series of steps or tasks. It is simple, straightforward, and very efficient.

The checklist is an old dependable partner for a lot of us. It can be used for many things, one of the most common being to record the results of a performance test of psychomotor skills. Suppose you want to discover whether new employees can perform a task. You might ask them to do it while you document whether the task was done well and completely with some sort of checklist.

Checklists vary in complexity from a simple two-step or three-step process to one that may contain hundreds of steps. The checklist used to determine whether underground miners have their equipment before going on shift only has three or four entries (important though they are). The one used to prepare for the liftoff of a space shuttle has thousands and takes days to complete.

The format will vary. Some checklists are highly structured like this one.

Worker _____			
Gang _____			
Shift _____	Date _____		
Item	Cor.[a]	Prep.[b]	Auth.[c]
Light and battery Coverall Hard hat Boots Gloves Tool kit			

[a] Whether the items fit, are in good repair, and are clean.
[b] Whether the worker is prepared for the job to be done.
[c] Whether the equipment is authorized for this job.

The checklist above is an example of a measure of preparedness. Rigor is attained through use. The third column in the checklist has more room for responses because the supervisor has to initial it, which tends to encourage care on the part of the supervisor. If a worker is injured and equipment or clothing is found to be a contributor to the injury, the company will know who authorized it.

Checklists normally have three parts:

• A heading specifying the nature and use of the checklist.
• The body, the part that has the items to check.
• Space for someone to indicate acceptance or rejection of each item.

Checklists may have other elements such as space for the date, instructions for use, signature lines, or a provision for a special requirement such as a caveat to discourage litigation. Following is a sample checklist meant to qualify divers for a dive:

1. I have been informed of the dangers of diving, including marine life, currents, and other potential life-threatening phenomena.

2. I certify that my equipment is sound and has been checked. It is in good working order.

3. I am in good health and have no problems, health or otherwise, that would place me or other divers in danger.

4. If, for any reason other than personal carelessness on the part of others, I am injured, I will hold *Wonderful Dives, Inc.,* completely harmless.

Signed _____

Date _____

This checklist has neither identification nor a place for someone to check each item, but it is still a checklist. Those who might use it would read each item, respond to it in some way, and consider its importance before signing and dating the document.

As you may have noticed, the separate elements of a checklist perform the same function (more or less) as items on a test. In effect each respondent is being asked whether each item is true or not. Normally, a checklist is dichotomous (has two choices per item); however, they can have more, although instruments with more than two appropriate responses are often not considered checklists. The drawbacks of dichotomous items on tests are not as apparent for checklists. In fact, a checklist that is *not* dichotomous often is not as definitive or useful as one that is. This is because most checklists test for the presence or the absence of an item or a process. The nature of the inquiry is dichotomous; therefore, the instrument (checklist) should be dichotomous, too.

Checklists are very important, particularly in the development of job aids and performance documentation. Unfortunately, there is neither space nor mandate to explore them further in this book. Further information about them is available in Harless (1983).

Multiple-Choice Results

> **internally referenced**
> Related directly to the stem of the item.

The alternatives to a multiple-choice or matching item often describe a scale or continuum, but that is *not* a requirement. They can represent anything as long as they conform to the standards for good items discussed in Chapters Two and Eight. They do, however, have to be *internally referenced*, that is, related directly to the stem of the item. Internal referencing means, simply, that the alternatives are anticipated by the stem. The stem tells respondents what to expect in the alternatives. Of course, the alternatives may relate to more than one item or to an entire test, but they are only required to relate directly to the stem of the item in which they are found.

This is an important attribute of any multiple-choice item. Unless the alternatives make sense, they should not be allowed. The next example shows internal referencing as it should be.

1. What food does *not* represent the same basic food group as the others?
   a. Green peas.
   b. Peanuts.
   c. Pinto beans.
   d. Soybeans.
   e. Wheat germ.

Now look at this rendition of the same item:

1. What food does *not* represent the same basic food group as the others?
   a. Peanuts.
   b. Hair.
   c. Pintos.
   d. Soy.
   e. Whiskey.

Two of the alternatives are not foods (hair and whiskey) and one (pintos) could as easily be a horse as a bean. The key to the appropriateness of the alternatives is found in the stem. The stem says the alternatives will be foods. Therefore, they should be foods. Otherwise, internal referencing is suspect. Internal referencing can be invalidated in three ways.

1. *Poor setup.* The item writer can fail to include elements in the stem that anticipate the answers.
2. *Poor communication.* Alternatives may inadvertently deviate from respondent expectations.
3. *Tricks.* Alternatives can be designed to be misleading or inappropriate.

Poor Setup. In writing the item, the item writer sets the respondents up to answer. The good writer will do this for every item, but there is a tendency among writers to make the stem either too complex or too simple. Results, therefore, don't reflect respondent skills as well as they should. Here are examples of each:

1. From the following historic eras in American history, identify the one that provides the most eloquent parallel with the events of the period from 1970 to 1980.
   a. The populist movement of the 1900s.
   b. The economic instability of the pre-Hamiltonian era.
   c. The labor unrest of the 1880s.
   d. The expansionist movement at the turn of the twentieth century.
   e. The beginning of the Industrial Revolution in America.
2. What is best?
   a. Formic acid followed by cold water.
   b. Acetic acid with a light abrasive.
   c. Ammonia with a mild detergent.
   d. Aqua regia applied sparingly.
   e. Sodium bicarbonate followed by vinegar.

   In either case, the item can be made much more friendly with a simple edit. You may wonder why the items weren't written better in the first place. The easiest answer to that question is the mind of the item writer. All of us are used to writing in a style we have evolved over years. Your writing style tends to dictate your choice of words and patterns in everything you write, even test items.

   The items above could be rewritten in the following ways:

1. What American historical era most closely parallels the events from 1970 to 1980?
   a. The economic instability of the pre-Hamiltonian era.
   b. The expansionist movement at the turn of the twentieth century.
   c. The labor unrest of the 1880s.
   d. The populist movement of the 1900s.
   e. The beginning of the Industrial Revolution in America.
2. What is recommended to clean excess grout after laying ceramic tile?
   a. Formic acid followed by cold water.
   b. Acetic acid with a light abrasive.
   c. Ammonia with a mild detergent.
   d. Aqua regia applied sparingly.
   e. Sodium bicarbonate followed by vinegar.

Poor Communication and Alternatives That Deviate from the Expected. There are examples of poor communication and deviations on almost every test, including standardized exams such as the SAT or GRE. Many times, deviations are done on purpose, but usually not. It normally happens when the item writer fails to review each item from the respondents' point of view. Either deviations seem OK and therefore don't arouse suspicion or they're put in deliberately (like jokes). Sometimes they are invented by a frustrated item writer who can't think of more appropriate alternatives.

Most deviations are fairly innocent. They don't upset the respondents and tend to test fairly well, but they can be pretty ugly. Check these:

1. What writing convention helps the reader understand the flow of a narrative?
   a. Circumlocution.
   b. Indentation.
   c. Polymerization.
   d. Canonization.
   e. Characterization.

Pretty funny, eh? Not to the person trying to figure out what all those $10 words mean.

2. What communication tactic is most valuable for a writer of technical manuals?
   a. Providing a fog level (readability) at or below that of the reader.
   b. Composing the page so the reader's attention is directed to key elements.
   c. Relating key elements to events in the reader's own experience.
   d. Inserting anchors to *hook* readers and keep their attention.
   e. Making sure illustrations and figures are easy for the reader to find.

On the surface this one seems OK. But hold on! Alternative b is a graphics concern, c is a device employed in public speaking, and d is used in therapy sessions. The item writer has done the respondents in. Because all of the alternatives seem somewhat appropriate, respondents are likely to continue to associate them with writing skills in years to come. The item writer has made them seem legitimate by using a form of the word *reader* in each one.

3. How was James Fenimore Cooper's writing style described by his contemporary Samuel Clemens (Twain, 1938)?
   a. "Cooper is a paragon of sweet virtuosity."
   b. "A foulmouthed rendition of European wrongheadedness."
   c. "A clumsy imitation of an educated baboon."
   d. "An elegant forthright example of what's good in contemporary writers."
   e. "Cooper's style is always grand and stately and noble."

Because the stem sets the test taker up to look for a quotation, all of the alternatives must have quotation marks to be plausible. But four of the supposed quotations are fictitious. (The correct answer is e.) The distractors here are supposed to be funny, and perhaps they are. However, the respondent is led to believe that Mark Twain said all those things when he did not. Once again the test taker is taken by the test maker.

Tricks, Misleading Statements, or Intentionally Inappropriate Alternatives. Test writers often doll up incorrect responses to tempt respondents into choosing the wrong one, even when they know the correct answer. Test writers may even contrive to make the best answer look wrong. The Twain example could be classified this way. History teachers love this expedient. Consider the next item.

1. On page 238 of your text there is a picture of General George Washington crossing a river. According to the picture, during what season of the year did this take place?
   a. Summer.
   b. Autumn.
   c. Winter.
   d. Spring.
   e. Not enough information.

The correct answer is e. The ice on the river and the snow on the ground could be there during later autumn or early spring. The river isn't frozen over, as it probably would be in the dead of winter. Most respondents will know Washington's attack came during the Christmas holidays so they will probably choose alternative c. The teacher thinks he's clever. I think he's a stinker.

2. What floor covering is appropriate for a heavily used rest room in a metal-processing plant where acid is often spilled?
   a. Ceramic tile.
   b. Paint.
   c. Industrial carpet.
   d. Heavy vinyl.
   e. A or d.

The respondents read through the alternatives until they come to one that is correct, a. They mark it without even reading the rest of the alternatives. Unfortunately, d is also correct. Gotcha!

3. What adjective is most often used as superlative?
   a. Excellent.
   b. Best.
   c. Shiniest.
   d. Most.
   e. All of the above.

In this case, the writer has disqualified the correct answer, e, with the wording of the stem. "All of the above" is always a bad alternative. It demonstrates its incompetence in this item. The point to be made here is that alternative e does not answer the stem. It is not an adjective and it is not singular.

More will be said about the combinational alternatives (as in alternatives 2e and 3e) in Chapter Eight. Between now and then you will see other examples of how they mess items up. The key is to remember that *tests are for respondents*. They give respondents a chance to show off.

Multiple-choice items are the most popular kind of item. A big reason for this is that each item can stand alone because of internal referencing. Items can be stored in an item bank. The test maker can then randomly select items for use in a test. Some teachers and professors have accumulated great numbers of items from which to choose. They keep them in a file and when they come to the point

> **item bank**
> A database containing an assortment of test items dedicated to a particular use.

at which testing that content or skill is appropriate, they simply take a sample from their item bank and administer it. The same technique has been expanded and is commonly used by testing companies to produce unique versions of the same test three or four times per year.

Certification exams rely on this expedient. Each item in an item bank is identified through the content it covers, its level, its domain, and its difficulty. A computer selects items randomly through these conventions. Every administration of the test is equivalent in content, level, and difficulty. But the items used to make it up cannot be predicted, so respondents are presented with a new challenge on each iteration.

As with any kind of item on any kind of test, multiple-choice items generate results. Those results are used by the test evaluator to estimate the skill levels of respondents. If the results represent respondents adequately, the test is considered a good measurement instrument—one that yields useful data.

Much more can be said about measures and about tests as measures. Two excellent sources as starting points are Gilbert's *Human Competence, Engineering Worthy Performance* (1996), which presents cogent arguments to support the ideas presented here, and Shrock and Coscarelli's *Criterion-Referenced Test Development* (1989), which provides a broad discussion of applications.

Summary

In this brief discussion of tests as measures, we have been involved in diverse inquiries. The chapter began with an examination of what a measure is and how that relates to tests and testing.

Testing is imprecise. No one has ever measured the total repertoire of a human being for even the smallest skill set. It cannot happen. Therefore, we are forced to sample those repertoires. The value of our tests depends primarily on our ability to select the best things to sample and to sample them well.

Testing and measurement are synonymous. We do the first to attain the second. A key to success is the pursuit of rigor in our work. Results are what we have in hand when a test is complete to use as we see fit. One would hope to use them constructively for the benefit of the respondents.

To gain a better understanding of what results are and how they can be used constructively, the chapter explored three kinds of measurement instruments and the way the results for each differ. Attitude items that often use scales to present results were described. We saw how checklists, which are usually dichotomous, function. The chapter ended with discussions of multiple-choice items and the kinds of results we can generate when using them.

We can measure anything. Our goal, however, is usually to discover if a respondent is competent—if that person has mastered a skill. This will be discussed in Chapter Four.

MEASURING COMPETENCE: DEFINING PERFORMANCE AND MASTERY

Almost every center of American productivity is feeling an increasing requirement to define and ensure competence. Whether they work for a small church or huge conglomerate, managers want better ways to determine how efficient and effective their people are.

Pressure is building. Schools are under increasing pressure from government and parents to teach more skills, better, in less time. Government agencies are urged by Congress to spend less while delivering more. Manufacturers have to cut profit margins to stay competitive.

It is becoming more apparent every day that the key to success will be more productive people. Technology is doing a lot, but the foundation for productivity will always be people. People run the machines. They negotiate; they sell; they maintain. They make decisions about what must be done and why.

The steel industry provides an interesting example. Not many years ago, the doomsday prophets were predicting the imminent demise of America's steel industry. Today America is producing more and better steel than before. Old plants have been abandoned; many workers have been laid off. However, steel manufacturers are healthy again, basically because they're working more competently than before.

The purpose of this chapter is to give you some basic decision-making tools. Often, requests for tests are poorly thought out or prompted by an external stimulus for a nontesting purpose. The CEO of Company A decides to start performance testing when he hears his chief competitor, Company B, is doing it. That may be sufficient reason for him, but it doesn't give you, who will develop the test(s), much to go on.

Two important questions must be answered before initiating a test-development effort:

- What will the test accomplish?
- Why is that important?

An important theme here is captured in the term *competence*. We will begin with it and return to it often. Performance testing and competence are closely allied, although other terms must also be explored. Among them are *efficiency, effectiveness, quality, mastery,* and *performance criteria*.

This section will also provide another view of performance. You will see how a diagnostic model developed by Brethower (1971) and Rummler (1984) provides insights into performance by organizations or individuals. And you will sample some of the thinking of Tom Gilbert (1974), the originator of performance engineering.

Competence

> **competence**
> The ability to do what should be done efficiently and effectively to the quality standards established.

Consider the term *competent*. What does it mean? A competent person is one who does what should be done efficiently and effectively to the quality standards established. This definition requires us to know what *efficiency* and *effectiveness* mean in this context and how they affect quality. I used the word *requires* because, without such an understanding, you won't be able to develop performance tests well.

A performance test often looks like a norm-based test. It has similar kinds of questions asked in similar ways, and it is scored in similar ways. The basic difference lies in how the test is used. The difference is tied closely to the three terms. Let's consider them in turn.

Efficiency

Common usage has caused most people to think efficiency is associated with economics. It is true to an extent, but an "efficient" operation does more than save money. In fact efficiency is basic to people's productivity. To understand why, think of efficiency as Chester Barnard (1938) did.

Barnard said *efficiency* is the ability of people to do what they are supposed to do. The more productive effort a manager can obtain from his people, the more efficient his operation. The fact that such productivity leads directly to increased return on investment prompts the association of efficiency with financial gain. An operation is efficient if it makes as much money as it was designed to make—or more. That means people produce as much as or more than they were supposed to. Efficiency has to do with how well people do what they are asked to do.

Effectiveness

Similarly, an operation is effective if it can deliver as expected on time, that is, the process does what it is supposed to do. It produces what it's supposed to produce and it does so in the amount of time given by management. Efficiency is tied directly to people, but effectiveness refers to mechanical processes, support systems, and materials. Think of effectiveness as it is used in this sentence: "Plastique is more effective than dynamite because of the properties it has as an explosive."

An effective work group produces results that meet specifications. Suppose a work group develops computer software. The group's work will be considered effective if the software does what it is supposed to do.

To be effective, an operation must be supported by appropriate processes, materials, and equipment. Otherwise, its products could be substandard. Therefore, there is a direct link between effectiveness and profits. An ineffective operation may be profitable, but it will be more profitable if it can become more effective.

Barnard (1938) said that efficiency and effectiveness are the keys to good management. He felt that a manager who could balance them well would succeed in any setting. Perhaps he was being overly confident, but the point remains. In almost any operation, efficiency and effectiveness are important ingredients for success and they apply universally to every aspect of the operation. They certainly apply to testing. Together they ensure the quality of the results of a test.

Quality

> **quality**
> A measure of the extent to which a process or product meets or exceeds the specifications set for it.

Quality involves both completeness and elegance. It is a measure of the extent to which a process or product meets or exceeds the specifications set for it. High quality is close conformity to expectations and requirements. Low quality is present when those expectations and requirements are not met. Of course the person or group that sets the expectations sets the standards.

Top-quality products meet specifications set for them by their producers. To advertise a product as being a high-quality product is to say it met or exceeded the manufacturer's specifications. It infers that the customers' expectations will also be met. This may not be true if the customer doesn't have the same expectations as the manufacturer.

If you are unsure about the term *quality*, pursue it further. Quality is crucially important. Understanding what it is and how different agencies interpret it can be of immense value. For this discussion, it's important to grasp two aspects of quality: (1) high quality is attained through a carefully managed process and (2) quality can and must be measured. Specifications for quality must be developed and validated. Results have to be compared with the standards.

Balancing Efficiency and Effectiveness to Attain High-Quality Products and Processes

Barnard suggested that managers have one basic responsibility: to maintain or increase productivity. He believed that they do so by maintaining a balance between efficiency and effectiveness in pursuit of production goals.

If such a balance is not found, quality will suffer as seen in Figure 4.1. Too much emphasis on efficiency will beget good relations within the work group, but may result in inferior products. Too much emphasis on effectiveness will guarantee good products but may damage the morale and, subsequently, the productivity of the work group.

Consider a man in a rowboat. If he pulls harder on the left oar than he does the right, the boat will turn to the right. If he then lifts the left oar and pulls with the right, the boat will turn to the left. Beginning oarsmen often leave a zigzag wake until they learn to pull evenly with both oars at the same time. When they learn to use their oars well, the boat will go where they wish, along the course they choose, at a speed controlled by them.

If an organization leans too much toward efficiency, it will produce poor quality products, but the people will be well treated and content. An organization that emphasizes effectiveness will produce good products and bad tempers. It will have a good process and unhappy (sloppy or uncaring) workers. Consequently, a productive organization must be both efficient and effective. Yin and yang—it's a bal-

FIGURE 4.1. BALANCE EFFICIENCY AND EFFECTIVENESS.

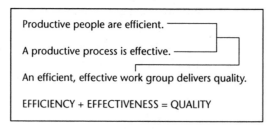

Productive people are efficient.

A productive process is effective.

An efficient, effective work group delivers quality.

EFFICIENCY + EFFECTIVENESS = QUALITY

ancing act. The manager who balances these attributes will probably produce quality products and services.

Such managers are called competent. So are their people. The problem is how we can discover if competence is being developed. How can we use the label *competent* with confidence? The key is in how we measure, in how we test.

Competence Again

The term *competent* implies "able to do." A person who is competent is able to do whatever is being discussed. A competent tax accountant is able to prepare appropriate tax forms and statements. A competent truck driver can drive a truck. Competence subsumes a set of criteria in which quality is assumed. Competent people produce quality.

Competent professionals are able to perform their duties and meet the standards of their professions. A competent doctor can diagnose, prescribe, and treat patients to maintain and promote health. Competent teachers can promote learning so their charges progress from grade to grade in a manner congruent with the standards set for them.

Tom Gilbert (1996) was very concerned that people, especially managers, were more concerned with behavior than they were with accomplishments. In his book *Human Competence* he devoted several pages to the issue. To paraphrase what he said, "It really doesn't matter how someone does something. What matters is whether s/he accomplishes what s/he sets out to accomplish." Use any appropriate process as long as you accomplish the results intended. Of course, you may have concerns about use of resources and so forth, but the basic reason (in Gilbert's mind) for competence is accomplishing what is expected in a reasonable amount of time using the resources you have available. If you can do this, Gilbert says you are competent—able to do it.

The question "Able to do what?" is the most pressing question in the beginning of any effort to certify competence. That brings up the critical concept of mastery.

Mastery

I have studied mastery since I was twenty-eight years old (centuries ago). The concept itself is ancient. There were master builders in ancient Egypt, and there was a felt consensus among Egyptians about what that meant. A *master* then was someone who knew what he or she was doing as well as or better than anyone else. Their definition worked for them, and, for most issues, it continues to work for us today. The problem is being able to tell one when you see one.

> **mastery**
> A level of competence; unquestioned skill.

Mastery, in this context, refers to a preferred level of competence. Mastery implies unquestioned skill. An obvious analogy comes from the trades. A beginner is called an apprentice, someone who has to be coached and taught, but who is familiar with the work. A journeyman is felt to know enough and be skillful enough to be trusted to perform well. A master practitioner knows the whole field with enough depth to operate competently anywhere within it. This doesn't suggest lack of specialization, as some masters will be more competent in some areas than others and vice versa. It does suggest a basic set of skills, a foundation, that all who wish to be called masters must have.

> **exemplar**
> One who is superior at what he or she does.

There is a very important caveat. A master is *not* necessarily an exemplar. Exemplary competence is the domain of those who are superior at what they do—who excel far above the level of simple mastery. They are competent and they have attained mastery, but they are more than that, hopefully much more.

Masters are identified through certification or, more often, through their rise to a place of eminence in their field. Usually a course of study, by itself, isn't felt to be definitive enough. Therefore, academics must pass comprehensive exams, be certified, publish, and establish good reputations. Medical doctors, lawyers, accountants, and other professionals are all certified, but those who are considered the best in their field (exemplary) have done something to mark them as better than almost any others.

Now consider the effect of mastery on a certification process. Assume there is a test of some kind as a basis for certification. The concept, mastery, will affect the test in at least three ways:

1. The test must measure both scope and depth of knowledge and skills.
2. It must do so in a way congruent with the practice of the profession.
3. It must discriminate those who can from those who cannot, and it must do so in a valid reliable way.

A hypothetical example shows how these three conditions apply. Assume that a group of people who do a certain job for a living assemble to be certified. They all take a certification test. They should expect the test to cover the whole job from beginning to end. They should expect the test to test not only their knowledge of the job, but also their ability to apply that knowledge in practical ways and their ability to solve problems associated with the job. If all those who take the test are competent, they should all pass it easily. If some are not competent, they should fail without question.

In the example, there is no indication of the number who pass as compared with the number who fail. This is important. All who are competent should pass.

If 100 percent of the applicants are competent, 100 percent should pass. If 100 percent are unqualified in one way or another, they should all fail.

Although this makes sense, it can be confusing to us because formal education uses a different set of premises. We are used to being compared with others, to having our performance rated in reference to what others have done or are doing. *The premise of mastery is a comparison with standards set to define competence on an individual basis.* A competent practitioner shouldn't have to worry about how others have scored on the test. Every individual is judged according to the same set of criteria. Either they can perform to standard or they can't. There are no conditions or exceptions.

Interesting analogues occur at track meets. The athletes in the field events compete with each other, but they do so by attempting to better a standard. High jumpers, for example, try to jump over a bar. If they are successful, they are said to have mastered the height. The standard in this case is dynamic; it moves up as the jumpers clear each height, but it remains a standard. Either they clear it or they don't. If they do, they have mastered it. If they don't, they have not. An important element of mastery is demonstrated by the jumpers. Some are elegantly graceful. Some are a bit awkward looking. Some jumps look smooth, even effortless. Some are accompanied by a grimace, a yell, or a flop. It doesn't matter what they look, sound, or feel like. All that matters is whether the jumpers go over the bar without knocking it down.

The high jump analogy also gives insight into the difference between competence and mastery. A competent high jumper can jump over the bar. He or she can execute a jump within the rules of the contest. However, he or she may or may not be able to master the height.

A person with a master's degree is said to have mastered the subject matter of an academic field of study. A person who has fifteen years' experience as a bricklayer may be considered a master of his or her craft. Basically, a person is considered a master if he or she can do a task (or know a field) competently.

One of my favorite professors in graduate school once told us he didn't want his daughter to go to biology class to study biology. He wanted her to become a biologist. His point was that anyone who takes an interest in a subject and works with it is a practitioner of that discipline. The question was not whether the daughter was a biologist but whether she was accomplished enough in the content for the purpose at hand, whether she had mastered enough of the discipline to be called one of those at her level.

A critical point is: mastery is relative. Consider the ancient Egyptian master builder. He was probably proficient with only a handful of tools. His work took years (sometimes centuries) to complete. He was dependent on unskilled laborers. A builder today with his skills couldn't make a living in the field. Yet the ancient was a master of his craft. Monuments he built have survived through millennia. He was a master of his trade because he clearly demonstrated his ability to meet or exceed every standard of that time.

No conception of mastery has been able to stand the test of time. A plumber who was considered a master of his or her trade in 1980 is probably out-of-date today. Engineers who graduate today can expect their skills to be obsolete in five years. Certification of teachers or doctors is no longer a once-in-a-lifetime challenge. They must continue to study and work in their respective fields or face having their licenses revoked.

If you have begun to think that mastery and competence are very closely tied, you are on the right track. A master must be competent. It makes sense, doesn't it? Yet many of us try to separate the two. However, you might even consider them different aspects of the same thing. The idea is appealing. We can say, with confidence, that a master must be competent. Otherwise, his or her mastery is a myth. The question is, How competent must a person be to be called a master?

Webster (1987) had trouble defining the term *competence,* but the definition is instructional. Webster says, "requisite or adequate." I interpret this to mean a person must be able to exhibit enough skill to do a task, but he or she doesn't have to be elegant about it nor do it better than everyone else. *The person merely has to be able to do it to the specifications given.*

Competence can exist in small increments. I am competent in several ways around a kitchen. I can competently open a can of beans. I'm competent enough to read a recipe and do what it tells me to do almost every time. I can cut up a chicken. I can make a very good gravy. But (there's no doubt) I am *not* a master chef. Although I'm competent in some of the aspects of chefdom, I know there are hundreds, perhaps thousands, of aspects in which I am not competent. Being a master chef depends on being competent in the whole endeavor, not just bits and pieces of it.

To be a master, a person must competently accomplish all (or a vast majority) of the standards associated with mastery. Those standards depend on a well-articulated set of specifications. A competent person can know of his or her competence only if the specifications are clear. He or she must be able to say, "Yes, I can do that." Two things bring clarity: a well-developed set of specifications and a test.

An entire profession, performance technology, is built around developing specifications. A pioneer in the field, Tom Gilbert (1978), wrote *Human Competence: Engineering Worthy Performance.* In performance technology, setting specifications is called *developing criteria.* To define *mastery,* you should do so by stating the criteria a person must satisfy to be considered a master. After you have done that, you can write a good fair test to discover whether people who claim to be masters are.

Every manager should have a copy of *Human Competence* close at hand. Gilbert discusses a whole gamut of concepts associated with human competence. Three are of particular importance for this discussion. I paraphrase them this way:

1. Competence can and should be measured.
2. A person's potential for improvement should be established.
3. Results must be measured to be of real worth.

Before we look at these three ideas and how they relate to tests and testing, consider performance criteria. Before we can begin to test whether or not a person is competent, we must define what competence is as it relates to that person. We must discover the criteria to be used to define the adequacy of the performance.

Performance Criteria

Gilbert (1978) describes performance criteria as *the devices employed to signal when a performance is done well enough to be called worthy.* Gilbert goes to great length

> **performance criteria**
> The devices employed to signal when a performance is done well enough to be called worthy.

to explain that performance and behavior are two very different concepts. A *performance* is undertaken to accomplish a worthy goal; *behavior* is simply how a person acts and may or may not have a bearing on the worth of what the person accomplishes.

As an example, consider an employee of a large corporation. He comes to work late most days. He might take a day off now and then without explanation or excuse. His suits are usually rumpled and his tie may or may not be appropriate for the suit. He wanders around the plant without preamble or explanation asking people questions about what they are doing. He doesn't explain his actions nor seem to have any plan. All in all you could say he is *not* a model employee. Yet he's one of the highest paid people in the company, and the company is highly pleased with his contribution. His job is to come up with ideas for improving products and for identifying new products to expand the company's markets. He does that very well. His behavior has little or no relevance as far as his worth is concerned.

Consider a young lady who works in a secretarial pool with five other people. She chews gum and pops it almost continuously as she types. She is fired because her habit annoys her boss. The output of the secretarial pool subsequently falls by almost 30 percent.

Look at a more complicated example. Suppose a clerk wishes to print a computer file. Suppose also that the clerk doesn't know how to run the computer. Several alternatives are open to him. He can learn to run the computer well enough to print the file. He can randomly strike keys on the keyboard until the file prints. He can call the company that manufactured the computer and ask someone how to print the file. He can ask a coworker to print the file. Any of the alternatives will accomplish the goal (of course, the second one may not be efficient). When the file is printed and in the hands of whoever asked for it, the goal is reached.

The behaviors are very different, yet each would produce the file. The clerk would seem to have performed no matter which tactic he used to produce the file. Because the performance requested was, "Print the file," and the clerk accomplished it, his performance was worthy no matter how he behaved.

The caveat is that a particular performance should not hurt the performances of others. If the clerk strikes keys at random, he could damage the computer or cause it to crash or do other kinds of mischief. If he asks someone else to print the file for him, he may be interrupting that person's work. Neither of these alternatives, therefore, is as appropriate as one of the other three. They might not qualify, in Gilbert's definition, as worthy.

Which of the clerk's alternatives would be best? It depends. If the clerk could assume that he might have to print many computer files in the future, it might be best for him to learn to run the computer. If the colleague who can print the file has little else to do and it is a one-time event, that could be the way to go. Other possibilities suggest themselves. Again, worthiness depends on the circumstances.

As you examined the clerk's alternatives, your mind was comparing them with your notion of what might or might not be appropriate. Perhaps the most efficient and effective way to do this is to have a set of rules or goals against which to compare the performance. One could say, "The clerk will cause the computer to print the file in twenty minutes." Obviously, taking time to learn how to run the computer is no longer a viable alternative. Now suppose you add, "The file will be easy for the engineers to use. The engineers will consider it easy to use if the conclusions are mentioned first, followed by the data and an explanation of how the data were interpreted." Our clerk now has to make sure the format and information in the file conform. None of the alternatives above will suffice without adding a process to format the file.

In this case, criteria were established for the clerk. His performance will be judged according to them. It still doesn't matter how he accomplishes them. His behavior won't be a factor. What counts is whether the engineers receive their file on time and if they can use it when they get it.

Performance testing is directly related to performance definition. If the clerk is asked merely to print the file, he can take years and produce almost anything as long as it is the file in question. The more detailed the specifications for his acquisition of the file and its contents, the more likely he will be to produce a satisfactory (worthy) result.

Detailed specifications are called *criteria*. The notion has been around for many years. It was given its present definition and impact by Robert Mager (1963) in his book *Preparing Instructional Objectives*. Mager was writing for teachers and trainers, but the work has had far-reaching implications and has had fundamental influence on performance technology. In effect, Mager said any objective has to have three parts to be useful:

- It must name the specific performance the learner (or whatever) will accomplish.
- It should specify the conditions under which he or she will be able to perform.
- It must have criteria to judge the success of the performance.

It must have criteria to judge success. If it does, the practitioner can be tested to determine if the criteria have been met. It may seem like a simple idea, an obvious conclusion, but without it, tests are much less efficient and effective than they could be.

Competence Cannot Be Assumed

Managers are learning that the key to success is competence. Competence can be attributed to a person, a team of people, or the whole organization. The problems managers face are threefold: (1) What defines competence in a competent person? (2) What is missing if a person is not competent? (3) How can the missing skills be taught? This book addresses the first question: How can a manager know if a person is or isn't competent?

The definition of a person's competence requires testing. Otherwise, competence must be assumed. Such an assumption can be a grave error. It's equally problematic to overlook competence when it is present. The conclusion is easy. If you want to know if people are competent, you must test them in some way. You must measure their ability.

This is a critically important problem for most managers today. They are finding that they must measure competence and that they must do it well. Obviously, they should test, but how do they find a good fair test, and how will they know one when they see it?

We can't discuss competence and testing for competence until we've examined critical elements of testing.

Needs and Respondents

> A need in this context is defined by the gap
> between what is and what should be.

I haven't mentioned *need* because some of you wouldn't know what I was talking about. Now, I believe, you are better prepared to think about some basic prerequisites for testing. Those prerequisites break down into two broad categories. First, you must know what the need is and why a test is being considered. Second, you must know the capabilities of your audience. Can the people who are to be tested understand and respond to the test being considered?

We have to understand both the performers and their performances. *Performers* are people who do the specific things necessary to accomplish something. The things they do are called *performances.*

Many people think of actors or musicians when they hear the term *performer.* It's OK. Those people *are* performers, but other people are too. Actors provide a nice analogy. They study their profession, practice doing it, and (in time) provide the skills to portray, to act. They are performers. But so are accountants. They, too, study, practice, and provide skills. The only real differences are the skill sets involved and the services provided.

It may take some getting used to, but we must learn to think of performances as actions taken by anyone who has a purpose, not just actors or musicians. It's sometimes convenient to think in terms of the performance of a service. A truck driver performs a service by driving a truck. An attorney performs a service for a client. A doctor performs a service by treating patients. When you think of it this way, you can see that any competent individual can and does perform a service. We are all performers.

Some of us perform better than others. Some doctors are wonderfully skilled and widely respected. Some do their jobs well and earn the trust and (perhaps) the admiration of their peers. Others don't do so well. They perform less ably and (again perhaps) tend to cause problems for patients and peers. Somewhere within the practice of medicine there is a line. Those above it can do their work satisfactorily; they are able to perform well enough to meet patient and peer expectations. Those below it are not trusted to perform to those same expectations. In other words, some doctors are competent, some aren't. That competence or lack of it is defined by their performances. If they perform well, they are considered competent. If not, they aren't.

The ability to perform is important in any line of work. Whether a person delivers papers or presents evidence before the Supreme Court, his or her success depends on the efficiency, effectiveness, and quality of his or her performance.

We have returned to the earlier discussion of efficiency, effectiveness, and quality. At this point, the connection between those concepts and how they relate to tests and testing should be clear. They are critically important.

Tests Define Competence

Consider this statement: every psychological test is, or should be, a test of human competence. Remember the two young men playing basketball? One dared the other to execute a particular shot. That was a test of competence. How about when the teacher gave students the pop quiz in algebra? That was a test of com-

petence. Those are easy to classify, and so are most of the other examples we have
seen so far.

Part of the problem with understanding this concept lies in our thinking that
competence is, in some way, special. Well, usually it isn't. Competence is merely
the ability to do something well enough to satisfy whoever establishes specifications or standards. If the standards are low, competence is easy to achieve. Competence can be difficult to pin down. It changes as perceptions of the performance
change and as time passes. So how can we test competence with confidence? We
do it by concentrating on effectiveness, efficiency, and quality.

Standards of performance are stated through estimates of efficiency, effectiveness, and quality. *Efficiency* depends on people doing their jobs within the process constraints imposed by conditions or management. *Effectiveness* requires
production of the right product. *Quality* depends on the product meeting user expectations. A test of competence would, therefore, sample the performances required to produce the right product on time to meet user requirements.

The Brethower-Rummler Model

A model was developed by Dale Brethower (1971) that allows us to visualize how
these three elements interact in a process. It was used and modified by Karen
Brethower and, later, popularized by Geary Rummler (1984). Figure 4.2 shows its
basic elements.

The model has three operational elements: *inputs, processes,* and *outputs.* The support elements are process control (management) and formative and summative
feedback. People control how and when inputs are used in the process. They make
the process work and control the basic nature of the outputs. It is important to note

FIGURE 4.2. THE BRETHOWER-RUMMLER MODEL.

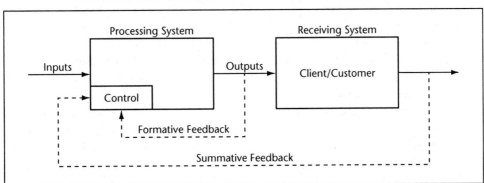

that, if a process is properly defined, competent performance by the people involved is also defined.

This model can be used to define any process. It has *inputs,* whatever the performer must have (tools, materials, and environment) to perform. It has a *process,* the actual performance. It has *outputs,* the results of having performed. The outputs are perceived as appropriate and valuable by a receiver.

Consider a singer. She uses her voice, the musical composition, and the accompaniment as *inputs.* Her *process* includes the working of her larynx, her thoughts as she sings, and the feelings she develops to project the song. Her *output* is the music as it is heard by herself, her accompanist, and the audience.

Now think about the Brethower-Rummler Model as a model of worthy performance. It defines competence. A competent person or organization will have the *inputs* required to perform, will have the *skills and guidance* that make the performance possible, and will produce *outputs* to satisfy both internal and external criteria. Competence depends on satisfactory accomplishment in all areas.

Testing Competence

The message to the test maker is clear. To test competence, we must consider all aspects of the Brethower-Rummler Model. If any of the foundational elements are poorly done or missing, competence can't exist.

Inputs. Without proper inputs a performer is forced to improvise. There are three basic inputs for any performance: tools, materials, and environment. A performer must have all three to demonstrate competence.

Tools. The tools for a performance are the devices used to perform and the skills of the performer. *Devices* include physical implements, mental constructs, and processes. Mental constructs and processes are devices because the performer uses them to do a job. The Brethower-Rummler Model is a device. It's a construct that allows a manager to apply his or her skills—to perform a job. Almost any performance requires devices found in all three domains (physical, mental, and emotional). A shovel is a physical device used to dig ditches. The determination to dig a ditch is a coping mechanism, an attitudinal device. The procedure for using the shovel is a mental construct. The test maker must discover if appropriate devices are available and in use.

Obviously, *skills* must be present before a process can happen. They are also tools because they enable people to do work. A skilled musician uses his or her skills to produce music. Accountants use their skills to audit. In this sense, skills are implements. Like other tools, they are used to perform tasks. The test maker can check the adequacy of the skills people have to accomplish a performance.

Materials. Materials are the resources required to do a job. Some are consumed by the process. Some aren't. When a gasoline engine runs, it is, in itself, the performer. It draws in air and gasoline and uses oil and water, which are the material inputs for the process.

People also have to have materials to do work. Sometimes those requirements are simple—paper and pencil or just the food and water necessary to keep people functioning. At other times the materials can be complex and widely varied. A chemist, for example, may use complex reagents to accomplish his or her goals.

Quality is important for all inputs. This is most apparent when we think of materials. Poor-quality materials (or other inputs) usually beget poor quality products. Good-quality materials make good-quality products possible. In testing materials and their use in a process, the test maker must often be as concerned with quality as he or she is with sufficiency.

Environment. Most of us don't think of the environment as an input to a process. In many ways the environment is a critical input. Consider tasks that require penetrating thought or good judgment. The place where such a task takes place can have a huge effect on the product. Noise levels, air quality, movement, light, and other aspects of the environment impact performance directly. They are inputs. Sometimes the environment is basic to the process. A singer can't *perform* without an audience. An athlete can't play a game without an arena of some sort. An office worker can't accomplish much without a desk and a chair. Many tests do more to test the environment than to test the performers.

Process. Look at the model in Figure 4.3 (p. 90), a rendition of Figure 4.2. The Processing System has three parts: the overall process, the control area, and a feedback loop. These three elements serve to define Mager's term, *performance.* When we ask someone to do something, we're asking for a performance subject to some type of control and communicated through some sort of feedback.

Although the three parts are separate in the model, they really are not. Any time anyone does something, controls are in place and information is generated about the performance. Even so-called mindless activities have all three attributes. I suppose there are activities that seem to be out of control. If so, there are controls that would be appropriate, even if they aren't in use. There might be activities for which feedback doesn't happen. For example, I once cut myself and didn't realize it for quite a while. However, the information was available.

This is important to you and me. We can test performances by testing the nature of the controls or information generated through feedback. We don't necessarily have to test the performance itself. Consider a daunting example. How can trainers know whether would-be soldiers or police officers are willing to shoot at an

FIGURE 4.3. THE BRETHOWER-RUMMLER MODEL: PROCESSING SYSTEM.

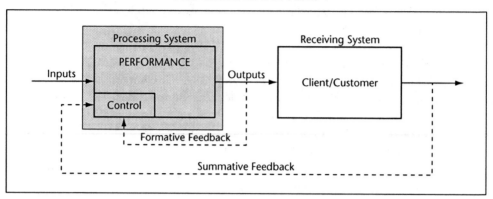

enemy or criminal? It's difficult to produce an enemy to check this out. Yet, for the most part, trainers are able to spot people who are reluctant to shoot and to recommend a different line of work.

How do they do that? They review the candidate's background, religious life, records, education (especially sports activities), and other information. More to the point, they administer a test, a psychological profile, to discover whether such a reluctance might exist. They test the controls for the process.

They also interview the candidate, asking how the person feels about physical conflict, death, and other relevant topics. They might also simulate battle conditions on a firing range. In these ways they sample information from the *formative feedback* system.

This sort of testing occurs for many activities, such as executive management, nursing, law, and fire fighting. It is legitimate. The caveat, of course, is that it must be done well. Tests of this sort are often very important to the respondents. Ergo, the more you and I can do to make such tests for respondents, the better our test results will be.

Feedback. Rummler (1984) spent a great deal of time and effort moving his clients from an examination of formative feedback to summative feedback. Summative feedback is *not* directly associated with the performer. Rather, it comes from the user—from the person or organization that receives the outputs from the process as inputs. In the model shown in Figure 4.4, Brethower and Rummler call this the receiving (or client) system.

FIGURE 4.4. THE BRETHOWER-RUMMLER MODEL: RECEIVING SYSTEM.

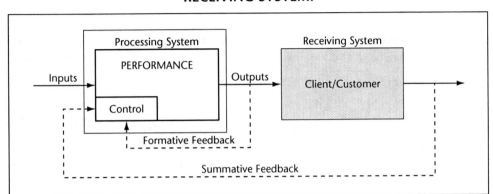

Everything we do or are goes somewhere or is noted by someone. Good, bad, or indifferent, everything about us is manifest in some way. Client systems are influenced by their inputs in much the same way that our processes are influenced by the inputs we receive. They are impacted in some way. They are changed. Those changes can be measured and reported. Contrary to what some people believe, feedback is always there, whether we ask for it or not. The client observes and develops the feedback; then the client informs us.

In most test situations, the emphasis is on feedback. This is usually sufficient because the feedback will directly reflect the adequacy of a performance internally and externally—but not always. If there is doubt, check the other areas.

One final, crucially important observation about the Brethower-Rummler Model: *it cannot be taken apart*. The four basic pieces belong together. We can discuss them separately. In fact, we must. But we can't separate them. *None of them can exist without the others.* They are an integrated system, a gestalt. Brethower's first conceptualization of the model has been proved through many years of practical application. The model represents what Brethower (1971) called the Total Performance System.

In his book titled *Strategic Planning Plus*, Roger Kaufman (1991) makes it clear that the best way to approach a situation or problem is through the mega perspective. By mega he means that you must examine and deal with the total environment before considering macro or micro elements. His contention, very much in line with Margaret Wheatley's in *Leadership and the New Science* (1992), is that you cannot deal with the whole problem by examining pieces and parts.

Gilbert's Directives

Let's return to Gilbert's three directives.

Competence Can and Should Be Measured. In general this book is about how competence can be measured. There are two important reasons for measuring it:

- To document the truth of its existence.
- To discover its extent.

Existence. I could say that I am competent as a lawyer. But society isn't going to accept my word for that. The state I live in will insist that I pass its bar exam before I'm allowed to practice law. My saying so isn't enough for me to become a lawyer. Even if I'm the best who ever was, I must still pass that exam. Passing the bar exam supposedly documents the competence of would-be attorneys. Other professions are regulated in the same way. It's easy to see the importance of documenting competence in sensitive areas such as medicine and the law.

How about reading? Is it important to document a person's competence as a reader? What is a competent reader? Someone must know; otherwise we wouldn't see news stories about the rate of literacy in this country. At any rate, let's say there are times when it is important to document people's ability to read, that is, their competence as readers. Universities have found they can't assume this competence from the evidence that a potential student has graduated from an accredited high school. It's a major reason they require candidates to take the SAT to qualify for admittance. Candidates must be able to read and comprehend complex questions in a given amount of time. You must be a competent reader to do well on the SAT.

Extent. I once had an argument with a colleague about this. My position was that people either are competent or they aren't. There is no middle ground. He insisted that there are levels of competence—a continuum that begins with a smidgen and ends with superiority.

My colleague reasoned that competence lies in a person's ability to do something well enough to accomplish a *worthy* performance. He illustrated his point by citing a young man's ability to climb a tree. It seems a kitten was stuck in the tree too frightened to come down. The lad found a small ladder to reach a low branch and proceeded to climb the tree one laborious foot at a time. It took him an hour, but he eventually reached the kitten and rescued it. Compared with other climbers, our hero wasn't very good at climbing trees. But my colleague insisted he was competent because he accomplished what was supposed to be accomplished and he did it well. It was a worthy performance.

The whole story depends on the way you define *criteria*. If the goal had been to climb a tree fifty feet high in ninety seconds, the young man would not have been called competent. However, the goal was to return with the kitten and himself without injury. Under those criteria, he was competent.

I now believe my colleague was correct. One person can be barely competent while another is exemplary, but both are competent. Of course, one is clearly better at it than the other. I suspect a fireman trained in such things could have rescued the kitten more quickly than our hero did.

Gilbert emphasizes how the *extent* of competence is important in many ways. For now, simply remember that *competence ranges do exist*. Although two people may be able to do the same thing, usually one of them is better at it than the other. Because this is true, the test maker is put in the position of having to decide how much competence is enough. Many times I don't feel competent to make that decision, which is a major justification for establishing a cut-score through an objective study such as the Contrasting Group Method (see Chapter Ten).

A Person's Potential for Improvement Should Be Established.
Whether competent or not, everyone has potential for improvement. As time passes, competence decays or new ways of doing things makes old ways less appropriate. The person who isn't competent can become competent. The person who is barely competent can become exemplary. Gilbert (1978) established a procedure for determining competence and measuring the gap between where a person is and what he or she can become. He called it a PIP, "potential for improved performance." It's the ratio of the current ability of a performer compared with the ability of an exemplar.

> **potential for improved performance**
> A ratio of the current ability of a performer compared with the ability of an exemplar.

Gilbert provided two important reasons for establishing a PIP. First, the PIP defines the gap between what a person can currently accomplish and what is possible. Having this information puts us in a better position to determine whether the person is competent or not and what to do about it. Second, the magnitude of the PIP helps us decide if reducing it would be worthwhile, whether it would pay to increase a particular person's competence in a particular area.

Either of Gilbert's reasons provides motivation to test. Both are reasons why testing should be done as well as possible. The consequences of poor testing to both the organization and the individual can be ugly. For example, suppose we are testing to establish PIPs for a group of engineers at an aerospace manufacturing company. A poor test could spell disaster for the engineers *and* for the company. Whatever example you could provide, you should come to the same conclusion: a poor test is worse than no test at all.

Results Must Be Measured to Be of Real Worth. The fact that results must be measured almost goes without saying. When Gilbert uses the phrase *measured results,* he means some kind of device must be put in place *before* results are achieved to determine the worth of those results afterward. To measure results, you must have a measure you can depend on, a tool you can use to decide the worth of the results. Trying to develop that tool after the results are in hand is not a good idea. It happens, though, fairly often. People will run surveys, obtain the results, and then wring their hands over how to decide what the results mean. Usually all they accomplish is wrung hands.

You can use a simple process to decide what to measure and how to report the results. It has three steps:

1. Examine the objectives for the test and put them into performance terms.
2. Select the criteria to be measured, usually the ones that will mean most to the respondents.
3. Decide how the results should be displayed, which is dependent on who the audience is—who will use the report.

The result always will be measured results (no play on words intended).

Summary

The emphasis of this chapter has been to set the stage for your decision-making process as you develop tests. You must answer two critical questions before you begin:

- What will the test accomplish?
- Why is that important?

The basic definition of *competence* used here is: "a competent person is one who can do what should be done efficiently and effectively to the quality standards established." This definition contains three terms that must be understood when developing good fair tests: efficiency, effectiveness, and quality.

To be good at testing, that is, to develop good fair tests, also requires an indepth understanding of what competence is. Many views of competence were presented in this chapter, one of the most important being a discussion of how competence relates to and supports mastery.

Because competence begets mastery, we must decide how to examine a person's repertoire to discover where competence lies and how to use our knowledge to advantage. Chapter Five is devoted to the question of what sort of test to use for this purpose.

THE THREE PRINCIPAL USES FOR TESTS

This chapter is about what you can and perhaps should do with tests. How are tests used profitably? Tests are *not* preferred by most respondents. Given a choice, they would just as soon do something else. This is true even when they pay for the opportunity to take a test.

The test taker's distrust doesn't keep tests from being useful, so take your respondents' reluctance into consideration, but don't allow it to stop you from using a test if one is justified. This chapter is devoted not only to what uses are justified but also to how to get the best bang for your buck. A test can be useful; it can even be a preferred solution. If you can accomplish the tasks discussed in this chapter, your tests should become preferred solutions whenever such a testing situation comes up.

Tests are used for three basic purposes: to measure *achievement*, *accomplishment*, or *opinions*. The differences among the three can be stated simply. *Achievement* tests compare respondents with one another and are referenced to a set of norms. *Accomplishment* tests compare individuals with themselves and are referenced to a set of performance criteria. *Opinion* tests (opinionnaires) compare results to a priori thinking and are referenced by a common situation or problem area.

> **achievement tests**
> Tests that compare respondents with one another and that are referenced to a set of norms.
>
> **accomplishment tests**
> Tests that compare individuals with their past performance and that are referenced to a set of performance criteria.

opinion tests (opinionnaires)
Tests that compare results to a priori thinking and that are referenced by a common situation or problem area.

A large portion of this chapter is devoted to opinion tests. If your charge is to develop an opinion test (a survey, for example), you should find most of your fundamental questions answered here. Actual construction of items will be covered in Chapter Seven.

Achievement Tests

You and I are used to others deciding how a test should be used. The decision in school has traditionally been to measure achievement. Remember how it used to be? You would come into the classroom, accept the test, and do your best. Then the teacher would grade the tests. Your score would be listed with the scores of the other kids in the class. Kids who scored higher than other kids were given "good" grades.

Standardized achievement tests work in much the same way. The main difference is the size of the population against which scores are compared. Of course, standardized test scores are treated with more sophistication than your teacher used, but the process is the same.

Let's examine how the process works. It's based on human characteristics and how they accumulate. Consider a history test at a local high school. It will probably be taken by three or four classes, each with from twenty to thirty-five learners, so about one hundred students will take the test. Centuries of experience have convinced us that not all of those students will attain the same score (well, not very often). Some of them will know a lot about the content of the test. Some of them won't know very much. Most will know about the same amount, though, and will tend to receive the same grade.

Normal Distribution

When teachers talk to one another about children in their care, they might say something like, "I have a couple of dumb kids and a couple of smart ones. The rest are about average." They are acknowledging a basic tendency among human beings. They are referring to the *normal distribution*. The normal distribution looks like an anthill cut through the middle as shown in Figure 5.1.

The curve was developed many years ago by a German named Gauss. He came up with the idea from observing the natural way things pile up. For example, if you dribble grains of sand one at a time onto the same spot, they will form a hill. If the grains of sand are tiny, a cross section of the hill will look like the drawing in Figure 5.1. Human traits pile up in much the same way. They form the same curve.

Most of us have taken IQ tests sometime during our lives. The results of these tests show about 2.5 percent of the people to be very bright, about 13.5 percent to be bright, 68 percent to be average in intelligence, 13.5 percent below average,

FIGURE 5.1. NORMAL CURVE, SHOWING STANDARD DEVIATIONS FROM THE MEAN.

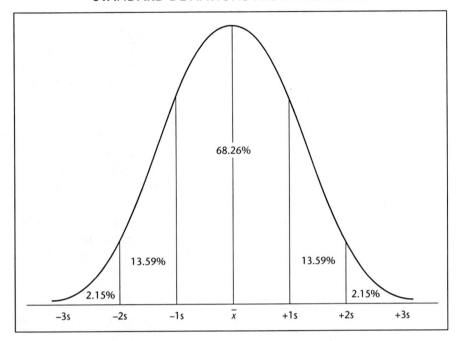

68.26%

13.59%   13.59%

2.15%   2.15%

−3s   −2s   −1s $\bar{x}$ +1s   +2s   +3s

Source: Downie & Heath, 1965.

and 2.5 percent to be slow. When all the scores are graphed, they form a "normal curve."

Whenever a test is given, the results tend to fall into the same pattern. Let me show you how it works. Let's say that fifty-eight scores were recorded for a test, as follows:

a. 65	b. 68	c. 57	d. 71	e. 52
f. 56	g. 60	h. 68	i. 63	j. 51
k. 64	l. 62	m. 63	n. 63	o. 60
p. 70	q. 61	r. 60	s. 64	t. 62
u. 59	v. 61	w. 61	x. 57	y. 53
z. 64	aa. 58	ab. 68	ac. 69	ad. 51
ae. 66	af. 59	ag. 60	ah. 70	ai. 65
aj. 61	ak. 60	al. 63	am. 62	an. 61
ao. 61	ap. 57	aq. 64	ar. 56	as. 57
at. 61	au. 67	av. 58	aw. 60	ax. 60
ay. 58	az. 62	ba. 62	bb. 63	bc. 61
bd. 62	be. 53	bf. 59		

If we record the scores by placing a hash mark beside the score for each time it was attained, it looks like Figure 5.2. You can see that the curve described by the history scores tends to look like the normal curve standing on end. It isn't an exact copy. The more kids there are who take the test (assuming they all have the same preparation), the more the curve will look like the normal curve.

This tendency extends to almost any human trait. If you counted the number of hairs on the heads of one hundred people, for example, the results would look something like the normal curve.

What does it mean when a teacher awards scores based on the normal curve? *The teacher is comparing each individual to all the others who have taken the test.* In Figure 5.2 those kids who scored 70 or 71 did significantly better on the test than those who scored 62. The teacher feels justified in awarding the high scorers significantly higher grades than the lower ones. They might, for example, receive A's, and those who scored 62 would receive C's.

Achievement testing has a serious drawback. The teacher is unable to specify whether any of the children (or all of them) have learned enough about history. Because the teacher is comparing the kids against other kids, the amount of history they have learned is of secondary importance. What is important in

FIGURE 5.2. DISTRIBUTION OF HISTORY TEST SCORES.

71.	/
70.	/
69.	/
68.	///
67.	/
66.	/
65.	//
64.	////
63.	/////
62.	//////
61.	////////
60.	///////
59.	///
58.	///
57.	////
56.	//
55.	
54.	
53.	//
52.	/
51.	//
50.	/

achievement testing is where a particular respondent scores in comparison to others who have taken the same test. The assumption is that by achieving a score as good as or better than others, a respondent has done well. This may be a safe assumption, but often it is not.

Assume you are a personnel director in a large corporation. You develop a test to sample the skills of people who operate word processors. Suppose that you give the test to two job applicants. Jane scores 66 and Betty scores 73. Should you hire Betty and not Jane? Should you refuse to hire either? Should you hire them both?

You cannot make a good decision without more information. Suppose you have administered the same test to 117 applicants over the course of two years. The average applicant has scored 70 on the test. Now can you answer the three questions? Perhaps. It appears Betty is as good as or better than the average applicant, so perhaps you should hire her and pass up Jane. But you can't be sure.

Why not? Because it doesn't matter what the average applicant scored. You want to be able to forecast an applicant's chances for success on the job. To do that you need to know what a competent word processor would score, no matter where that score would be on the curve.

Suppose you give the word processing test to all the people at your company who are considered good at their jobs. Their average is 74. Now you can compare new applicants to people who can do the job. Would you hire either Jane or Betty? Neither one is as good as the average competent person. If you're like me, you would still have trouble making a decision. How competent do new hires have to be? Surely they don't have to be as competent as seasoned veterans.

OK, so you look up the records of all the word processors who regularly received satisfactory job evaluations after they joined the company. Their average score on the test was 69. Now we seem to be getting somewhere. You should hire Betty, but have reservations about Jane. Right? Wrong! If the average score of those who were successful is 69, surely many of them scored 66 or even lower. Therefore, you should hire both Jane and Betty. Right? Well, maybe.

We could continue to play this game of comparisons, but the point has been made. Comparisons with others (whether they are successful or not) leaves questions that are hard to answer. The easiest way to avoid this problem is to compare the scores with a standard.

Accomplishment Tests

Accomplishment tests may not look much different from achievement tests. They can have the same kinds of items. They can be formatted or written in the same way (good fair tests). They can have the same kind of instructions. They can be scored in the same way. The differences lie in how their results are used.

What you, the personnel director in the situation above, wanted was a cutoff score. You wanted a score you could rely on to separate those who could do the job well enough to succeed from those who could not. Accomplishment tests can help.

Accomplishment tests are usually evaluated through a standard. The test maker decides, *before the test is administered,* what successful people will score. For example, a college basketball coach I know has determined that to be competitive, college players must be able to convert (make) 70 percent of the free throws they attempt. So he has the youngsters who try out for his team shoot free throws under game conditions. If they make 60 percent of their attempts, they have a good chance to make his team. (The coach expects everyone to improve with time.) It doesn't matter to him how many free throws other players convert. His requirement is for any individual player to convert 60 percent. That is his standard.

The idea with an accomplishment test is to measure what a person has accomplished. Let's return to the example of the history test. How sure will the teacher be that learners have learned enough history to be called competent in the content tested? Given the method of scoring, it would be hard to defend any of them as competent or incompetent. One might decide the highest scoring students (those who received 70 or 71) must be competent. Indeed, that is what the teacher will decide. But the teacher cannot be sure. It could easily be that 75 is an inadequate score or that 45 is just fine.

A story is told about Colonel Gabriel Ofiesch (1972), who was in charge of training bomber pilots during World War II. When he took command, potential pilots had to score at the average or above on a test to be certified to fly bombers. This turned out to be a score of about 70 percent. Ofiesch was troubled. What if the 30 percent they failed to learn was something as essential as how to land the plane? In fact, he had evidence that some so-called certified pilots had crashed trying to land the planes. They were not really competent to fly. Ofiesch solved the problem by ordering pilots to perform at the 90 percent level to earn their wings. He set a cut-score. Subsequently, the number of pilot trainees killed in crash landings decreased dramatically.

Ofiesch pioneered the concept of *mastery learning* as it's used today. Before his time, most evaluation was done through achievement testing or through the judgment of an expert. Setting cut-scores has become common practice for many certification tests, and it's becoming more common in other areas.

The other difference between achievement tests and accomplishment tests is best illustrated by how the scores look in a distribution. The scores in Figure 5.3 are fictitious results of a performance test given to people in a management course. Sixty-three people took the test over a period of several months. Fifty-seven of them met or exceeded the cut-score. The fact that two of them did relatively better than the others is of no concern. The only consideration is for the six who did not pass. Those six, for one reason or another, did not make it. In the mind of the test administrator, everyone else received the same score: passing.

What happens with most accomplishment tests is that the test givers don't ask people to take the test *until they have somehow qualified themselves to do so*. Therefore, the expectation is that everyone will pass. This doesn't happen in real life (which is why Ofiesch set his cut-score at 90 percent rather than at 100 percent). What happens is that some of the people the test giver thinks are qualified really aren't. They may not have learned as much as they seem to have. They may have had a fight with a colleague or been ill and, therefore, could not perform well. You can see how this affects the scores in the distribution. Six people were not qualified to take the test and, therefore, they failed.

The fact that so many passed does not mean the test is easy. On the contrary, it could be very difficult. For example, how many people in the world could pass the preflight test for astronauts? Not very many. Yet most of the people who take it pass it because only qualified astronauts are allowed to take it. Most of the people who take comprehensive examinations for doctoral studies at most universities pass the

FIGURE 5.3. MANAGER PERFORMANCE IN EXIT INTERVIEWS.

```
34.   //
33.
32.   /
31.   /////
30.   ////////////
29.   /////////////
28.   /////////
27.   ///
26.   ////
25.   ///
24.   ///
23.   ///        *****cut off*****
22.   /
21.   /
20.
19.   //
18.   /
17.
16.
15.
14.
13.
12.   /
```

test. Take my word for it—it isn't easy. The students have to meet rigid standards before they can stand for the test.

This trend is good news for business and industry. Organizations hire people with the expectation that those people will succeed. If a company hires 200 people, it expects all of them to be productive contributing members of the organization. Assume the 200 people are given training for a job and told they must pass the final exam to stay in the company. If an achievement test were used for the final, 5 of the people would be labeled superior, 27 would be above average, 136 would be average, 27 would be below average, and 5 would be total failures. Using the same kind of judgment teachers use, the personnel director would be instructed to terminate 32 of the 200 and put 136 on probation.

Now, suppose the same 200 people are asked to take an accomplishment test under the same circumstances. Chances are 180 would pass and 20 would fail. The company has just avoided terminating 12 people and putting 136 on probation. The implied savings to the company are enormous. The caveat is that the test must be performance based. (Chapter Four contained a discussion of performance-based tests.)

Opinion Tests

Many people in America respond to opinion tests often, sometimes every week. Such tests are a common way for organizations to do market research. They can look like the other kinds of tests, but usually not. They are often composed of either scaled or ranking items. An item might be similar to this:

1. Put a 1 by the kind of bleach you use most often, a 2 by your second choice, and a 3 by your third choice. Mark other brands you have tried with a check mark.

___ Brand A

___ Brand B

___ Brand C

___ Brand D

___ Brand E

___ Brand F

___ Brand G

___ Brand H

Or an item might look like this:

2. Rate each of the candidates for mayor. In your opinion, how honest is each person?

Winston Churchill

Very Honest	Honest	Not Sure	Dishonest	Very Dishonest
1	2	3	4	5

Adolph Hitler

Very Honest	Honest	Not Sure	Dishonest	Very Dishonest
1	2	3	4	5

Franklin Roosevelt

Very Honest	Honest	Not Sure	Dishonest	Very Dishonest
1	2	3	4	5

Joseph Stalin

Very Honest	Honest	Not Sure	Dishonest	Very Dishonest
1	2	3	4	5

You may not be interested in market analysis, but there are many other uses for the opinion test. It can be used to sample opinions about almost anything. You could discover employee feelings about corporate policies. You could find out how training is perceived by attendees, instructors, or both. You could investigate needs. In almost any situation in which you might want to test values or attitudes, you can do so through an opinion test.

Many people feel opinion tests are unreliable. They can't really be trusted. This is true for many such tests, but the basic difficulty usually doesn't have much to do with the instrument itself. Usually, the problems come from one of two sources: either the sample (people selected to respond) or the coverage (how many people respond) is faulty.

Opinion testing can be important to you. If you can do it well, you will find many useful applications that can provide measurable benefits. Therefore, you probably need detailed information about opinion testing and how to do it. One area, in particular, is very important in opinion testing: sampling.

Sampling

Many books are devoted to sampling. They usually have many pages of statistical derivations and other technical information. The purpose here is not to make you an expert on sampling theory but to give you enough information and guidance to do it for yourself with accuracy and confidence.

The basic problem that sampling addresses is the size of populations. Most surveys (or opinion tests) are directed at very large groups of people. Approaching each person and soliciting responses can be a time-consuming, expensive process. Sampling is used to avoid these constraints.

Statisticians have been able to show that, when it comes to opinions, one carefully chosen person can and will speak for many others. For example, a well-chosen sample of 1,200 people can accurately represent the opinions of 98 percent of all the people in the world. A good sampling process must control variables caused by language and cultural differences, but it can be done. This may seem ludicrous, but large polling firms such as Roper and Gallup have been able to operate profitably for many years because it is true. The keys lie in how the sample is chosen and in whether the people chosen actually respond.

Choose a Sample. The basic technique for choosing a sample is *randomization*, the process of selecting people at random from the population. It requires four steps:

1. Define the population so all who are part of it are included and those who don't belong are excluded.
2. Document the population so random selections can be taken without difficulty for the sampler or for the population.
3. Select a sample using a technique that is, in fact, random.
4. Protect the integrity of the sample.

Here's an example to show how the procedure works.

Define the Population. Suppose you are the manager of a large division of an international organization and you want to find out how your people (at all levels) feel about a newly instituted policy change. Let's also stipulate that there are 2,213 people in your division. You decide to use a survey to get their opinions.

You have three choices. One, you can send the survey to people whose opinions you value above those of others (opinion leaders) by identifying the opinion leaders and sending them a copy of the survey. Two, you can send the survey to everyone in the division, thereby giving them all a chance to express their opinions. Three, you can sample the population and send your survey to the people in the sample, knowing they will accurately reflect the wishes of the whole group. (*Note:* the choice you make here will solidify your definition of the population. Consider that as you read on.)

Choices one and two have obvious drawbacks. The first choice will not represent everyone. Although opinion leaders are supposed to be representative, it's only true if everyone agrees with one or more of them. Too often opinion leaders are people who have imposed their opinions rather than made themselves representative.

The second choice is too cumbersome. If you send out 2,213 surveys and everyone replies, the pile of responses will be huge. The job of recording the responses and then analyzing them will take time and effort. Usually such expenditures are too high to justify.

So you're left with the third alternative. This isn't bad, as it is a viable way to obtain the data you want.

Document the Population. Here's how to select a random sample from the 2,213 employees. First, label the people in the population so each one has a unique designation. The easiest way is simply to number them 1 through 2,213. Then randomly select 26 of the people for your sample. Two questions must be answered before I can continue with the process. First, why 26 people? Where did that number come from? Second, why select them randomly?

Representative Samples. Statisticians and others who deal with the problems associated with sampling try to develop *representative* samples for their studies. To be representative a sample does *not* have to represent the ideas and opinions of every person in the population totally. To do that, you would have to include every person in the sample. What a representative sample does is provide an *opportunity* for each person to be represented. The laws of probability help us here.

> **representative sample**
> A sample chosen to represent the values and inclinations of every member of a population.

Twenty-six is a representative sample of 2,213 because there is an excellent chance it will represent every single person in the population. If we choose a sample of 1 person, the odds against being representative of the other individuals are 1 in 2,213. Not good. For a sample of 2, the odds would be 2 in 2,213, or 1 in 1106.5. Better, but still awful. Before we try 3 people, take a look at how the people chosen relate to the total population.

When there is a sample of one, that one attempts to represent each person in the population. Picture one person with a string attached to each of the other people in the population. It's like a congressman representing everyone in his or her district. Each constituent is tied to the representative. Each constituent has a voice in what the congressman does and is directly affected by the results of his or her actions.

If there are two representatives, it's analogous to each state having two senators. Because both senators are supposed to represent the whole state, ideally both are tied to every citizen of the state. Visualize 2 people tied to everyone in a population. Picture 2 people with strings attached to all 2,213 of the people they represent in our example.

OK, now think about adding a third person. The third person will also be tied to all the people in the population. The strings will cross each other even more. Each person in the population will have three chances of being directly represented by the people in the sample. Think of it this way. Each person in the population has a 1 in 2,213 chance of being the first person in the sample. Each has a 1 in 1106.5 chance of being either the first or second person. When we add the third representative an interesting thing happens.

Each person in the population has a chance to be the first person chosen for the sample. If he or she is not chosen for the first person in the sample, there is a chance to be chosen to be the second. Again the chance is equal. When we add the third possibility the chances are much better. Why? Because each choice must consider all people in the population in relation to the three in the sample. Each person has a chance to be either number 1, number 2, or number 3. This is because all people in the sample are chosen at the same time.

Most people don't think about this process as it really happens. They think about the sample being chosen one at a time. If that were the case, a representative sample would be very large. But the sample will be chosen simultaneously. That is, all the people in the sample will be chosen at the same time, so everyone in the population has an equal opportunity to be any of those chosen for the sample. There isn't a first, second, or third. Because no one is chosen before anyone else, there is no priority. Now (and this is the difficult part to visualize), in addition, everyone in the group is simultaneously available for selection for any of the three representative positions. A random selection means all members of the group are equally likely to represent the group. Each of them can be the first, second, or third one sampled. Or they could be the second, third, or first. Or they could be the third, second, or first.

Let me show you how it works with numbers. When the sample is drawn, each member of the group has an equal chance to be part of any of these sequences: 1, 2, 3; 1, 3, 2; 2, 3, 1; 2, 1, 3; 3, 2, 1; or 3, 1, 2. There are *six* chances to be selected. Mathematicians have developed a shorthand way to say this. They represent it as 3!, which means "three factorial." Operationally, it is 1 x 2 x 3. 1 x 2 x 3 = 6. Yes, it's true. This idea is what makes Roper and Gallup successful. The confusing part for most people is that they don't understand representation. Ideally, each person chosen for a sample would represent everyone in the sample.

Consider the representatives for a mythical state. Say the state is small and there are only three of them. Each one feels responsible for every person in the state. Each representative will consider the people in his or her home district first, but in broader debates, he or she will try to represent every single person in the state. When national security is threatened, that same representative will feel responsibility for each and every person in the country. That is part of the meaning implied by the term *direct representation.*

Now think about those three representatives. They ran for election, but they could have been anyone from their respective districts, as all qualified voters are welcome to run for the House of Representatives. Anyone in the country can run, so in a sense, they are a random sample of the population. They aren't, of course, but think of them that way for a moment. Suppose there are 145,000 people in the state in question. Each representative is personally responsible for the well-being of every single one of those citizens. Even though they come from different districts, in most matters they are responsible for the whole state. They are also accountable. If they don't represent their constituents well they can be voted out of office.

The election process in the United States is not part of the day-to-day life of the nation. It is a special event. Because of this, the people who are elected are much like those selected in a random sample. It doesn't matter which one is first, second, third, and so forth. All of them have the same job. All receive the same pay. All are responsible in the same kinds of ways. All are tied directly to every citizen in the state. So the people in our mythical state aren't represented by one representative. Each one is represented by all three. The chances of their being represented fairly by those three is 3! (or 6) in 145,000. Those are not good odds, you may say, but it's twice as good as 3 in 145,000.

Now let's return to our example. Using the same logic, if the sample size is 4, the number of chances for any person to be represented is 4! or $1 \times 2 \times 3 \times 4$. That equals 24: $1 \times 2 = 2, \times 3 = 6, \times 4 = 24$. Most people think that when four people are being randomly selected, the chances of anyone in the population being chosen is the size of the population divided by 4. In reality, the chances are the population divided by 24. So, for our example, if you chose four people at random, the chance for any single person to be represented by that sample would be 1 in 92.2 ($^{2,213}/_{24}$), not 1 in 553.3 ($^{2,213}/_{4}$) as most people would think.

Notice that we are talking about the chances of being represented. The chances of one person actually being part of the sample is still 1 in 553. But we're not concerned about whether each person is physically asked questions (responds to the instrument). We are very much concerned that each person has a very good chance of saying what he or she wants to say. Because everyone can't do that personally, each has to be represented. Random selection can virtually guarantee that representation. If we pulled a random sample of four people, 1 in 92 of the population would be represented. Those odds aren't good enough. We need a larger sample.

Let's skip forward to twelve people randomly selected. By selecting twelve, we give each person a 1 in 12! chance of being represented. $1 \times 2 \times 3 \times 4 \times 5 \times 6 \times 7 \times 8 \times 9 \times 10 \times 11 \times 12 =$ more than 479,000,000. Now, since the number associated with representation is much larger than the number in the population, the chance of each person being represented is very good.

It still isn't enough. We are dealing with the real world. In the real world not every person in the sample will feel responsible for all the people in the population.

He or she may restrict responsibility to a small minority or even to a group of one (himself or herself). Statisticians have been able to consider these problems and come up with a number for a random sample that provides a very good opportunity to all to be represented fairly. That number tends to be twenty. Twenty people chosen randomly can usually represent almost any size population.

One problem remains. The sample must be guaranteed. If you lose one, you've lost him or her and you can't simply draw another at random. To do so is to ruin the integrity of the original sample. But people get sick, have babies, go on vacation, quit their jobs, or are unavailable for a plethora of reasons. One or two are bound to not be available when the time comes. The expedient is to pick more than you really need in the first place. If you must have twenty, pick enough to virtually guarantee that total. For most situations, the number you should pick for a sample is twenty-six. If you have doubts, you're justified in choosing even more. But be careful; if you choose them, you must use them.

Suppose you choose thirty-seven people for your sample and all of them show up? You must use them all. The twenty you need are embedded in the sample, and you can't tell one of them from any of the others. So you must use all thirty-seven. You have increased your administrative problems without increasing the validity of your work. My advice is to stick with twenty-six as the sample size. It has been shown to be adequate for most applications.

As you have already guessed, my explanation is not complete. My goal was not for you to become proficient in statistical control. It was to assure you that twenty-six people in a random sample can easily represent a large population.

Of course, I have simplified the process here for sake of illustration, but the point is important. A sample of 26 is more than adequate to represent everyone in a population of 2,213. In fact, if we could demonstrate that it's truly representative, a sample of that size could represent all the people in the United States.

The random sampling process is discussed in depth in textbooks on statistics and sampling. Probability theory is fascinating to some, and you might like to pursue it elsewhere.

You must be sure, when choosing your samples, that they are truly random. Most statistics books have tables of random numbers you can use or you can make the selection using a computer. My preference, for most samples, is to use a deck of cards. Just be sure the process you use is unbiased. Find a procedure and use it rigorously. All three of the processes above (random number table, computer programs, and a deck of cards) are described in detail in *The Competent Manager's Handbook for Measuring Unit Productivity* (Hale & Westgaard, 1984). They are also available from many easily obtained measurement texts.

Now that you have drawn your sample, how do you make sure that those people will actually respond and that all who are supposed to respond actually do?

Coverage. Pollsters have virtually surrendered to the problem of coverage. So many things can happen. If they send a survey to 100 people through the mail, experience tells them that only about 35 of them will respond. If you do the same thing with your sample of 26, only 8 or 9 will reply. What does that do to the sample? Ugly things.

Why do people fail to respond? They may be too busy. They may not like surveys. They may not like the people who are conducting the survey. They may be afraid they'll be taken advantage of in some way (that is, end up on another mailing list). Whatever the reason, when a survey respondent fails to reply, all the people he or she is supposed to represent are not heard from. The integrity of the sample is destroyed.

In the example above, 26 people are selected to represent 2,213. If 1 of the 26 does not reply, some of the population may have lost the ability to impact the outcome. Usually, if 1 or 2 don't reply, the results are not seriously compromised. If someone is ill or out of town, the survey is still a reliable source of information, but if more than half the respondents fail to respond, the problem is serious. Such a small representation would, in all likelihood, be biased, first, because people who are more accessible are more likely to reply and, second, because some people are more motivated than others. So, if the response rate is low (less than 75 percent), chances are the results will be biased. Data will represent some portions of the population better than they do others.

Consider a common situation. Some of a company's workers have voiced an interest in organizing to become unionized. The company conducts a survey of the employees to find out if the majority wants a union. Should the company be satisfied with a 30 percent response rate? No way! Nor should you, for any sampling. You may think, "Well this isn't that important. I'll be happy if 30 percent reply." If you take that attitude, you're just looking for people who like surveys. They are the ones most likely to be motivated to reply.

How many is enough? For a mailed instrument, the response rate should be 75 percent or more. If you receive fewer, you should not feel confident of the results. After all, 25 percent of the population is not being represented, even though 75 percent is a very high response rate. Most mailed surveys result in even fewer than that. Leading survey companies are content with as little as 35 percent.

So how can we make the response rate better? The following three approaches work well.

Ask managers to be responsible. In the example above, it would be very important to make sure that as many of the twenty-six people chosen respond as possible. The best way I have found to do so is to make the survey the responsibility of management. Send the survey to the respondents' supervisors or managers with a letter explaining how important it is and why a particular person must fill it out. The managers are directed to collect the completed surveys personally and return them. Voilà, response rates approach 100 percent.

Conduct a parallel data-gathering effort. This approach means to conduct the survey in more than one way. Perhaps two samples can be chosen. One group would be sent the mailed survey. The other would be interviewed by phone using the same questions. If the response rates are appropriate, the results of the two efforts would be highly correlated.

Conduct the survey orally, either in person or by phone. This method works well if respondents don't feel rushed or in other ways constrained by the personal contact. However, some employees don't react well if they are being interviewed by someone they think represents management.

When the survey must be conducted by mail and there isn't a viable way to back it up with interviews, there are ways to combine and recombine results to achieve confidence. This is what happens in polls such as those conducted by Roper or Gallup. That is why they need large samples (as many as 1,200). In most cases this should not be a concern for you. One of the three methods above should work well for most of your needs.

A final note about coverage. If you have it, you have it. There's no need to use more than one of the three methods, because any of them will provide the confidence you want.

Using Opinion Tests

Let's consider how opinion tests can be used to advantage. Not long ago a small manufacturing company was considering expanding. They had been very successful and were thinking about building a new plant. The new facility would more than double their capacity. However, the CEO was concerned that employees would not want to move or that they might not be as productive in a larger company.

The CEO had his personnel manager prepare a survey to discover how the employees felt. The results were encouraging, so the company built the new plant. Productivity increased; quality increased; and the company became even more successful than before. Of course, it would be foolish to say the survey had anything to do with all that. Still, it was important. Through the survey, the employees had a direct say in corporate plans. They were able to commit personally to the plan and, therefore, supported it when it was put into motion. Naturally, other steps were taken to secure these benefits, but the survey was a key element. It was a small effort, but the return on that investment was huge. What happened there can happen anywhere.

Perhaps you're still not convinced. Let's try an experiment. Complete the following survey. Be serious about it. Respond for yourself—the way you feel personally. As you work with each item, be as honest as you can be about your own beliefs and feelings. Select the statement that most closely matches your own feelings. Choose only one answer for each item. If you want to add a comment, write it in the space below the item.

1. How do you feel about tests used to qualify people for employment?
   a. Most of them are OK. They provide a fair, unbiased selection method. Anyone who is qualified for the job has a good chance of being hired.
   b. Some are OK, some aren't. The good ones do a good job. Unfortunately, there are bad ones that hurt qualified people.
   c. Most of them are bad. They discriminate against people for the wrong reasons, such as inability to read well. People are usually nervous, so they don't respond as well as they could.

   Comments: _____

2. If a test is being used for hiring purposes, who should have to take it?
   a. Everyone. That includes people who are applying for the job *and* people who presently do the job.
   b. All people who are applying for the job.
   c. Only people applying for the job who are marginal, that is, those who might not be qualified to do the job.

   Comments: _____

3. What should be done with people who take a test for a job and fail, indicating that they cannot do the job at all?
   a. All but the worst of them should be hired and given a chance. Most people will learn a job and be able to do it if they're given adequate training.
   b. They should only be hired if they seem promising. Then they can be trained to do the job.
   c. They should not be hired. The company can't afford to take a chance on nonproductive people.

   Comments: _____

4. What should be done with people who take a test for a job and barely pass, that is, score just above the cut-score?
   a. They should be hired without reservation. They passed the test.
   b. They should only be hired if they seem promising.
   c. They should not be hired. The company can't afford to risk employing nonproductive people.

   Comments: _____

5. What should be done with people who take a test for a job and do very well, that is, "ace" it?
    a. They should be encouraged. They will probably advance rapidly in the company.
    b. It might be a good idea to encourage them. The company needs the best people it can find.
    c. They should *not* be treated differently from anyone else.

    Comments: _____

6. What do you think a test to qualify people for a job should contain?
    a. Performance items that test ability to perform, to do the job.
    b. Performance items and items that test basic knowledge of the job.
    c. Items that test basic knowledge of the job.

    Comments: _____

What happened as you were answering the questions? If you are like a lot of people, you began to form opinions about the content. There is a good chance that your attitude about testing job applicants has changed and that the change has been influenced by this little opinion test.

Because you could answer the questions any way you wished, the survey helped you form your opinions a little better and, perhaps, gave you food for thought about some of the issues sampled. There is a good chance you are more in favor of such tests than you were before, even though the survey doesn't favor a particular viewpoint. Now take one more item.

7. How do you feel about tests to qualify new hires?
    a. More positive than before.
    b. About the same as before.
    c. More negative than before.

You probably chose b for item 7. If not, you are more likely to have chosen a than c. Now review your answer to item 1. Are you more positive now than you were before?

When an opinion test is implemented, respondents are usually influenced to react positively toward the topic under consideration. This usually happens because the test maker has a preference that is reflected in the test. Choice of words and style reflects the bias subtly, but surely. Consequently, opinion tests can be used to influence the public. Advertisers and propagandists use this fact to encourage acceptance of their products and ideas. Many of the surveys we receive in the mail or see on television are produced for this reason.

You can do the same thing. It isn't unethical or immoral. The test above doesn't try to push you one way or another. It is *not* subliminal manipulation. It simply articulates a stance and gives you an opportunity to support it. The fact that historically Americans tend to be more positive after taking an opinion survey than before is a reflection of their tendency to be optimistic. The result is a more concrete expression of that optimism. Naturally, if the ideas promoted by an opinion test are repugnant to those being surveyed, they will *not* react positively. In such a case the test will substantially reinforce former negative feelings.

Opinion tests tend to polarize respondents. Therefore, be careful. If the test was about unionizing a plant and management had recently done some things to alienate workers, the effect of the test would be to consolidate and reinforce negative feelings toward management. It could easily aid the cause of the union. Union leaders know this and often use surveys for this purpose.

Polarization

> **polarization**
> The movement of people with no opinion or with a weak opinion to either the positive or the negative side of a situation or a condition.

Tests of any kind can cause polarization. People who pass a performance test are more likely to favor the performances tested than those who don't. But this tendency is more obvious with opinion tests, so test makers must consider it before developing and implementing the test.

Suppose, for example, you want to find out if people who attended a seminar responded well to the experience. You develop and administer a *smiles test,* asking people how well instructors knew the content, used audiovisual aids, organized the experience, and so forth. By choosing these items, you cause respondents to think about all these things as being either positive or negative. When the respondents select responses, they reinforce the attitude being expressed. Chances are the test will amplify feelings that existed before the test was implemented. Such amplification can be a mistake.

> **smiles test**
> An opinionnaire or a survey designed to get people to report favorably about an experience.

Consider the seminar. If it is the first of a series and the same instructor will be leading the remainder of the sessions in about the same way, your test will affect the rest of the sessions. It will polarize the audience. Those who were positive will be more positive. Those who were negative will be more negative.

To summarize, there are many uses for opinion tests. Generally speaking they can be used:

- To sample opinions about a product, a new plant, a political candidate, and so forth.
- To discover attitudes about ideas or plans.
- To reinforce or establish bias toward a product or process.

Opinion tests are often used with a sample of a population rather than the entire group. A sample should be random in nature and ensure coverage of the total population.

Now let's discuss how you can treat the data from a test of any type to ensure that your conclusions are appropriate.

Treatments

> **treatment**
> A method for dealing with data to garner results.

Let's begin with another look at the last example, the opinion test about entry-level tests. How can we analyze the results of such a test?

Figure 5.4 shows how sixteen people may have responded to the test. The number of respondents was chosen arbitrarily to fit the page layout. In real life there would be twenty-six or more, unless the total population were smaller. The scores are fictitious.

Displayed in this way, the a's, b's, and c's don't tell us much. We can get an idea of what the respondents wanted to say, but we won't be sure. For example, it looks as though they much prefer b for item 2. How about item 3? They chose a three times, b four times, and c nine times. Is nine enough more than four or three to be called significant? Should we assume they are against hiring people who fail the test? We really can't be sure without analyzing the data.

FIGURE 5.4. RESULTS OF HIRING TEST SURVEY.

Item	Respondents A B C D E F G H I J K L M N O P																Totals a	b	c
1.	a b b b c b b c b b a b b b c c																2	10	4
2.	a b b b b c b b b b b b b b b b																1	14	1
3.	c c a b b a c c c c a b b c c c																3	4	9
4.	b a c b b a a a a b a a b b c a																8	6	2
5.	b c c c b a b c c c b b c c c c																1	5	10
6.	b a a b a b a b b c a a a c c b																7	6	3
7.	a a b a a a a b c a a a a a c a																12	2	2

Chapter Eleven is devoted to solving these sorts of dilemmas. For now let's look at one way to treat the data from the hiring survey. Let's suppose we gave the test to the eight executive managers who know what the company wants to do. Their scores are recorded in Figure 5.5. Although some might argue that the troops are better judges of this sort of thing than their officers, we might assume a need to see how well the employees agree with their executives.

In the matrix in Figure 5.5, the results are shown to the right of each item. Item 1, for example, has six a's, one b, and one c. If we change these to percentages, they become 75 percent, 12.5 percent, and 12.5 percent.

If the employees have about the same opinions as their bosses, their percentages should be similar. Perusal of Figure 5.4 shows that the employees chose a twice, b ten times, and c four times. The percentages are 12.5 percent, 62.5 percent, and 25 percent. Obviously there is *no* agreement here.

How about item 3? The percentages for the executives are 25 percent, 12.5 percent, and 62.5 percent. For the employees they are 18.75 percent, 25 percent, and 56.25 percent. They appear to be in agreement, but we can't be sure unless we run some kind of statistical analysis.

For this example, we would run a test called the Chi-Square Goodness of Fit Test. It would show significant disagreement for item 1 and agreement for item 3. Therefore, we could say with confidence that the executives and their employees disagree about whether such a test would be OK, but they agree about who should fail if it is offered.

As you can imagine, these are important pieces of information. To have them gives the organization an advantage. Decisions can be made with more confidence. Evaluation, in my opinion, should be based on statistical treatments simply because users can have so much more confidence in the results.

FIGURE 5.5. SURVEY RESULTS FROM EXECUTIVES.

Item	Respondents								Totals		
	A	B	C	D	E	F	G	H	a	b	c
1.	a	a	a	b	a	a	c	a	6	1	1
2.	b	b	b	b	b	b	a	b	1	7	–
3.	a	c	a	b	c	c	c	c	2	1	5
4.	b	a	a	a	b	b	c	a	4	3	1
5.	a	c	c	b	c	a	c	c	2	1	5
6.	b	b	b	c	b	b	a	b	1	6	1
7.	a	b	b	b	b	b	a	b	2	6	–

You don't have to be a statistician to use statistics. In fact, with the computer programs now available, almost anyone can use statistics to help them make decisions. But you do have to know what statistical treatment to use for what. Why, for example, did I decide to use the Chi-Square Goodness of Fit Test for the analysis above? Once you decide what treatment to use, you have to prepare the data for use by that treatment. I counted the letters to get numbers. I changed the numbers to percentages. Why?

This topic will be discussed thoroughly in Chapter Eleven, after we have covered enough background material and reached a point at which a discussion of statistics will make sense.

Summary

Chapter Five began with a discussion of the three basic uses for tests. *Achievement tests* compare people with other people. They provide information about how individuals and groups compare with others who have taken the same test. Comparisons are usually made via the normal curve, which is a statistically appropriate way to make comparisons fairly.

Accomplishment tests look like achievement tests. The basic difference is that respondents' scores are compared to a standard of some sort. The difference seems almost trivial, but it's very important. Instead of relying on the normal distribution for comparisons, accomplishment tests use a cut-score, which represents the score a competent respondent should receive.

Opinion tests look and *are* different. Their effect is mostly in the affective domain and they have special aspects. Their effectiveness often depends on sampling. Two aspects of sampling are critical to the integrity of an opinion test: representation and coverage. Opinion test results are usually displayed in a matrix of some sort. The matrix allows the test evaluator to use statistical treatments to analyze results. Treatments are statistical devices that manipulate the data without harm to its basic nature. They provide vital information to make results useful.

This discussion of the types of tests has taken time and, I hope, careful consideration on your part. At this point, we're ready to work on the "how." Let's do it. Part Two of this book is devoted to a systematic process for designing, developing, producing, implementing, and evaluating tests. Everything you should know and do to produce a good fair test is there. Use it well.

A SYSTEMATIC PROCESS
FOR TEST DEVELOPMENT

In Chapter One you were introduced to a process for test development and it was explained that the fifteen steps take place whether the test is formal or informal. The chapters in Part Two give the process for using each of those steps.

Whatever your needs, these are the basic chapters of the book. They present the process, discuss the reasoning used to develop the process, and provide guidelines for implementing it to produce good fair tests. You will find some repetition, which was done deliberately so you won't have to review earlier chapters to remember important points.

As you saw in Chapter One, the test-development process has fifteen steps.

1. Identify and qualify potential respondents.
2. Justify the test.
3. Identify performances to be tested.
4. Set criteria for each performance.
5. Select the type of test that best fits the desires of respondents and provides a valid assessment of the criteria.
6. Design test presentation and administration.
7. Design and select the evaluation process.
8. Write the items.
9. Review and qualify the items.
10. Pilot the test; revise and rewrite.

11. Set respondent and qualification scores (cut-scores) or other parameters.
12. Produce the test.
13. Administer the test.
14. Evaluate the results.
15. Use the results.

Each step ends with a decision—whether to go on developing the test or to stop.

CHAPTER SIX

JUSTIFYING THE TEST

Step 1: Identify and Qualify Potential Respondents

I have to laugh at times at the thinking of some test makers. For example, a physicist at a well-known university developed a new theory about an aspect of the nature of the universe. He was so excited that he wrote a long test on its properties and salient aspects. Because the theory was unproven, and, indeed, turned out to have serious flaws, it was discarded. The test was never used (thank heaven). The professor never encountered students who would have profited by taking the test.

How many people should be tested on their ability to identify $1 bills? How many people should be tested on their ability to punch a time clock? The vast majority of people won't ever have to be tested for those skills. They either have them or can acquire them without much effort.

Problems stem from the test maker not considering the target audience. Everyone has repertoires of knowledge and skills. Testing is a way to discover the extent of those repertoires. But it's not the only way. In fact, testing should be considered the final expedient—the last thing you should use as a way to find out what you want to know about people.

It may seem strange to say such a thing at this point. After all, I've spent pages telling you testing is an OK thing. But that doesn't mean a test should be used in every situation in which it could be used. There are three very good reasons for this:

1. Other methods of assessment are less expensive and less time consuming.
2. Evaluation doesn't have to depend on measurement.
3. Some skills should *not* be defined well enough to allow a definitive test.

Use of Resources

Tests are generally expensive. Developing even a relatively brief test, such as a twenty-item, multiple-choice exam, takes a lot of time. A proficient item writer can produce about five good items in an hour, so the test would take four or five hours to write. Then it would have to be edited, pilot tested, and produced. Administration takes about an hour. The little test would take at least a day's time, not counting the time used by respondents to take it, scorers to score it, or administrators to document the results.

Evaluation Without Measurement

Some people judge situations and other people continually. Others are less prone to this, but all of us do it. It is a necessary and useful trait if it isn't carried to extremes. In some ways, tests are ways to channel judgment, to make it better. Sometimes, though, tests are superfluous. For example, if a manager is fairly sure of the skills and loyalty of his or her employees, there is no justification to test for either. It's highly appropriate, in most instances, to accept the judgment of someone who is familiar with a person or situation and who has a track record of making good decisions.

Skills Not Defined

Most of our lives are based on our acceptance of situations and other people. We're usually satisfied with our perceptions of others and find progress easy enough to accomplish without specific information about them. The test maker must avoid testing everything that can be tested. We must ask ourselves about the possible negative consequences that could arise.

Qualification of Respondents

The people who are going to be tested are usually not much of a problem. They are easy to qualify. They will have three characteristics: (1) a personal desire to display their skills; (2) a mastery of prerequisites; (3) an untested repertoire.

Personal Desire. Test takers should want to take the test. They may feel hesitant, but the desire should be there. Sometimes it's easy to see. People take driving tests to become qualified to drive their cars without risking fines or jail. Others take bar exams to obtain the right to practice law in certain jurisdictions. But what about the people who will take your tests? Maybe their desires aren't as easy to pin down. They may want to pass the test to advance their careers. They may want to show they can operate a computer program or whatever. They may want to pass the test simply to build more confidence in themselves. In most cases they will be taking your test to display skills—to show they can do something well enough to be trusted to do it.

Whatever these people's desires are should drive the test maker. The test should be specifically designed to measure skills in a way that satisfies the test takers. Of course there will be organizational and other objectives to be attained, but those should be secondary. The test, if it is for respondents (as it should be), will consider what they can derive from it—how they will profit from the experience.

Some test takers will claim that their most pressing desire is to avoid the test. They will claim that they don't want to take a test. That may be what they want. However, for the circumstances prompting the test, it probably isn't what they need. The test maker must specify how the test takers will gain and articulate it so respondents are less likely to resent the test when they do take it.

Consider a test to see if workshop attendees learned the skills covered in a workshop. They may not feel like taking a test. They may try to avoid it or to resist in some way. The test maker must ask himself or herself a serious question: "Why should these people take this test?" Unless that question can be answered with assurance, there is a strong possibility the attendees are correct in thinking that they won't gain anything from it. If, however, the results will be used to evaluate the *adequacy of the instruction,* tell them this. Perhaps their remarks will help you improve the course.

Let's say the workshop teaches workers how to use a new procedure in a manufacturing process and several opportunities to practice are included. If all the attendees demonstrated they could use the process within the standards set, they have already been tested and shown competence, so there is no rationale for a formal test. Or maybe there is! They may want to show off. It's OK to give people a test for their own satisfaction or to help provide closure on their learning experience, especially when that test qualifies them to do a job or to attain certification. They want to demonstrate to the world that they are proficient in the skills.

This is the case in almost any good performance-based learning situation. The learners begin by examining the performance objectives of the training. They know what they must be able to do at the end of the training to be certified as competent. They go through the training. They learn the skills. In the end they must be given a chance to demonstrate their competence because, if that opportunity isn't afforded them, they must depend on gut feeling or on informal feedback from their instructor and fellow trainees. That may suffice in most cases, but it's still not nearly as satisfying (to the trainees or their bosses) as a passing score on a performance-based exam.

Now consider a university course introducing graduate students to a professional field. Perhaps it could be titled Introduction to Performance Technology. If this is an introductory course and students successfully complete the readings and projects assigned, there may be no justification for a final examination. They have been introduced to the material.

Now suppose a company wants its salespeople to be more proactive in their dealings with potential and ongoing clients. The company provides training in using tactics that promote proactive interactions. An important aspect of the training is to encourage people to use the tactics with clients. How much confidence will the employees have in their ability to use the tactics? How well will they actually be able to use them? What will be the effect on day-to-day operations? The answers to those questions and others are very difficult to pin down without a test.

Notice that the justification for giving a test in the first place tends to dictate the nature of the test to be developed.

Mastery of Prerequisites. When qualifying people for positions, for specific training, or for formal or informal tests, we sometimes assume more than we should. The workshop for salespeople mentioned above assumes that attendees are competent in the use of oral expression—that they can speak well. But what if they can't? All the proactive tactics in the world won't help the ones who cannot to build client confidence and loyalty. Perhaps there should be a test to see whether applicants for sales positions can use language well.

A pretest, or a diagnostic test, is sometimes extremely valuable in determining whether and what kind of training is required. Training is expensive. If people don't have the prerequisites that enable them to benefit from training, it may be a waste of time and money. Pretests also help us avoid assigning people to training they don't have to have. Inappropriate training can develop negative feelings in trainees that could have been avoided.

Let's assume that a repair shop hires people to service several kinds of electronic equipment. They hire people who are supposed to know something about electronics before they come on board. When new hires report for work, their supervisor takes them on a tour of the shop. During the hour, the supervisor points to various components and test equipment and asks the new hires how they are used. This qualifies as a test because it is a deliberate attempt to obtain information about people. It's very effective, because the supervisor can determine whether they require training, what kind of training, and whether it would be worthwhile to keep them on staff.

Determining prerequisites helps define *need*. In the best of all worlds, people take the final exam for a course or training *before they begin*. That way they know exactly what they have to learn to make good use of the training they're about to receive.

Performance tests measure respondents' possession of a set of skills. The skills don't have to be the result of a specific training episode. Making training a prerequisite for taking a test is often an error. Consider this example. This manuscript was written on a computer. If I applied for a job for which I would use the same software, I wouldn't have to be trained. I could pass a fair performance test on the software without training. To force me to take training before taking the test could cause resentment, severely hindering my ability to do well on the test. More important, it could make me resent the whole job and lose respect for my superiors. I might not be as motivated to do well on the job.

The prerequisites for an opinion test are different from the prerequisites for performance tests, but they are equally critical to its success as a measure. Suppose you wish to learn about the market for disposable diapers. Your target would be parents of young children. You wouldn't want to know the opinions of retired army officers. Knowing who will be responding should have a profound effect on the test. Would you use the same items for young parents as you would for retired army officers? If you did, could you expect good results?

Professional occupations often require a prescribed course of education and/or experience before a candidate can take a certifying exam. Some jobs require membership in an association or union. In this way a certification test is restricted to qualified people. Such prerequisites have a profound effect on the nature of a test. Professional certification that requires experience in the field doesn't have to test candidates' knowledge of normal facilities or equipment. They can be assumed to have acquired the knowledge through experience.

Untested Repertoire. When my oldest son was in the third grade, his teacher asked him to take a prepared reading test. It was a test he had taken four times, once that year and three times before in other schools. He refused. He had passed the test the other times, so why should he take it again? The child was correct. Unfortunately, the teacher didn't credit his explanation and tried to force him to take the test. When he continued to resist, she sent him to the principal. The principal called me. I agreed with my son. The teacher refused to allow an exception. My son was branded as uncooperative. Other teachers in the system treated him as if he were a bad kid. The boy lost respect, trust, and faith in the school system.

Fortunately, our family moved. The next year my son regained a sense of the fun and challenge of school. The point is that the teacher should have made sure that what she was testing had not been tested adequately before.

The military used to be a consistent abuser of this type. They would make soldiers take the same proficiency exam every six months. It makes sense that soldiers should be retested on how well they fire a weapon. But once they know how to hold their rifles, to aim them, and to take care of them, they shouldn't have to be tested on those skills again.

Some tests help to establish the extent of individuals' repertoires. IQ tests, attitude surveys, value inventories, and others are like this. Once a person takes such a test (and evaluators have a fairly accurate estimate of that person's skills), further testing is not required.

The psychological impact of repeating this sort of testing can be ugly. Marketing organizations know, for example, that if they persist in testing about certain types of products, respondents will often change their minds. So they keep doing it. A company has been sending me an opinion test every three or four months for about five years. Each time I put down the same answers I put down before. They continue because they want me to question my preference for a competitor's brand. Once that has happened, they can follow up with offers of their own.

Suppose you have taken, and passed, a test on a skill you have in your repertoire. Now suppose you are asked to take another test on the same skill. What is your reaction? You may learn to doubt your own ability in an area in which you thought you had proved yourself.

It's usually a simple matter to determine the repertoires of potential respondents. You have only to ask. If that isn't possible, you can use a caveat to negate the psychological impact of testing. You can simply acknowledge that some of the people may have already shown the skill, but (for whatever reason) they should respond to the items presented.

Step 2: Justify the Test

Although the second phase seems self-evident, it's often done poorly. Many tests are developed and implemented simply because someone in authority expects tests to be used. For example, some universities expect professors to give midterm exams whether they are justified or not.

A better example comes from the business world. A manufacturing company hired a consulting firm to develop training for its order-entry employees. The resulting training contained a great deal of practice and supervision of trainees while they were actually doing the work. By the time trainees had completed the training they were already doing the job. They were certified as competent by their supervisors, but before they could actually go to work on their own, they had to take a test.

When I asked the order-entry manager why, he said, "That's the way it has to be. Besides, they should have a way to show they are competent." Why? They had already shown they were competent. The test was a good fair test. It had been developed by the consultants who produced the training, but its use was not only superficial, it was damaging. It caused doubt where none existed before.

This kind of muddleheadedness happens a lot. People often decide to test others for the wrong reasons. Two of these justifications should be made federal crimes: testing to punish and testing to provide a challenge.

Testing as Punishment

Years ago my job was to supervise student teachers. In that capacity, I often observed classes conducted by master teachers. More than once such a teacher, when confronted by an unruly class, would say something like, "If you kids don't behave, I'll give you a test." The threat was bad enough, but they would do it: "OK, you asked for it. Take out your tablets. Now list the fifty states and their capitals." Did this ever happen to you?

"Well," you might think, "that was school. It simply doesn't happen anymore." Are you sure? What about the order-entry manager in the example above. What other reason could he have for forcing his people to take a test? It was a chance to show superiority, and the manager wasn't going to let it pass. He had the same motivation as the teacher. It allowed him to demonstrate that he was the boss. In my opinion he simply demonstrated his incompetence as a manager. The practice is ugly. It should be exposed wherever and whenever it takes place.

Tests as Challenges

Actually, tests *are* challenges by nature. If they don't challenge respondents, they aren't valuable. For skills to be measured, skill holders must be challenged to display those skills. So it's OK for a test to be a challenge, but not if that is all the test is.

"I'll bet you can't spell the names of the first three presidents." This is obviously a dare. So are many tests. The test maker or test administrator is saying in effect, "I dare you to pass this test." For example, the people in the customer service department mentioned earlier take a test every six months. If they beat the others, they get three days off with pay. The test is a contest. The winners can brag. The losers are shamed.

Physical education teachers use this tactic often. Footraces, throwing contests, and similar exercises are set up as contests. They have no other redeeming function. It would be different if the coach (or order-entry manager) used the results to diagnose possible problems and arrange for people to get help, but they don't. Once the test is complete and the victors (and losers) are announced, no further action is taken. Such a test is simply a challenge. Unfortunately, the poor victims have no choice; they must participate.

Perhaps the worst example of this abuse of testing happens in graduate schools across the nation. Tests are used as hurdles. Qualification exams, final exams, comprehensive exams, and orals are all used this way by some academic departments. The justification for these exams is to qualify students to remain in the program. The only rationalization I can see for this approach is that neither the students nor their professors are qualified to judge the adequacy of their preparation and potential to accomplish the goals of the program. Of course this is nonsense. Both the students and the professors are examples of the best talent in the nation. Either group is exquisitely prepared to make such a judgment. Both, working together, could do it with ease.

A caveat: tests are important to the process of education. They have a critical role to play in academia. My objection is using them simply to challenge students, to rank them when a ranking isn't appropriate, or as a way to dare them to continue.

Failure to Test

The other end of this spectrum is the failure to test when you should. We may hesitate to test because we have experienced tests administered as punishment or challenge. We don't want that to happen again. We develop an abhorrence of tests and testing, so, even when a test is appropriate, we tend to avoid giving it or water it down so it doesn't hurt so much. The reluctance to test can lead to grave errors.

Consider the CEO of a software company. Her firm produces programs for computers. The software performs critical functions in many companies. She hires programmers. She trains them to develop products. If she fails to determine whether they can actually do what she wants done, the business will fail. Customers won't buy software that has bugs in it or doesn't do what it's supposed to do. She must test those people one way or another.

Often, companies test new employees by giving them work to do that won't harm the company badly if they fail. The computer software company could do that. They could ask new programmers to build programs for use in the parent company. Then when bugs are found, they will only inconvenience the company's own people. That seems kind of dumb. Why not test those people to be reasonably sure they'll perform competently?

Another kind of failure also exists. Sometimes a manager or expert decides a task is so rudimentary (or obvious) that it doesn't require testing. A typical intersection in a busy city provides a good example. City drivers don't have any trouble with such an intersection. They know where to look, what to look for, and the usual tactics to use to negotiate the intersection without mishap. What about a young truck driver? This kid can drive a huge truck from one end of the country to the other without fear or concern, but if he has never taken his rig through a city intersection, his chances of a serious mistake there are very good. At least one commentator advocates a test for truck drivers to certify that they can negotiate a cross-country rig through a city before they are allowed to try. I must concur. An incompetent truck driver can cause a lot of grief.

The point is that failure to test when you should test is as bad as testing when you should not. It's very important to justify testing before it happens and to ensure that it does happen when appropriate.

A test is justifiable if three conditions are met: (1) knowledge about the presence of a skill is absent; (2) the skill can't be assessed by simply looking or asking; (3) the skill is required in the present context.

Knowledge Absent

If you have no other way of finding out whether someone can do something, you may have to test. Sometimes the respondents aren't sure either. They will welcome a test as an opportunity to find out.

Ask for information. It seems crazy, but we often test when we could have found out what we want to know simply by asking. This is particularly true of terms and policies. People may not know the precise definitions of terms, but they generally know where and how they're applied. For example, what if you want to know if people know how to use a rheostat? They may not know that a *rheostat* is a register for regulating a current by means of variable resistances, but they know to turn the knob to the left to reduce the heat. All you have to do is ask them.

A young woman applied for a job as a secretary. She had three years' experience doing the same job at a similar company in a distant city. Her former boss gave her a glowing recommendation. Yet the personnel director directed her to take a standard test to see how fast and error-free she could type. As it said on her application, she could type more than seventy words per minute (closer to ninety). Enough said. Don't test when you can find out more easily another way.

Can't Tell by Looking or Asking

Professional football players must be able to run forty yards in less than five seconds. Their ability must be tested, even if it was tested earlier. Physical skills atrophy or change through lack of conditioning or injury, and one should not judge by what a player says he can do. The temptation to exaggerate is too strong. He may truly believe that he can do it, but that doesn't make it so.

How good is your reading comprehension? How much of what you read do you retain? Can you analyze problems without having to apply some tool such as a matrix or mathematical formula? These questions and many others point to areas in which testing should take place simply because the potential respondents aren't sure enough of their abilities.

This becomes even more important in arenas such as management where people often give themselves credit for a skill they aren't proficient in. Yesterday I listened to a talk by a young man. He showed confidence and presented himself well, until he started to speak. In less than three minutes he used the phrase "ya know" more than twenty times. He thought he was communicating well, but he was not communicating at all. The audience didn't boo or throw things at him, but they didn't hear his message either.

The Skill Is Required

A small company near Chicago refused to hire people who couldn't speak and write English. Turnover in every department except shipping was less than 15 percent. In shipping it was close to 300 percent. They went broke. They couldn't find people who spoke English, were honest and dependable, and would work for minimum wages in shipping. It was a good little company. They would have done well.

Another company hired anyone who applied who had a record of honest hard work. That was a fine idea except the company manufactured signs. A young man named José did very good work. His fellow workers liked him. He advanced quickly. Eventually, his supervisor recommended him for a job in quality control. José could do every part of the job except check to see if words on the signs were spelled correctly. If they had been written in Spanish, he wouldn't have had any trouble at all.

Four Steps to Justify a Test

The steps are simply stated:

1. Identify the skills to be tested.
2. Establish the need.
3. Discover whether the skills are known to be present at the desired level of expertise.
4. Set a time and place for the test to happen.

Let's look at a possible situation, a regional, fairly large retailer that has 151 retail outlets in a four-state region. All outlets are serviced by a centrally located distribution center. The company has twelve people who respond to and expedite requests from the outlets for merchandise, promotional materials, and other support services. Ninety percent of their work is with a computerized order-entry processing system. Through it, orders are received, processed, assembled, and shipped to the outlets. The clerks also manage returns (damaged, returned, end-of-code, or seasonal merchandise, as well as reusable promotional materials).

The skill repertoires required by these people are large and important. They must be able to deal with store managers efficiently and effectively on the phone. They must be able to operate the order-entry system well. They must be alert to potential problems such as shrinkage or pricing errors. It would seem to make sense to test the skill levels of these order-entry clerks in several areas. Let's look at the four steps for justification as they apply here:

1. Identify Skills. Although I won't provide a list of the skills, the description above leads me to believe they won't be hard to describe. We must be as comprehensive as possible, but some skills may seem to be so obvious they don't have to be listed. For example, the clerks must be able to use the English language in oral communication fairly well. Seems obvious, but what about the young man who used "ya know" so often? Are the skills important enough to be tested? If you can't say yes, you can't justify a test.

2. Establish the Need. The term *need* is a noun and, in this context, it means the difference between what you can do and what you should be able to do. It defines a gap between what is and what should be. We often use the word as a verb to describe wants or emotions, but for purposes of this book, it will normally indicate something missing or inadequate.

You may want an expert to help with this step. Some of the skills listed in Step 1 will be basic to the job, some won't. Go through the list and specify those important enough to be on the proposed test, being careful not to qualify the skills as you look at them. Some will be easier to test than others. You may shy away from difficult-to-test skills such as "maintain composure under pressure." But if the skill is important enough to show up in the criteria, you must test it.

3. Discover Whether Skills Are Present. Do what you can without resorting to a test. For example, if the order-entry people are doing their job without complaints or problems, they wouldn't profit from a test. But suppose three of the order-entry people are about to quit or retire? Their manager hires three new people. The natural tendency is to put the new people into training immediately to prepare them for the job, but that may not be necessary. The manager can take steps to find out. For some of the skills, finding out can be fairly simple. To see, for example, whether the new people can interface with the order-entry system, the manager can simply ask them to try. Other skills may not be so easy to sample, for example, their ability to interact with store managers. A pretest may be appropriate for the new hires.

4. Schedule the Test. By being scheduled, the test becomes a reality. It is no longer conjecture. You say, in effect, "We are going to do this." You put the wheels in motion. For the order-entry example, the test should be given as soon as possible, as there is no justification for delay.

There is an obvious caveat. What if no test exists? The order-entry manager had no use for a test until the three new people were hired. This, unfortunately, is a common occurrence. In the best of all worlds, the requirement for a test would have been projected, and it would have been developed well in advance. Our order-entry manager can't schedule a test that doesn't exist, can she? Of course she can. The importance of scheduling is obvious when you look at it from the order-entry manager's point of view. By scheduling the test, she mandates its development.

The justification process brings the test maker to the first go/no-go decision. After a test has been justified, work can begin. The decision must be deliberate and systematic. This saves countless resources by eliminating indecision.

Step 3: Identify Performances to Be Tested

Normally, performances are identified during justification. The task now is to look at the skill lists you developed with the express purpose of selecting those to be tested.

First, decide what skills should be tested. In the case of a skill set such as those possessed by order-entry clerks, the answer is fairly obvious. The skills tested should be those most essential to competent performance of the job. Identification of those skills, though, sometimes presents a problem. It's appropriate to go through the list and to examine the nature of the skills to check:

1. Whether the skills are direct application (the main objective) or enabling skills (prerequisites or components of other skills).
2. How complex the skills are.
3. The skills' relative importance to competent practitioners.

Application

Basically, skills either have a direct bearing on the performance of a job or they support the effort in some way. They are either *directly applicable* or they *enable* skills that are directly applicable. Direct application is sometimes difficult to pin down.

It is best to look for enabling skills first. If you can find the enablers, the rest must be direct application skills.

> **enabling skills**
> The fundamentals or building blocks for more complex skills.

For example, in seeking skills that have a direct application to order entry, you find "able to maintain an objective outlook." The skill is soft, but it is directly applicable because it does not enable another, higher-level, skill.

How about "speak plainly and concisely"? Is this directly applicable? You might have trouble deciding, but ask yourself, "Does it enable any of the other skills?" Yes, it does. It supports the skill to interact orally with a store manager and others.

Let's take a moment to look at an example from education. There is a mandate for teachers to bring their students into a discipline, to allow them to become historians rather than simply to learn history, and to allow them to become mathematicians rather than just learn mathematics. Teachers can look at skills much as the order-entry manager would. Which ones are enabling? Which ones are directly applicable? It is easier to spot the enablers here. Learning multiplication tables enables students to use multiplication to solve problems. Knowledge of the multiplication tables is an enabler.

Enablers for some tasks may be directly applicable for others, so one can't expect a skill to keep the same label. For example, computer keyboard skills are enablers for the entry of orders, but they are directly applicable when the skill sought is tutoring new hires. Knowing how to spell words enables a person to write, but it is directly applicable in a spelling bee.

Complexity

Task lists are most useful when broken down into components. An order-entry clerk may "post the order." This would entail listing separate items with quantity and price, calling up a screen on the computer, filling in the blanks, checking for errors and oversights, and sending the order through. The application contains many enabling skills. Break the complexity down so you can complete the next step of the process: setting criteria.

If you aren't familiar with a process for breaking complex skills into their basic components, you should find one and use it. Complexity brings uncertainty, and uncertainty can lead to tests that do not yield useful information.

I recommend the process developed by Briggs and Gagné (1977) or a similar one by Mager and Pipe (1984) or, more recently, Carlisle's work (1987). All can help you isolate skill areas with confidence. Once this is done, you can easily identify the skills you should test.

Importance

The next basic question is, "Is this skill important enough to include on a test?" The success or failure of a test often rests on the answer to this question. Given skills that are directly applicable, should you test all of them? Probably not. Often there is neither enough time nor resources to test them all. To decide which belong on the test, remember these cautions:

1. Don't test skills you can safely assume to be in place.
2. Don't test skills that resist testing.

> **assumed skills**
> Skills required for a person to be where he or she is.

Assumed skills are those easily deduced from the evidence available. For example, the new hires for the order-entry positions were screened before they were hired, and it should be safe to assume the new hires know how to do simple arithmetic and write simple reports. This isn't always true, but for that position, such an assumption should be safe.

You will also be able to assume skills more directly related to the task. People promoted from within a company will know things about the company and have skills they've developed in other positions. A simple investigation should reveal what those skills are. College graduates who majored in an area can be assumed to know something about the area (be careful not to overestimate this, though).

Because of the complexity and scope of jobs in these times, you will have to assume many things about the potential test takers. Be cautious, but don't be afraid. Usually, when a respondent lacks an assumed skill the lack is reflected in the person's ability with other aspects of the job that are being tested. If new hires can't interpret a computer screen, they'll have trouble sending an order through the system.

Skills that resist testing may be difficult to articulate. They may require considerable resources. They may be *one-time-only* skills. If this is the case, you may choose to avoid testing them directly. Be sure you think the decision through in terms of their impact on the process. You may want to test them anyway. It costs the U.S. Army several thousand dollars each time a soldier fires a missile. The cost of testing is justified, however, because those people have to be able to fire the missiles. Lives depend on their skills. On the other hand, what if order-entry people must have "warm personable relationships with store managers?" Testing will be so cumbersome and time consuming that you will probably choose not to test it.

Now you're down to the nitty-gritty. What skills will you choose to test? Basically, decide which ones are most important and test those. Importance is subjective. What you think is important may not seem so to the client or the test takers. You should check your perceptions after making the choices.

Because importance is a matter of judgment, I will leave it for you to determine. However, don't be tempted to drop skill areas that are difficult or expensive to test for reasons other than importance. Although it is true that some skills are expensive to test, that doesn't mean that they should not be tested. Consider the bottom line. If you don't test a skill, people who lack it may be asked to perform it. What will be the net effect on the organization if they are unable to do so?

Suppose you are testing the order-entry people. Suppose, also, you decide not to test their ability to fill out the forms correctly because it would require using the computer, and perhaps interrupting current operations. What would happen if, on the job, they entered an incorrect order or several incorrect orders? Store managers would not receive what they ordered. Their customers might become upset and stop shopping at the store. Inventories would be out of whack. Just-in-time supply would be thrown off. All kinds of trouble could result from not testing a necessary skill.

Step 4: Set Criteria for Each Performance

This is a key task. Without adequate criteria, your test is bound to fail. The evidence points that way. There are so many ways a test can fail. One all-too-familiar way is for the test to test the wrong thing.

Before you set performance criteria, you should have decided on and expressed the skills to be measured as performance statements. A performance statement specifies the performance, conditions, and criteria. Develop complete performance statements. There is an added benefit. If you have a performance statement, it's easier to decide whether the skills tested are the right ones.

For example, suppose your boss asks you to develop a qualification test for soft drink route drivers. The drivers deliver soft drinks to stores, resorts, corporate facilities, restaurants, school campuses, and brokers. They handle seventeen brands in cans, bottles (including plastic), and syrup. They are responsible for:

- Driving safely and courteously.
- Presenting a good image of the company and its products.
- Maintaining their trucks.
- Unloading the merchandise and arranging it when necessary.
- Sales and route development.

- Service and maintenance of dispensing machines.
- Delivery on time in the right quantity with courtesy and good humor.
- Inventory control through the LORAN system.
- Billing and revenue collection (where appropriate).
- Marketing and promotion of the product at the point of sale.

These statements about the route drivers' duties are informative. In fact, at first glance, you may think they're just fine. They pretty well tell the reader what a route driver must do to be successful. You might not see any problems until you begin to build a test for potential route drivers. Then you begin to see that the statements are insufficient. For example, look at the first one. The route drivers are responsible for "driving safely and courteously." What is safe? What is courteous? Can you tell when you see a soft drink truck moving down a highway? Probably not. The statement is important. Route drivers should drive well; after all, it's a major part of their work.

It may be good for the company to tell the route drivers they must be "safe and courteous." However, the drivers would not receive much guidance about what safe or courteous means. I suppose they could look the words up in a dictionary; sometimes that helps. The point is that statements like the ones above don't really provide enough guidance to be useful. This is particularly true when it comes to testing people to see if they are conforming.

Suppose you have been commissioned to develop a performance test to determine whether route drivers at the company are competent. The statements above are the ones you have to use to build the test. Would you be able to do it? Probably. Would the test test what it should? Probably not. You would have to guess about major variables. What is safe? What is courteous?

Safe and courteous are fairly easy. There are state and national guidelines that could help you. There are other sources for them, but how about another of the statements in the job description? How are you going to test whether drivers fulfill their responsibility to "service and maintain dispensing machines"? The policies and procedures for this are internal to the company.

This clearly illustrates the problem of deciding what to test. How will you know whether any driver is any better than any other in performing this activity? What you should have is a clearer statement about what drivers do and about how they should do it.

Performance Statements

A performance statement contains three parts. (1) It gives the conditions under which a performance can take place. (2) It states the performance. (3) It specifies criteria to be used to measure accomplishment of the performance. These may

performance statement

A statement of the conditions, activity, and criteria used to define a performance.

sound familiar to you. They are the three parts of Bob Mager's performance objectives (1963, 1997): conditions, performance, criteria. With those in place you can measure anything.

Conditions are what should be in place before a performance can happen. They include things like where it will happen, the materials and equipment, who will support it, and so forth. Consider the route drivers. What conditions are required for them to drive safely and courteously? They must have a truck in good condition. They should have been given the government regulations and company rules. A good performance statement about driving safely and courteously would include these things. Of course, some things don't have to be stated. These *safe assumptions* include things that are commonly available, normal conditions, and other conditions you might ordinarily expect to be in place, such as this: The trucks will have rearview mirrors and they will perform on appropriate streets and roads.

Performances say what people are expected to do—the activity that will take place. Performances can be cognitive, affective, or psychomotor. We tend to think of them as being physical activities, but they can be thoughts or emotions as well. In a performance statement, the performance is usually indicated by a verb phrase.

Criteria are the standards to be used to judge the adequacy of the performance. They can say how many, how much, or when. They can state who will be

criterion

The measurement to be used to judge adequacy.

satisfied. They can be detailed or general. However they're stated, they prescribe the measurement to be used to judge adequacy. They are the part of a performance statement the test maker is most interested in. The more specific they are, the easier they are to measure.

Let's look at an example: "On a sunny day the lumberjack will use a double-bitted axe to chop down a mature (at least twelve inches in diameter) pine tree in less than fifteen minutes, leaving a stump no more than six inches high." The three elements are easily identified. Look at the conditions: *on a sunny day the lumberjack will use a double-bitted axe.* We know what kind of light is appropriate, who's going to do it, and what he or she will use as a tool. We know what type tree is to be chopped. The performance is simply expressed as *chop down.* It doesn't take a lot of verbiage to say what will happen. Now look at the criteria: *mature (at least twelve inches in diameter) pine tree in less than fifteen minutes, leaving a stump no more than six inches high.* The criteria do two things. First, they tell us what to look for (size of tree, time, and size of stump). Second, they prevent us from looking for something else. The stump doesn't have to be smooth or level on top. The chips don't have to be a certain size. There's no requirement for an undercut or accuracy in directing the fall of the tree. Of course, these things may, indeed, be important. They could be stated in a second statement, but they are absent here, and *if this is the only statement about this activity, no other aspect of the work should be tested.*

Respondents are often judged in unexpected ways. This happens whenever criteria are not spelled out. It's a way a test maker can play "Gotcha!" However, if particular criteria have not been prespecified, they should *not* be used to judge adequacy of performance. This is true even when both respondents and test givers know the criteria should have been supplied. But if they are not, the test scorer must not count them in scoring.

Another example: "Given simultaneous quadratic equations, the student will select techniques to be used to find correct solution sets." The *conditions* are a set of quadratic equations. The *performance* is selection of techniques. The *criteria:* we will know the students have performed well if they select techniques that lead to appropriate solution sets. This statement does not provide as much detail, nor is it as clearly written as the lumberjack example. It does the job, however, because both the students and the scorer will know from reading it what is required for success.

Now let's return to the route drivers. A performance technologist (PT) examined the job description and wrote performance statements for each of the requirements. The conditions were stated as givens for the entire set:

Route drivers are provided:

- Delivery trucks in good working condition.
- Adequate descriptions of their routes and established customers.
- Adequate supplies of all products.
- All tools required to service and maintain equipment.

The conditions were followed by the performances. Each performance carried its own criteria. For example, one of the descriptions was, "Service and maintain dispensing machines." When the PT rewrote it as a performance statement (under the conditions above), it looked like this:

The driver will service soft drink dispensing equipment to:

- Freestanding vending machines.
- Syrup tanks for fountains and other over-the-counter locations.
- Carbonation equipment.

The driver will perform these duties so that:

- Equipment performs as designed without inconvenience to operators or customers.
- Equipment is well stocked, and out-of-stock conditions occur less than 2 percent of the time.
- Revenue is maintained at current levels or increased.

The driver will maintain soft drink dispensing equipment (see givens above) so that:

- Downtime is limited to less than 5 percent of time in service.
- No machine is allowed to remain out of service for more than twenty-four hours.
- Customer complaints about delivery of product from machines amount to no more than two per month.
- Machines meet corporate standards for cleanliness.
- Machines present an appealing appearance to customers (that is, customers don't complain about how the equipment looks).

The magic words are *so that*. They signal criteria. The test maker is interested in the complete statement, but the *so that* portion is the critical part. These are the words that direct measurement and, therefore, mandate the test. Not only do the criteria specify what is to be measured. They also forecast test conditions, test type, and the kind of items to be used. More important, they specify what the test items should test and how they should be tested.

As was stated earlier, *criteria are the key to development of good fair tests.* If the criteria don't represent the intended results well, the results won't be as intended. Double-talk, yes, but the message is clear. Without good criteria, you can't expect to develop a good test. A lot of your success will depend on your ability to develop and interpret criteria.

All of the *so that* statements above can be measured. How this is done is discussed in the next chapter. Let's return for a moment to developing performance statements. How did the PT do what he did to the route drivers' job description?

The process comes from what Joe Harless (1983) calls *front end analysis*. It is a needs assessment process, which, when done well, provides three things:

- What should be, that is, how things would be if conditions were totally acceptable.
- Current conditions, that is, how things are now.
- The gaps between the two. These are the needs.

If you are interested in being able to do this yourself, there are several sources you can consult. Perhaps the most efficient is Joe Harless's workshop. Many books have been written about it. I heartily recommend *Instructional Design Principles and Applications* by Briggs and colleagues (1992) or *Strategic Planning Plus* by Roger Kaufman (1991).

Whether you develop them yourself or obtain help from others, performance statements must be the foundation for your tests. And they must have criteria. Criteria enable you to ask good questions. In Chapter One, I stated that anything can be measured. Remember that this is only true if criteria have been developed.

Unfortunately, criteria are often developed without consideration for respondent preferences. This is particularly true in formal education. The teacher decides what the criteria are without thinking too much about what learners might prefer. This tendency can be illustrated through a tactic often employed by teachers. They develop so-called *behavioral objectives.* You may have seen some of them, such as, "The students will be able to name the capitals of the fifty states." The criteria are unstated, assumed. The teacher *assumes* the students know how fast they have to work, whether they have to spell the names correctly, and how they will display their skill. If they were stated, students would know whether they would be responding orally or in writing. If in writing, they would know whether spelling counts. They would know how much time they have in which to respond and whether they would be writing capital names beside the names of states or writing capital names on a map of the states.

You can find similarly sketchy criteria for performances in business. Supervisors expect workers to recite the steps of an assembly process, or managers ask their people to specify regulations governing certain activities. The recitation (besides being a poor predictor of success in application) puts some workers at a disadvantage.

The way criteria are stated determines the nature of the test. The results of this step determine the basic thrust of the test and, therefore, are the keys to developing a good fair test.

Summary

The first two parts of the test-building process involve the theoretical considerations and the basic thinking through of the testing process and results. In essence, you will have decided what kind of test to use, how to develop it, who will benefit from its use, and what those benefits will be.

Now you can plan the test with confidence.

CHAPTER SEVEN

PLANNING THE TEST

As we begin to discuss the next group of steps, keep in mind that the processes suggested here are not, by any means, the only feasible ones. In fact, other test makers prefer other procedures. However, these steps work well, and you will find them useful and dependable.

There is an important caveat. *This process is a system,* that is, the steps fit together. Each depends on the others for consistency and elegance. If you leave one or more out or if you substitute a step from another paradigm you run the risk of the system breaking down. The gravest risk you run is that the test you build will become less effective as a performance measurement instrument.

Therefore, if you use this process, use the whole thing as it is presented. Of course, you can modify the steps to fit your personality and your situation, but please conform to the intent and stick with the process. Carefully consider any modifications before you implement them.

The steps presented in this chapter focus on the important choices you must make before actually writing your test. The following questions will be answered as you work through these steps: What type of test will give respondents the best opportunity to respond well? What test will best fit the constraints of your organization? What will the test look like? and How will respondents react?

Step 5: Select the Type of Test

You must now decide which type of test best suits the criteria you have developed. If this seems difficult, review the ideas in Chapter Two.

Basically, there are two item formats: either respondents supply the answers or they select from answers you supply. There are many item types within these overall formats. In this book serious consideration is given to four kinds of items: essay, short answer, multiple choice, and matching.

There are also three kinds of tests: achievement tests, which are usually norm referenced; performance tests (including diagnostic tests), which are usually criterion referenced; and attitude or opinion tests. The tests you build can be any of these kinds and use any of the types of items. You could also use different types of items within a test. I wouldn't recommend this, but it is an option you will find appropriate from time to time. For example, you might develop a hard-skills performance test, but also have respondents answer a few multiple-choice items to discover learner attitudes about training they have just undergone.

The goal is to design the specific test that best measures what you want to measure. You want the best possible way to satisfy the criteria you developed in Step 4. Figure 7.1 illustrates the choices you have.

Look again at some of the criteria presented for route drivers. I've added numbers to identify each *so that* (each criterion).

FIGURE 7.1. ITEM TYPES AND KINDS OF TESTS.

Kinds \ Types	Essay	Short Answer	Multiple Choice	Matching
Achievement				
Accomplishment				
Opinionnaire				

The driver will service soft drink dispensing equipment to:

- Freestanding vending machines.
- Syrup tanks for fountains and other over-the-counter locations.
- Carbonation equipment.

The driver will perform these duties so that:

1. Equipment performs as designed without inconvenience to operators or customers.
2. Equipment is well stocked, and out-of-stock conditions occur less than 2 percent of the time.
3. Revenue is maintained at current levels or increased.

The driver will maintain soft drink dispensing equipment so that:

4. Downtime is limited to less than 5 percent of time in service.
5. No machine is allowed to remain out of service for more than twenty-four hours.
6. Customer complaints about delivery of product from machines amount to no more than two per month.
7. Machines meet corporate standards for cleanliness.
8. Machines present an appealing appearance to customers (that is, customers don't complain about how the equipment looks).

First, decide what kind of test and type of item would be best for each criterion. One way to do this is to place the number for the criterion in an appropriate cell of the kinds/types matrix. Look at criterion 1.

1. Equipment performs as designed without inconvenience to operators or customers.

Where will the answers be found? The people who operate the equipment (client stores and locations) and customers would have the answers. The kind of test most often used to find this sort of information is the opinionnaire. Neither an achievement test nor an accomplishment test is appropriate.

How should the criterion be tested? Essay is not a good choice. Customers aren't likely to respond well. Short answer would be OK (except collecting the answers would be time consuming). Multiple choice would work well. Matching would not. You could call customers on the phone and administer either a short-answer or a multiple-choice test. Such an approach might save time and money. You could simply ask people, "What, if any, problems have you had with this machine?" The traditional survey is appropriate, but it has drawbacks (such as the risk of a poor return).

Or you could write a short-answer item like this:

1. Have you had problems with this machine? Please note the kind of trouble you have had in the space below.

Or perhaps you would prefer a multiple-choice item administered via a survey:

1. Have you had any problems with this machine? Please circle all appropriate answers.
   a. No problems caused by service or condition of the machine.
   b. Leakage from product.
   c. Coin mechanism jammed.
   d. Soft drinks not falling into delivery chute.
   e. Soft drinks too cold or too warm.
   f. Cans damaged (dented or marred).
   g. Other (please indicate other problems in this space).

These samples illustrate that either short-answer or multiple-choice items would be appropriate for the criterion. (If you aren't sure whether an item type would work, try writing one.) Because either type would work for the criterion, place the number of the criterion (1) in the appropriate cells in the matrix (Figure 7.2).
     Look at the second criterion.

2. Equipment is well stocked, and out-of-stock conditions occur less than 2 percent of the time.

FIGURE 7.2. SAMPLE MATRIX.

Kinds ╲ Types	Essay	Short Answer	Multiple Choice	Matching
Achievement				
Accomplishment				
Opinionnaire		1.	1.	

Again the answers will be found with clients and customers. You could check client stores or locations for complaints, but the information would probably be more dependable if you went directly to the users.

This time, short answer wouldn't do the job well because it would be difficult to categorize the answers. However, multiple choice would work well if you supplied respondents with a scale, as in the following example:

2. How often during the past three months has this machine been sold out of one or more kinds of soft drink?
   a. More than once a day.
   b. At least once a day.
   c. More than once a week.
   d. At least once a week.
   e. More than once a month.
   f. At least once a month.

Because multiple choice seems to be the only type of item that would work well, place a 2 in the appropriate cell in the matrix, as shown in Figure 7.3.

Have the idea? First, visualize the kind and type of items that could be used to test each criterion. Then enter the number of the criterion in all appropriate cells in the matrix. Let's look at criterion 3.

3. Revenue is maintained at current levels or increased.

Oops. Just when things were going along so well. Clients or customers would not know the answer to this one. The finance officer would, but so would the route

FIGURE 7.3. SAMPLE MATRIX.

Kinds \ Types	Essay	Short Answer	Multiple Choice	Matching
Achievement				
Accomplishment				
Opinionnaire		1.	1. 2.	

drivers themselves. Why not ask them? You are not limited to a single test. If two distinct populations are involved, it makes sense to develop two separate tests.

What sort of item would work best for criterion 3? Again, short answer would work fine, but so would multiple choice. Because the response doesn't have to be specific (the criterion specifies current or better levels of revenue), the alternatives can be stated generally. However, with this criterion you're no longer asking for an opinion. You want data you can check if necessary. So the *kind of test* has changed to performance. Now place the number 3 in the matrix, as shown in Figure 7.4.

Criteria 4 through 8 are repeated below. Criterion 7 should be tested through direct observation; that is, someone should look at the machines and decide whether they meet the criterion, or perhaps you can test it by use of a short-answer item. Examine each of the other criteria (4, 5, 6, and 8). Decide what cell it should be in. Then check against my choices, shown in Figure 7.5.

The driver will maintain soft drink dispensing equipment so that:

4. Downtime is limited to less than 5 percent of time in service.
5. No machine is allowed to remain out of service for more than twenty-four hours.
6. Customer complaints about delivery of product from machines amount to no more than two per month.
7. Machines meet corporate standards for cleanliness.
8. Machines present an appealing appearance to customers (that is, customers don't complain about how the equipment looks).

The completed matrix (Figure 7.5) helps us decide that a multiple-choice test would be best, or perhaps two of them—one to measure driver performance and the other an opinionnaire to use with clients and customers.

FIGURE 7.4. SAMPLE MATRIX.

Kinds \ Types	Essay	Short Answer	Multiple Choice	Matching
Achievement				
Accomplishment		3.	3.	
Opinionnaire		1.	1. 2.	

As is usually the case, I would have to compromise. Some of the criteria are measured better by items other than multiple-choice. This is almost always true. But, in the real world, we aren't always in a position to use the best kind of item for each criterion. The best possible item has to be forgone if it results in respondent indifference, too much elapsed time, or unjustifiable expense.

Respondent Indifference

Respondents usually want to respond. However, they can be turned off. One way to turn them off is to keep showing up with tests or surveys. I once proposed a survey for a job we were doing with a manufacturing company. Management thought it was a good idea, but when I asked the employees who would be responding, they weren't enthusiastic. It seems they had responded to five surveys in the past month. I found another way to obtain the data I wanted.

Another way to generate indifference is to use essay items. People are not fond of writing long explanations. When faced with a comprehensive report or long letter, many times they will procrastinate or comply without enthusiasm. Even when they agree that there is a need, many people simply don't want to write long explanations. You may want to avoid essay items for this reason, especially on opinion tests, because they are designed primarily to help the test maker, and respondents know that.

Too Much Time

Bulky tests can turn people off. The moment they see several pages of items, they become restive. Sometimes you can counter this tendency by telling them how long the test will take. If you do, be sure your estimate is accurate for the audience you're addressing. People with average reading skills can work three or more

FIGURE 7.5. COMPLETED MATRIX.

Kinds \ Types	Essay	Short Answer	Multiple Choice	Matching
Achievement				
Accomplishment		3. 5. 7.	3. 5. 6.	
Opinionnaire		1.	1. 2. 4. 8.	

multiple-choice items per minute. A fifty-item test, therefore, should take less than twenty minutes. On the other hand, it often takes people an hour or more to do just three essay items.

The critical element about use of time is how the respondents perceive it. For example, one of the disadvantages of a true/false test is that, even though people can respond to as many as twenty true/false items per minute, they generally have the feeling the task is taking a long time. This happens because a true/false test has to have a lot of items to measure anything accurately. To counter the guess factor the test must have at least one hundred items. That's quite a few. Respondents often feel the test is taking a long time, even though they may finish it in ten minutes.

Expense

Tests are expensive. They take time and, for most of us, time is an expensive commodity. A simple example illustrates how expensive a test can be. Assume that you ask the managers in your company to complete a survey. Assume, also, that they can complete it in about thirty minutes. If there are one hundred managers, they will use a total of fifty hours. Your company will have paid them for that time. If their time is worth $20 an hour, the cost of the time used is $10,000. Now add your time to develop, administer, and evaluate the test. Add the costs of duplication and distribution. Add administrative costs. Your company's total outlay for a simple survey could easily exceed $20,000. "Well," you might say, "that isn't a fair estimate. They can take the survey when it won't interfere with their other duties." True, but they will still be paid for the time.

One often overlooked expense is the cost of lost opportunities. This is a major problem for many bureaucracies. While managers and workers are filling out forms, conforming to administrative mandates, and obliging the desires of others (by completing surveys, for example), they aren't generating ideas or watching the shop. In some organizations, the costs of lost opportunities are huge.

As you select the type of items and the kind of test, consider the risks. Indifference, poor use of time, and excessive costs can make or break a test.

Step 6: Design Test Presentation and Administration

A test is a test. They all look about the same, so design shouldn't be a big deal. Right? If that's what you think, think again. The way a test is designed and administered has a critical effect on how well it will succeed.

A lot of the fear and trepidation associated with tests has to do with how they look and how they're handled by the test giver. Consider a test I took in graduate school. I was herded into a big room with the other respondents and told to seat

proctor
Someone hired to administer and oversee a test situation.

myself so at least two desks separated me and my nearest neighbor. The proctor, a serious young man, gave a short lecture on how we would be summarily executed if we cheated. He then handed out test booklets. They were severe in appearance, printed officiously, with warnings like, "Do Not Open Until Told to Do So," on every page. We were given one hour to complete each section. When finished, we were instructed to put down our pencils and sit silently. It was not a pleasant experience.

Tests don't have to be like that. They can be fun. They can look nice. Of course, a bit of decorum is necessary. Respondents must be given a decent opportunity to respond; laughing and carrying on aren't appropriate. But the scene I described should be an exception. Was my ability to do my best enhanced by the way the test was presented and administered? You're shaking your head. What was wrong? What could be done to make the task of the respondents easier?

Let's explore that. You are going to give people tests. It's appropriate that they should have a fair chance to do their best. How you present your test and how you administer it will bear directly on how fair that opportunity is. I won't try to explain everything there is to know about presentation (appearance, size, composition, and format) and administration here for three reasons: (1) this topic is a book by itself; (2) many of the details of presentation are better given in the development phase; and (3) most of the information about administering a test is in Chapter Nine, where it seems more appropriate.

I do, however, want you to think about these things during the design step. Otherwise, you will probably have to rework your design later. How the test will look and how large it will be (presentation) and how respondents will encounter it (administration) should be considered well before actual development begins.

Presentation

Two aspects of presentation will be covered here. One is *appearance*—how the test looks, how it's printed, the kind of paper, use of illustrations, formatting, and so forth. The other is the *size* of the test.

Appearance. A test can look like a test without scaring people. It should have a title and instructions for use. There is usually little doubt about its nature. Still, it doesn't have to intimidate respondents. If you take the time and effort you would on other important documents, a test can look less threatening to respondents. The difference is easy to illustrate. The first page of the Manager's Philosophic Value Inventory (MPVI) is shown in two different ways in Figures 7.6 (p. 148) and 7.7 (p. 149). Look at them and then decide which one you would rather encounter as a respondent.

FIGURE 7.6. MANAGER'S PHILOSOPHIC
VALUE INVENTORY (MPVI).

The MPVI is a new kind of inventory. It will tell you how your management style compares with your own feelings about yourself, the style of your executive management, the style of your peers, and the styles of the managers across the country.

It is a simple instrument. There are twenty-three multiple-choice questions with five alternative responses each. But it will take some thought. Every answer is correct, depending on how you personally feel about the situation described. So each response requires consideration.

The process is easy. If you are not a manager, put yourself in the position of a manager in your organization. Visualize yourself dealing with superiors, peers, and subordinates as a manager should. Respond to each item in the way you think best, whether you believe that tactic is viable for your organization or not.

Instructions for Use

In each of the items you will find a situation described. Some of these will be rather ordinary; some will be outlandish. Whatever the situation, you should have some kind of initial reaction.

Take a moment to note that reaction in the space provided if you wish. Think about it a moment or two before reading the responses provided.

Then look carefully at the five solutions or actions that follow. Choose the *one* that most closely matches your initial reaction and circle its letter. If none of the solutions or actions matches your reaction, choose the one that seems most reasonable. You must choose *one and only one* response for each item.

All of the responses are correct. Each has been used by a manager in a situation similar to the one described. Of course, you will not like them all. You may not like any of them. However, you must choose one of them.

FIGURE 7.7. MANAGER'S PHILOSOPHIC
VALUE INVENTORY (MPVI).

DO NOT OPEN BOOKLET UNTIL TOLD TO DO SO

The MPVI interrogates your management style compared with your own feelings about yourself, the style of your executive management, the style of your peers, and the styles of other managers across the country. There are twenty-three multiple-choice questions with five alternative responses each. First, if you are not already a manager, put yourself in the position of a manager in your organization. Visualize yourself dealing with superiors, peers, and subordinates as a manager should. Second, respond to each item in the way you think best, whether you believe that tactic is viable for your organization or not.

Instructions

In each of the items you will find a situation described. Whatever the situation, you should have some kind of initial reaction. Note that reaction in the space provided. Choose the *one* alternative that most closely matches your initial reaction and circle its letter. If none of the solutions or actions matches your reaction, choose the one that seems most reasonable. You must choose *one and only one* response for each item.

The rendition in Figure 7.7 saves a lot of space, but at what cost? In my opinion, it's a disaster. I would not want to take the test as presented.

Many tests are crowded affairs. Questions are jammed onto the page. Margins are narrow. Spacing is close. The type is small. Test makers have two basic reasons for using such a format: (1) to reduce the number of pages so the test doesn't seem big and (2) to save paper. Neither reason justifies the disservice done to the respondents.

I have found that another pair of eyes is helpful. When the test has been developed, ask someone with experience to look at it with the intent of improving how it looks.

Size. Of course, there is a good reason to reduce the size of the document itself if you can. People are often intimidated by bulky documents, particularly tests. There are things you can do to reduce the size of a test. One is to ask fewer questions. Don't use forty multiple-choice items if you can do the job with twenty. The secret is to avoid Level One Cognitive items, which tend to bulk up a test. If you can restrict your test to Levels Two and Three, you'll be able to test well with relatively few items.

Another way to reduce the size of the test is to use the space you have wisely. Look at Figure 7.8. It is OK, but you could save space with a few simple changes, shown in Figure 7.9. Figure 7.9 illustrates the effects of three changes:

FIGURE 7.8. WORKSHOP OPINIONNAIRE.

Name : _____

Department: _____

Training session: _____

For each item, circle the letter of the one alternative you feel is closest to your own experience.

1. Do you feel you possessed the knowledge and skills needed to begin the session?

   a. I did not know what to expect so I was not well prepared.

   b. I did a few things to get ready but not a lot.

   c. I'm not sure whether I was ready to begin the session.

   d. I was fairly well prepared, although there were areas where I could have done better.

   e. My preparation was complete and accurate. I covered all the bases.

   Comments:

2. How difficult was it to understand the materials used in the workshop?

   a. I could not understand them. They were practically useless.

   b. I understood some of them, but they were difficult.

   c. I could understand most of them, although it was not as easy as it could have been.

   d. I only had one or two minor problems.

   e. I understood them all very well.

   Comments:

(1) respondent identification has been reduced to two lines at the top, (2) the alternatives are now on a continuum, and (3) the margins have been reduced to five spaces on each side.

There is now enough extra space on the page for two more items. You could put four on a page instead of two. By the way, these changes also make it more user-friendly.

Another trick is to print the test on both sides of the paper, which cuts the number of pages in half. If you do this, be sure to use quality paper so the printing on one side doesn't show through.

There is a school of thought that declares people are turned off by tests with more than one page—that respondents won't bother with a test if it seems to impose on them. This may be most true for inventories and, especially, surveys. It's a catch-22. If you make the survey short to appease such people, you won't get all the information you want. The instrument will be much less valuable. If you make it as long as it should be, your returns may be so poor as to make it much less valuable. Either way, you lose.

FIGURE 7.9. WORKSHOP SURVEY.

Name: _____

Department: _____ Session: _____

For each item circle the *one* alternative you feel is closest to your own experience.

1. Do you feel you possessed the knowledge and skills needed to begin the session?

not prepared		satisfactorily prepared		well prepared
1	2	3	4	5

Comments:

2. How difficult was it to understand the materials and presentations during the session?

very difficult		some difficult; some easy		very easy
1	2	3	4	5

Comments:

Administration

The question here is not how long the test is but how it is administered.

Some time ago I had the opportunity to administer a survey for a large company. At the same time, unknown to me, an employee of the company was administering a very similar instrument. The rate of return for my instrument was just higher than 90 percent. Ninety percent of the people completed and returned the survey. His rate of return was less than 30 percent. The difference was in how the two surveys were administered.

The reason for the difference? He sent the survey to all the people in the company and asked people to return them in envelopes he included as part of the package. Essentially, he placed the responsibility for returning the instrument on the respondent. Think about it. Why should people help him with his problem when there isn't much in it for them? Even though the survey was designed well, it failed in its purpose because the return was so small. I did it differently. First, I selected a random sample of the population (twenty-six people). Then I contacted the manager or supervisor of each of the targeted respondents. I asked the managers to agree to be sure that everyone completed the survey and then return it to me. Because the managers had a vested interest in the results, they were quite willing to do so. Voila.

Test administration should be thought through during the design phase, but test makers usually should not be too specific until a test is ready for use. By then you will know much more about it and any special requirements you may encounter. I don't mean that administration is not very important. Indeed, I've devoted Chapter Nine to the topic. But you will benefit by having read that chapter before completing your design, just to be sure the requirements can be met through your design. If administration is your immediate concern, you may want to read Chapter Nine now. Administration is often the key element in the success or failure of a test.

◆ ◆ ◆

Formal Test Design: An Added Concern for Major Efforts

Most of the tests you design and develop yourself won't reach large or cosmopolitan audiences. They will be important but, for the most part, they will be limited in scope and impact. Perhaps your test will be a final exam for a course or a qualifying exam for a particular group of employees. For most of you, Step 6 previously mentioned and Step 7 to follow will be sufficient for your design work. However, if your test is more ambitious, your design must be thorough and comprehensive. For example, if you intend to use your test to certify people to do a particular job or belong to a select group, you must design it as carefully as possible. Otherwise, you could run into litigation problems as well as unhappy clients.

Let's take some time, then, to discuss how you can execute a foolproof design for a good fair test. Good design is an ongoing concern, not a onetime activity. The test design is your plan for carrying out the fifteen steps. If you have a good design, you can build a good fair test. If you do not, the task is uncertain and difficult. Design stabilizes test content by providing a framework and an outline for development.

Stabilizes Content

Design is a mental activity. You do it in your head, but to ensure that your testing process doesn't change over time, you must document the process. The documents you produce are evidence of your thinking. It's important to keep this in mind because design documents cannot fully represent your thinking. As good as they are, they will fall short of the total thought process. Many who are reading this will say to themselves, "That's true, so I shouldn't have to spend a lot of time on it or produce a pretty document." Please don't think that. Your design documents have to communicate your thinking not only to others, but to yourself later as you use them to produce your test.

Design is critical. Not only will your design specify the content and criteria to be tested, but it will also indicate how they will be tested and why they will be tested that way. Consider yourself and what you want to accomplish. If you have to develop a test, the chances are the task will take many hours over several days. What are the odds that your thinking about the test will be the same when you finish as when you began? Not good. In fact most of us tend to lose much of our original thinking as we progress with a lengthy task. Shortcuts are taken. Considerations are forgotten. Unanticipated problems cause loss of time and concentration.

Basically, without a design of some sort, we stand a very good chance of producing a second-class product, which is not a pleasing prospect. Probably, the more important the test is to the respondents, the more important it is for us to design it well. Thus, the only safe assumption is that every test is important—every one. So we should be conscientious in designing every test we develop, whether it's a pop quiz or a national certification exam.

The design describes the content to be tested. The design also specifies how it will be tested. By tying each item to a specific criterion, it tells why it will be tested. The content to be tested is analyzed, evaluated, and communicated. When the design is complete, the content is totally known and understood; you will understand what you are testing much better than you did before you began.

A Framework and an Outline for Development

A framework or outline is what most people think of when they hear the term *design*. It's analogous to an author's outline for an article or book. It provides a blueprint for the product, the test. A good design will consider all fifteen steps of the development process. It will address the tasks each step presents as comprehensively as possible, short of actually beginning test development. In fact, a *good* design will contain elements of the final product as examples or prototypes.

If you conscientiously adhere to your design for your test, you will make sure what you think should happen for respondents does, indeed, happen for them.

The Design Process

The fifteen steps are implicit to good design. To say that another way: A good design will contain all fifteen steps. In essence that's all there is to it. Easy to say and, usually, fairly easy to do. A test design is *not* a big deal. If you consider each step and how it will be accomplished and document that thinking, you will have a design. It doesn't take long, and the more you use the process the easier it becomes.

I recommend using the fifteen steps as an outline for your design. To illustrate, let's assume Figure 7.10 is a test design developed by a director of training at a large corporation. In the pages that follow, I will comment on what the director did for each step and why he did it.

A design is a working document. It's the blueprint for the test. It provides the specifications to guide developers and item writers as they work. The critical issues are centered in how well they can respond to it. If there is a rub, it's in how well others can respond. Let's consider the ramifications of the design illustrated in Figure 7.10, taking each step separately.

1. Identify and Qualify Potential Respondents. *Current and potential order-entry clerks at XXX Corporation. People who work full-time or part-time as order-entry operators. Generally, this will be restricted to those in the order-entry department, but probably should include others who have been cross-trained to do the work. At present, the audience includes the director, three supervisors, twenty-seven full-time operators, six part-time operators, and nine people from distribution who have been cross-trained for the function.*

This tells us who the respondents will be, how many there are, and some things about them. I would want a bit more information after the design was approved and work was about to begin. Basic demographic information, for example, would be nice.

FIGURE 7.10. DESIGN FOR ORDER-ENTRY QUALIFICATION TEST.

1. Identify and qualify potential respondents.
   Current and potential order-entry clerks at XXX Corporation. People who work full- or part-time as order-entry operators. Generally, this will be restricted to those in the order-entry department, but probably should include others who have been cross-trained to do the work. At present, the audience includes the director, three supervisors, twenty-seven full-time operators, six part-time operators, and nine people from distribution who have been cross-trained for the function.

2. Justify the test.
   Mandate from executive management. The goals are to reduce turnover in the position and the error rate among active order-entry people. The test is to identify weaknesses (if any) in individual performance so remedial action can be taken.

3. Identify performances to be tested.
   Current and anticipated order-entry job skills and attitudes about service and customers.

4. Establish criteria for each performance.
   Can use performance criteria from current job descriptions. Develop new criteria with training department.

5. Select the type of test that best fills the requirements of respondents and provides a valid assessment of the criteria.
   Accomplishment and opinion test. Items will be multiple-choice at levels two and three (see matrix).

6. Design test presentation and administration.
   - *Style—Informal, fog = 6, will provide opportunity for respondents to comment on their needs/wants.*
   - *Time in process—The test will be taken on the job so time in process must be kept to about twenty minutes (double break).*
   - *Environment—Test will be taken by individuals at their workstations during slacks in work. Will try to have others take respondent's calls while he or she is taking test.*
   - *Materials and support—Respondents can use any aids normally available at workstation.*
   - *Administration—Test will be administered by supervisor. Test itself must be self-administered, self-paced.*
   - *Appearance—Booklet. Separate answer sheet. Should be friendly, but not flowery. (See attached outline of first page.) Duplex and staple booklet.*

7. Design or select the evaluation process.
   Test will yield two sets of results.
   - *One: Scores on performance criteria items will indicate mastery of job skills. Cut-score must be established before administration.*
   - *Two: Scores from opinion items will be correlated with manager and supervisor expectations. Significant differences will be referred to management in report form.*

8. Write the items.
   Items will be written by myself and June Carrington. Our subject-matter experts are George Smith, order-entry director, and Maxine Marlow, senior order-entry operator.

FIGURE 7.10. DESIGN FOR ORDER-ENTRY QUALIFICATION TEST, cont'd.

9. Review and qualify the items.
   In addition to the four people above, two senior operators will be asked to review the test and perform a developmental test of it.
10. Pilot the test. Revise and rewrite.
    Pilot on August 12. Use current senior operators as experts and select people from other departments for control group. Pilot can be first administration of test.
11. Set respondent qualification scores (cut-scores).
    Yes. Use contrasting group method.
12. Produce the test.
    In house. June will arrange.
13. Administer the test.
    First administration August 12. Rest of order-entry department by October 14. Subsequent administrations as required.
14. Evaluate the results.
    Compare accomplishment test results with cut-score. Use rank correlation and chi-square for opinion test.
15. Use the results.
    Report to executive management on basic findings. Detailed report to director and supervisors. Recommendations should include training (if any) and specific areas in which improvement would impact the mandate (turnover and error rates).

ATTACHMENT A: PRELIMINARY ESTIMATE OF ITEM TYPES AND USES

DOMAIN / LEVEL	Cognitive — Thinking, ideas, opinions	Affective — Emotions, values, attitudes	Psychomotor — Physical acts & conditions
I Recall	1 Could have one or two items on key terms.	2	3
II Application	4 Should be bulk of test, about 65 percent.	5 Sample ability to be positive and helpful; 20 percent.	6 Could test process with simulation at work. Check time and $.
III Developmental	7 Ability to deal with the unexpected; 15 percent.	8	9

FIGURE 7.10. DESIGN FOR ORDER-ENTRY QUALIFICATION TEST, cont'd.

ATTACHMENT B: OUTLINE OF COVER

ORDER-ENTRY QUALIFICATION TEST

1. Short paragraph on purpose of test. Keep positive and informal.

2. Description of contents, where it will be taken, when, and who will respond.

3. Instructions for test, use of answer sheet, and so forth.

4. Strong statement about how results will be used. No one currently employed should feel threatened. To use the test for disqualification would open the company to litigation.

There is always a possibility management may want to expand the target audience. Normally, I resist this, because changing the intended respondents usually changes the basic nature of a test. To use an old cliché, it mixes apples and bananas. (If it does happen, your conceptualization must change to accommodate it.)

The important implications here have to do with potential worth to the organization. Although the number of people to be sampled is not large (a total of forty-six), their positions in the organization and their impact on the bottom line make this test important. Time and effort to develop an elegant test should be easily justified.

2. Justify the Test. *Mandate from executive management. The goals are to reduce turnover in the position and the error rate among active order-entry people. The test is to identify weaknesses (if any) in individual performance so remedial action can be taken.*

If you remove management and the three women who have been with order entry for so long, the average tenure drops below two years. Turnover is more than 50 percent per year.

The current error rate is a puzzle. There doesn't seem to be a pattern. Old-timers are almost as prone to making errors as new hires. It varies from 82 percent error-free operation (very poor) to 99+ percent (very good indeed). The company standard (goal) is to operate at 97 percent error free or better. The error rate is restricted to data entry and other computer operations. It does not include errors in judgment when dealing with customers. The director of order entry, Robin Jerkins, believes botched calls and poor interactions with customers cost the company much more than data errors.

Although a test should not have much impact on these figures, it can point to areas in which improvement can happen.

3. Identify Performances to Be Tested. *Current and anticipated order-entry job skills and attitudes about service and customers.*

4. Establish Criteria for Each Performance. *Can use performance criteria from current job descriptions. Develop new criteria with training department.*

Because we have discussed criteria at length in other parts of the book, I won't do it here. However, with a test as important as this one, the criteria should be listed. They should be reviewed by the key players to make sure they represent the skills to be tested in ways that make sense to management and the respondents. Be particularly sensitive that the criteria for the opinion items are what management wants to know and what respondents will be able to supply.

5. Select the Type of Test That Best Fills the Requirements of Respondents and Provides a Valid Assessment of the Criteria. *Accomplishment and opinion test. Items will be multiple-choice at levels two and three (see matrix).*

We already have a matrix showing what kinds of items will be used and approximately how they will be distributed. At this point, develop another matrix showing the criteria and how they will be tested. This is a standard part of test design for many people. It's particularly valuable when the test is being developed by a team and two or more people are writing items. Figure 7.11 is an example of the kind of matrix that can prove valuable for this task.

The matrix lists every performance to be tested, along with the criteria. The kind of item to be used is written in. The level the test maker feels is most appropriate is indicated. Of course, these are estimates. The numbers in the cells indicate how many items will be written for that criterion at that level. The actual numbers may vary on the finished exam, but the matrix provides a target. The test will obviously be a performance test done at a person's workstation. It could easily be presented through the computer.

This matrix, along with the one completed previously, should provide all the guidance you will want to begin actually constructing items.

6. Design Test Presentation and Administration

- *Style—Informal, fog = 6, will provide opportunity for respondents to comment on their needs/wants.*
- *Time in process—The test will be taken on the job so time in process must be kept to about twenty minutes (double break).*
- *Environment—Test will be taken by individuals at their workstations during breaks in work. Will try to have others take respondent's calls while he or she is taking test.*

FIGURE 7.11. SAMPLE TEST DESIGN MATRIX.

Performance/Criterion	Type (MC)	Levels			Comments
		1	2	3	
Enter customer identification data so there are fewer than three errors per 100 entries.	Short Ans.	5	2		Obtain information over phone from customer and enter it correctly.
Provide customer with prices, delivery information, and special circumstances on the basic product line. No errors.	Short Ans.	12	3		Call up on monitor and relay information to customer over phone. Send form letter.
Refer customer to sales whenever circumstances warrant. Decisions affecting commissions, scope of order, or nature of delivery are automatic.	Short Ans.		3	5	Must decide if sales should be involved and make referral smoothly, both on the phone and in writing (form). Must be documented to sales and management.
[And so forth. Be sure the criteria are all included, even the enablers, or those that resist testing at this time.]					

- *Materials and support—Respondents can use any aids normally available at workstation.*
- *Administration—Test will be administered by supervisor. Test itself must be self-administered, self-paced.*
- *Appearance—Booklet. Separate answer sheet. Should be friendly, but not flowery. (See attached outline of first page.) Duplex and staple booklet.*

This is fairly self-evident. The booklet provides a permanent record of what the respondents' answers were and how they were scored. There will probably also be a record in the computer, but legal implications and the possibility of data loss make hard copy desirable.

There is a tendency for some test makers to add detail to this part of the design. That should not be necessary. Of course, if these elements will be developed by someone else, you will want to be as specific as you can be. This is true for the entire design. If you intend to turn development over to others, you must refrain from assuming they know what you want. Make sure they will be able to develop a test that fairly represents the test concept you have in mind. If there is doubt, add detail until you're fairly certain there will be no mistake. Then prepare yourself for a small amount of disappointment. Others won't be able to replicate your thinking. There will be deviations. Make sure through your design that those discrepancies are as few and as minor as can be.

7. Design or Select the Evaluation Process. *Test will yield two sets of results.*

- *One: Scores on performance criteria items will indicate mastery of job skills. Cut-score must be established before administration.*
- *Two: Scores from opinion items will be correlated with manager and supervisor expectations. Significant differences will be referred to management in report form.*

The design tells us what the results will look like and briefly explains how they will be evaluated. Always specify how they will look. If respondents are supplying answers to short-answer questions, as in this design, explain how they will be scored and how those scores will be displayed. The same questions can be asked, no matter what kinds of items are used. For some tests a complete scoring process and guide should be developed. How will the test scorer know whether an answer is a good one? How many points will be awarded for each answer? Will all the questions have the same weight? These questions must be answered before respondents are presented with the test. Otherwise, confusion and misjudgment can (and probably will) mar an otherwise good experience.

This is a critical area for a good fair test. If the scoring and handling of responses have been thought out and described before the test takes place, responses can be treated objectively. Scores can be developed without undue bias.

These ideas will be discussed in detail in Chapter Eleven. You won't put all thoughts about evaluation in the design, but you must put in enough so others or you yourself will have proper guidance when scoring and evaluation take place.

8. Write the Items. *Items will be written by June Carrington and me. Our subject-matter experts are George Smith, order-entry director, and Maxine Marlow, senior order-entry operator.*

When I first began working with tests, I felt that writing the items was the only critical activity and that if a person could write good items, everything else was of secondary importance. I was mistaken. As it turns out, writing good items won't guarantee a good test. In fact, you can have a decent test with poor items.

Naturally, I want you to write delicious items: items respondents will understand and interact with easily and comfortably. But if you don't write the best, most elegant items possible, the world won't end. In fact there's a good chance no one will notice. The caveat is that everything else must be done well.

Now, what if there are missing or poorly done elements in the design? Can these be overcome with good items? You bet. Good items can save a test. In fact, that has often been the case. This is particularly true for multiple-choice tests.

Chapter Eight is about writing items. You will find yourself referring to it often. In fact, many people buy this book to use Chapter Eight. That's OK because it's important.

9. Review and Qualify the Items. *In addition to the four people above, two senior operators will be asked to review the test and perform a developmental test of it.*

I'm tempted to write a long dissertation about formative evaluation. This is it— or at least part of it. Reviews and critiques are essential. If they are done while the test is in development, you can save yourself much time and trouble later on.

The reviews will uncover typos, misspelled words, poor grammar, and other mechanical errors, but these problems are superficial. They are not important enough to prompt a formal review of the test. In the example, the key lies in using the senior operators. They will be able to spot items that sample poorly, sample the wrong thing, or sample the right thing in the wrong way. They make the review invaluable.

10. Pilot the Test; Revise and Rewrite. *Pilot on August 12. Use current senior operators as experts and select people from other departments for control group. Pilot can be first administration of test.*

There are two considerations here that may not be obvious: (1) a specific date has been set and (2) the pilot has been set up to develop cut-scores.

Setting a specific date is important because it gives all the development team a target date. It's a date that will be very difficult to change once it has been set, because people have been scheduled to show up for the pilot. Therefore, it is a very well-established deadline. The development team (even if you're the only person) must be ready by that time. Otherwise people's schedules will be severely disrupted. Make sure the date you select is reasonable. Give yourself time, but at the same time make sure the date *is* set. Otherwise, time will pass, tasks won't be completed on time or well, and you may face having to cancel the pilot altogether.

If the pilot is to provide the venue for setting cut-scores, make sure all the principals know it and have approved. Other managers won't understand the process or why it's important, so inform them and, if necessary, sell the idea. Make sure you have the time and support to do so.

11. Set Respondent Qualification Scores (Cut-Scores). *Yes. Use contrasting group method.*

12. Produce the Test. *In-house. June will arrange.*

13. Administer the Test. *First administration August 12. Rest of order-entry department by October 14. Subsequent administrations as required.*

These three steps are fairly straightforward. Setting the cut-scores will be accomplished through the process advocated by Shrock and Coscarelli (1989). Because their process is given in detail in Chapter Twelve, I will not discuss it here. Production is mostly administrative, simply making sure the test materials closely resemble the intent of the design and that they are all ready on time.

Administration of the test includes presenting the respondents with the opportunity to respond, monitoring as necessary, and collecting the results. These things should move smoothly and are safely left to people on the scene (supervisors) who have an interest in the outcome of the test. If you use people external to the developmental process, be sure to show them exactly what should be done. Don't just hand them the materials and say, "Here, give this test to the first shift order-entry clerks sometime during the shift." Make them a real part of the process.

14. Evaluate the Results. *Compare accomplishment test results with cut-score. Use rank correlation and chi-square for opinion test.*

This is the subject of Chapter Twelve, so we'll leave it for now. Don't be alarmed by the fancy terms. They're easy to use once you know what they mean.

15. Use the Results. *Report to executive management on basic findings. Detailed report to director and supervisors. Recommendations should include training (if any) and specific areas in which improvement would impact the mandate (turnover and error rates).*

It seems odd, but this is an area that is often shorted. We design and develop a good test. We administer it. We evaluate the results. Then we avoid telling anyone of consequence what happened. Perhaps it's human nature. After all, when we show our bosses information like this (especially stuff they don't understand well), we open ourselves to criticism. This can happen whether the news is good or not, so we avoid sharing the whole thing with management.

Your boss might say, "How did the test of the order-entry people go?"

Your response: "It went well. We're now in position to develop job aids that will bring both financial savings and better job satisfaction."

"Good." He nods his head and continues with another topic. You breathe a mental sigh of relief.

If that is what happens in your organization, you are missing a wonderful opportunity. Develop a report. Make sure it gets into the hands of people who can use it to good effect. Let them decide whether they want to use the information. If they don't read the report, that is sad, but even then the effort is not wasted. The fact that the report is available, the results published, makes the test official to the organization. Besides, it's a very good way to CYA. If something comes up later that reflects directly on the original reasons for the test, you will have your end of things covered.

There is a sample report in Chapter Ten based on the order-entry problem that has provided the examples in this section.

Summary of Special Section on Test Design

Test design is not difficult if you've worked through the steps beforehand. It is simply a matter of forecasting how the fifteen steps will be accomplished. Two matrices can prove useful. One is used to document the domains and levels. The second details the criteria, how they will be tested, how many of what kinds of items to use and, consequently, the type of test it will be.

Even though this task is almost mechanical to some of us, it is important. Without a design a test can be a hodgepodge of good or not so good ideas stuck together to present a challenge for respondents. This may not always be the case, but chances are that without a design you will forget something or test something incorrectly. Some problem from Murphy's vast supply will cause you trouble.

My experience has proven to me that a design saves time and effort. Without it I'm faced with rewriting items, correcting a scoring process, or making arbitrary decisions about criteria that were tested poorly. But that doesn't bother me nearly as much as the unnecessary fret and bother I've given respondents.

Michele Guest (1989) said, "At least 90 percent of the world's problems are the result of poor design." That may be an exaggeration, but maybe not. All I know is a good design makes the job of developing a test a whole lot easier and the product a whole lot better.

◆ ◆ ◆

Step 7: Design and Select the Evaluation Process

Researchers have known for centuries that the way a study will be evaluated should be known before the study is done. That doesn't mean the exact steps are chosen, but the style or kind of evaluation should be.

This is a good piece of advice for a test. Know how you're going to evaluate the test before you use it. In fact you should know before you write it. There are basically three ways to evaluate the results of a test. Any is OK, depending on the nature of the results and the uses to which they will be put. The three methods are to (1) read and discuss; (2) compile and describe; or (3) compile and infer.

Read and Discuss

This is what happens with most essay or short-answer exams. The test giver reads the responses, considers their adequacy, and provides the test takers with a judgment about the results.

Read and discuss is a very valuable evaluation process for some tests. It allows professors, for example, to gain an understanding of their students' grasp of a discipline or specific elements within it. The discussion is usually a handwritten critique of the students' responses. It can also be done as a group exercise, in which students may or may not provide part of the critique.

In some circumstances this is the only viable alternative. If respondents are asked to be innovative or creative, for example, there's no way to predetermine correct answers. Each response must be judged on its own merit.

Compile and Describe

This is probably the most common method for evaluating tests in schools. The teacher *grades* the tests (marks correct and incorrect responses), counts the number right or wrong, and awards a score to respondents in light of the points each has accumulated. For example, a group may take a test that has twenty-five items. Each will answer a percentage of the items correctly, and the percentages will be used to illustrate the adequacy of their efforts.

Assume twelve typists took a keyboard skills test. Part of the test was to establish the number of words each could type in one minute (with a correction for errors). Their scores might look like

A. 73	B. 101	C. 131
D. 102	E. 88	F. 75
G. 112	H. 110	I. 61
J. 92	K. 108	L. 117

The numbers describe the results of the test. There are no criteria to determine whether they are adequate. They simply describe the typists' ability to type error-free. You can see typist A didn't do as well as typist C. But you can't say A is a poor typist or C is good. There are no standards associated with the test. However, a hiring official who wants two or three typists for a clerical position would probably choose C, L, and G.

Compile and describe is a valid way to evaluate results, but you must do so with care. Relying on such results to evaluate test takers can lead to trouble. You'll see why in the next section.

Compile and Infer

The difference between inferring and describing can be critical. To infer, you apply a statistical technique (or other valid inference tool) to make decisions about results. Look again at the scores from the keyboard test:

A. 73	B. 101	C. 131
D. 102	E. 88	F. 75
G. 112	H. 110	I. 61
J. 92	K. 108	L. 117

Now arrange them as shown in Figure 7.12 so that you can see how they are distributed.

Various statistical techniques can be used to determine whether one score is *significantly* better than another. The simplest technique is to compare each person's result with a standard. In this case, the hiring official doesn't get much help because the standard he has for keyboard skills is seventy-five words per minute. All but three of the candidates performed above that standard. Are the results definitive enough to select the top four scores? Probably not. How about the top five?

FIGURE 7.12. DISTRIBUTION OF KEYBOARD SCORES.

60	70	80	90	100	110	120	130

```
I.  61
A.  x73
F.  xxx75
E.  xxxxxxxxxxxxxxx88
J.  xxxxxxxxxxxxxxxxxxxx92
B.  xxxxxxxxxxxxxxxxxxxxxxxxxxxxxx101
D.  xxxxxxxxxxxxxxxxxxxxxxxxxxxxxx102
K.  xxxxxxxxxxxxxxxxxxxxxxxxxxxxxxxxxxxx108
H.  xxxxxxxxxxxxxxxxxxxxxxxxxxxxxxxxxxxxxxx110
G.  xxxxxxxxxxxxxxxxxxxxxxxxxxxxxxxxxxxxxxxxx112
L.  xxxxxxxxxxxxxxxxxxxxxxxxxxxxxxxxxxxxxxxxxxxxxx117
C.  xxxxxxxxxxxxxxxxxxxxxxxxxxxxxxxxxxxxxxxxxxxxxxxxxxxxxxxxxxxxxx131
```

There is a gap of six between D and K, the sixth and fifth best. Would it be fair to select K and not D?

A simple inferential test called Analysis of Variance tells us that the average typist scored 99.2 and the standard error is 14.7. The standard error of measurement is the degree of refinement below which the test is incapable of discriminating differences between respondents. To be significantly better (better than the others) a typist in this group would have to type 113.9 words per minute. L and C were able to do this. To be significantly worse, the score would have to be less than 84.5. Three of the people were in this group. By this method, it would not be fair to select K and not D. Some other criterion would have to be used to make that decision.

The value in this kind of evaluation lies in the relative certainty the evaluator can have in a decision that comes from it. Whenever the results of a test are critical, as for determining eligibility for employment or qualifying students for continuation in a program, inferential tools should be used.

Details about how to use these tools are covered in Chapter Ten. The point is, decide what kind of evaluation to use up front. It will help you determine the type of test to use. If you decide to compile and infer, you will have difficulty justifying the use of essay or short-answer items because the results are too prone to variability to treat that way.

Keep the Test Current. We often forget a very important reason for evaluation. Evaluation provides an opportunity to document the currency and nature of the performances being tested and, therefore, the test itself. If you're not going to use a test more than once, this isn't pertinent. If you are, however, you owe it to your respondents, your subject-matter experts, and yourself to make sure the test is still as appropriate as you can make it.

There are two areas for concern. First, the performances being tested will change. Significant changes often occur in a very short time. For example, what happens when OSHA mandates a new set of regulations for employee safety? This is an obvious example, but it is real. New information changes the nature of operations; new software releases change processes and interaction modes; new or different managers want to stress different elements of the performance to produce modifications in the outputs of a process. All of these are common. Any of them can affect the validity of your test.

The second area of concern lies with the test itself. People talk about tests they have taken. When they talk to others who have yet to take the test, they change the results. Although this is usually OK for a performance test, you should review your work to make sure such information sharing won't invalidate it.

These concerns are all design considerations. How well you take care of them will depend a great deal on how well the test was designed in the first place. By the way, these concerns are still another reason for avoiding Level I (recall) items. They become obsolete far faster than the other levels.

Summary

A good fair test is valid and reliable. It does what it's supposed to do and it does it every time it's used. Without good design both validity and reliability are very difficult to attain. Steps 5 through 7 do not take a lot of time. They don't take much effort. For some tests they can almost be assumed. For example, if you're going to test the keyboard performance of clerical workers, you can complete the matrices without reference to anything except the standards set for this kind of work at your company. But if you want a good fair test that is both valid and reliable, you must design it well.

You must select a type of test appropriate for the skills to be tested. You must consider how the test will look and how you'll administer it. You must decide how you're going to evaluate the results. Don't skip these steps.

When the decision process is documented, when you have a design, you should be ready and impatient to "get with it," to start writing the items for the test. Chapter Eight is devoted to this effort.

DEVELOPING THE TEST

It's time to start writing actual items—to begin developing the test. Many people who buy this book expect it to be dedicated to writing test items. After all, aren't the items the heart and soul of a good fair test? Yes, they are. For respondents they are all there is to a test. For you and me, though, they are a natural consequence of what has happened before.

Because the items are all they see, most people think they are the only thing the test maker should be concerned about. They don't see the criteria, the matrices, or the design. They see items and an answer sheet. Before you picked up this book, you may have had the same conviction. I hope by this time it has been modified. If the other steps are done well, the items almost write themselves.

Step 8: Write the Items

Many test makers write items as they go along. As they accomplish Steps 1 through 7, they think of new ideas or try out notions about the test. The items that result are often useful in the test itself. If nothing else, they provide prototypes for the bulk of the test.

But two questions must be answered before item construction actually begins: What is the nature of the items? How many items will the test have? The answers depend entirely on the decisions made so far.

Nature of Items

You have already decided whether the test will be essay, short answer, multiple choice, matching, or combinations of these. You know whether the items will be at Level One, Two, or Three. You know whether they will be in the cognitive, affective, or psychomotor domains. So what else is there? Consider this performance statement:

A. Given a breakdown on an assembly line, the supervisor will implement the process described in the troubleshooting manual.

Assume the test maker has designed a multiple-choice test involving various scenarios to discover if supervisors know the basic troubleshooting process. The test could have an item like this one:

1. Where, on the line, is the best place to begin the initial search for the problem?
   a. At the first checkpoint where the trouble could originate.
   b. Near the center between the first point where the trouble could be found and the last place on the line where it could be.
   c. At the last place on the line where the trouble could be.
   d. At the place where the reporting operator thinks the trouble is centered.

This is a fairly straightforward approach and, in most cases, it should work well. Perhaps, though, you might prefer an approach like this one.

1. Examine Figure 8.1 (p. 170). Assume the operator has reported a problem at point G. Where on the line would you begin the troubleshooting process?
   a. Point A.
   b. Point B.
   c. Point C.
   d. Point D.
   e. Point E.

This also looks like a pretty good item. It should work well. It's quite different, though. Look at another one.

1. Your shift is running normally. Product is moving well. Quality control indicates standard or better goods. Workers are doing their jobs at or

FIGURE 8.1. FORK ASSEMBLY PROCESS.

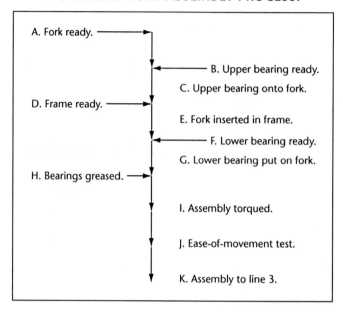

above expectations. Then you hear about a problem serious enough to cause you to shut down the line. What would you do as soon as the line stopped?

a. Interview the worker who noticed the trouble to find out what it is and where it's located.

b. Identify the areas on the line above and below where the trouble could not be located.

c. Use the troubleshooting manual to guide the troubleshooting process.

d. Go to the end of the area where the trouble could be located and systematically eliminate possible locations one at a time, working back toward the first possible location.

e. Go to the center of the problem area. Eliminate either the area above or the area below that point.

One more:

1. Use the checklist (Figure 8.2) to troubleshoot the assembly line. Indicate in appropriate spaces what you find at each checkpoint and the action you (or whoever is responsible) should take.

FIGURE 8.2. ASSEMBLY CHECKLIST
(REFER TO ASSEMBLY SCHEMATIC TO LOCATE CHECKPOINTS).

Checkpoint	Description	Action You Should Take
A		
B		
C		
D		
E		
F		
G		
H		
I		
J		
K		

All four items test the same performance statement. Yet they are very different from one another. Those differences come from two sources: the preferred style of the test maker and the culture of the organization. Often these are closely tied. Your item-writing style will be influenced a great deal by the culture in which you operate. As a result, the nature of the items you write may vary greatly from that of other item writers. This is usually only a problem if several people are working on the same test. If styles differ greatly, then one of the writers must direct the others because too much difference in the nature of the items can detract from the worth of the test.

That doesn't mean every item must look and feel like all the others. On the contrary, variety in the writing style of the items can stimulate respondents, but beware. Don't vary the nature of items too much.

Number of Items

The number of items required to test a criterion adequately depends on how important and how complex the criterion is. This is a matter best left to the judgment of the test maker. There is no magic number.

Taba (1962) and Woods (1960) recommend three multiple-choice items per criterion. My inclination is to vary the recommended number depending on the relative importance of the skill being tested. The more complex the skill, the more items you should use to test it. The key is to consider your purpose in asking people to take the test. How many items should you have to obtain the information you want from the respondents?

To decide whether a troubleshooter, for example, knows to make the first check near the center of the affected area, one *good* item is probably enough.

"What if," you might say, "the respondent makes a good guess or figures it out from the way the item is written? How can I keep that from happening?" You can't, of course, so you might want to include another item to double-check. You could use three of the items above to make sure of respondents' skills in beginning to troubleshoot.

As a rule of thumb, the more important the item is to the skill being tested, the more items you should use to test it. However, you probably won't need more than three items to test a single criterion.

This decision is yours. The nature of the items will help you. If you have used the items before (perhaps on a pilot test) and you know they are good discriminators, one is probably enough. Item analysis (discussed in Chapter Eleven) is a big help in this situation. Basically, item analysis tells you whether each item does what it's supposed to do. If it does, you only use one item for any criterion, no matter how important it is.

Why is this? Let's assume you are building a performance test. You are concerned with mastery. You want to know whether respondents have the appropriate skills. If they respond to good items successfully, they have demonstrated their skills. No further testing is required.

Good performance tests don't require a plethora of items. In fact, to be good, they should be elegant. Elegance assumes efficiency. How many times should a teacher require a fifth grader to spell the word *yacht?* Once is enough. How many times would you ask a swimmer to swim the length of a pool to find out if he or she could do it? Once. Any more repetitions should be classed as practice.

On the other hand, some performances require several items before you can find the information you want. Suppose, for example, you want to test a manager's ability to confront employees fairly and judiciously. Such a performance should be tested many ways.

A good test maker can easily decide how many items to use by considering whether the criteria are being sampled adequately. It's a judgment call, but it's one you should be able to make without difficulty.

Deciding how many items to write on any other basis is *not* appropriate. I had a teacher who always had either twenty-five or fifty items on her tests. It didn't matter if she was testing one criterion or twenty. It didn't matter how complex the skills being tested were. It didn't matter if the items were true/false, multiple choice, or short answer (her favorite types). There were always either twenty-five or fifty so she could score the test easily. Each item was worth either two or four points. This is a severe example of putting the cart in front of the horse, yet it happens.

People often decide how many items to use before they have completed Phase 1. They decide to build a test. Then they decide they have to have twenty items before they have thought about the respondents, the content, or the request for information. It would be amusing, except the respondents are often punished by the decision.

I'm reminded of a client who called several years ago. He wanted my company to design and develop a training program but did not know for sure which employees would be trained or what skills were to be taught. He was not sure about the nature of the instruction to be developed or the media to be used. About all he was sure about was how long the training should last: eight days. Unfortunately, it's a common story.

So is the one about the teacher who always used twenty-five or fifty items on her tests. It does not make sense. *Don't do it.* Let the content, the needs of the respondents, and your desire for information drive the decision. How many items should you have on a test? As many as will do the job. No more. No less.

Now, let's discuss how many items are enough to circumvent the guess factor.

The Guess Factor. Any time you provide the answers to an item (multiple-choice, true/false, or matching) you give respondents an opportunity to answer correctly by guessing. Normally, this is not a problem unless a passing score could easily occur through guessing.

Basic assurance is provided by a short trip into probability theory. The probability that anyone can guess correctly on any one true/false (dichotomous) item is 50 percent. The odds are 1:1. For every good guess there is a corresponding bad guess.

If there are three choices the odds change dramatically. You might think the odds of guessing correctly if there are three choices are 1:2. For every good guess there are two bad guesses. Although this is true, the bad guesses are not provided in a predictable way. They may be *a* and *b*, *a* and *c*, or *b* and *c*. Within each of those structures you could choose one or the other. Therefore, you have three opportunities to choose one or the other of the bad choices. (That's a total of six choices; two choices three times.) So instead of being 1:2, the odds are 1:6. If you guess on a multiple-choice item with three alternatives you have one chance to be right and five to be wrong. Even a *test-wise* respondent has trouble scoring 33 percent purely by guessing.

The normal distribution tells us that for any group of people there will be a certain percentage who do not possess a common trait. This percentage is about 17 percent (those more than one standard deviation below the mean). That is also about the number a person can answer correctly by guessing on a multiple-choice test with three alternatives in the items. So multiple-choice items with only three responses can provide an adequate test without having to resort to a fancy strategy to frustrate guessers.

So, 99 percent of the time, the number of items on a test doesn't have to be adjusted for a guess factor. You can do it if you wish, but you don't have to. Dorothy Woods (1960) suggests two good strategies for countering guesses. If you want to do this (the boss says so), I recommend either of her ideas. Perhaps the best way to discourage guessing is simply to ask people not to do it. Most respondents won't try to guess if you tell them it will harm the validity of the test. The second strategy is to modify the way the test is scored. For example, suppose a respondent answers 27 items on a 30-item test and leaves the other 3 blank. You could calculate her percentage score by dividing by 27 instead of 30. If she had guessed the answers of the other 3 you would divide by 30. Bad guesses would cause her score to be reduced. Some national testing services take away 1 point if an item is left unanswered, but they subtract 3 points if it is answered incorrectly. It doesn't pay to guess on those tests. You could end up with a negative total. If this scoring strategy is to be used, a fair test will make this information available to respondents as part of the test instructions.

Statistical Treatments. Another problem affecting the number of items on the test comes from how the scores will be treated. Suppose, for example, you want to set a cut-score. How many items should you use to ensure a strong enough estimate of a respondent's ability? The trick is to have enough items to eliminate false positives (people who pass who should not) and include false negatives (people who don't pass who should).

Sampling theory provides help. If you have at least twenty items, you can use statistical treatments to evaluate your results. Such treatments allow you to isolate and take into consideration both false positive and false negatives. These techniques will be examined later in this chapter.

So the basic answer to "How many?" is at least twenty. Of course you will write as many as your design suggests. However, try to have at least twenty so your analysis will be dependable.

We've already talked about test items in general. We know that not all items are questions per se (that is, they don't have question marks at the end). And we know that human brains respond more quickly and easily to questions than to other types of items. Because we will use questions wherever we can, we must know how to write good ones.

Writing Good Questions

Good questions are simply constructed, easy to answer, and congruent with the expectations of respondents.

Construction. A question is sometimes thought of as a statement followed by a question mark. But not often can you simply add a question mark to a statement to make a reasonable test question. Consider this example: "Jack and Jill went up the hill." If you replace the period with a question mark you have: "Jack and Jill went up the hill?" The symbol directs the reader to question the object, *hill*. The questioner is probably trying to ask where Jack and Jill went, so therefore the question should read: "Did Jack and Jill go up the hill?" or "Where did Jack and Jill go?"

The questioner must understand that a question is significantly different from a statement. Statements provide information. Questions do not. To repeat, *questions do not provide new information.* Remember that a person's mind goes into a different mode when he or she sees a question mark. People are *not* prepared to accept new information when they are in a search-and-retrieve mode. They have to change modes, store the information, and return to the search mode. The processing center in the brain is given two simultaneous tasks. It's asked to accept, interpret, and act on new information while simultaneously searching for an answer and formulating it for use. That's quite a bit.

If Gagné's model is accurate, putting new information in a question places an unfair burden on the respondent. Let's explore this. Suppose you find the following question on a test:

1. How might the social matrix change in an all-white Protestant church if the pastor invited a black gospel quartet to sing at a special service without telling the congregation about the quartet's race?

There are at least three chunks of information in this question that must be acted on before the respondent can begin to respond. The same question can be asked without mixing information with the query:

1. Consider the social matrix of an all-white Protestant church. Suppose the pastor invited a black gospel quartet to sing at a special service without telling the congregation about the quartet's race. How might the pastor's action affect the congregation?

The rewritten item allows the respondent to accept information, process it, and prepare for the question. The question itself does contain information. The critical difference is it doesn't contain any *new* information.

People who put information in a question may be trying to present respondents with a complete thought process. They may be saving space. Whatever the reason, they aren't doing respondents any favors. A period tells the respondents, "This is a statement." The question mark puts them into the search-and-respond mode. Here's rule number one: *questions should not contain new information.*

Use of Modifiers. Another useful rule for writing questions is to *avoid unnecessary modifiers.* This is especially important if modifiers imply an absolute. When you ask, "Why do all dogs pant?" you are implying that there aren't any dogs that don't pant. Because there are dogs that don't pant and because the respondent isn't sure how much open-mouth breathing is considered panting, the question loses its impact. Instead of preparing a response about cooling, the respondent is qualifying the question. The same kind of problem would pertain if the question had read, "Why do sheep dogs pant?"

You probably know it's not a good idea to use absolutes in a question. Words like *never* and *all* are fairly easy to spot and remove. Words like *sheep* aren't, but they can be just as confusing to the respondent.

Again let's refer to Gagné's model. Something special happens in the brain when a modifier is used in a question. For example, consider the question, "Why do sheep dogs pant?" The concept, *sheep dogs,* is a subset of a larger concept, *dogs.* Respondents have to orient their minds before answering the question. *Sheep dogs* is more complex than *dogs,* so the mental process of locating and qualifying it is also more complex.

The use of unnecessary modifiers is a favorite of the *dirty tricks* test maker. Testers who like to trick respondents into making the wrong response use modifiers often. There are classic examples:

1. What is the basic difference between the ranging omnivorous black bears of the upper Appalachians and the playful cinnamon bears of Yellowstone National Park?

The question is a trick in a trick. The modifiers are used to emphasize differences that don't exist. The word *basic* is used deliberately to mislead. American cinnamon and black bears are the same breed.

Test makers are tempted to use modifiers to remove ambiguity or fuzzy meaning from their questions. That is OK in theory, but it's often overdone. The result can be a question that is difficult for the respondent to read and understand. Here is an example:

1. As you approach the main, double-bin copier (it's beige in color) from the front, you will see a panel about six inches wide with four small square plastic cov-

ered windows in it. Each houses a green, yellow, or red colored light that provides internal information about the operational status of the machine. What action should you take when the ready light, the first indicator, the light farthest to the left, blinks on and off (it's green in color)?

The question is, "What should you do if the ready light is blinking?" Everything else in the question is either known or is useless verbal garbage. Respondents are being tested on their ability to analyze the question. Answering it is secondary. The test maker has tried to anticipate anything that could cause the respondent to misinterpret something about the question. All the modifiers and explanation are aimed at bringing precision. The result is hilarious to everyone but the respondents.

The point is that modifiers should be used only if the question won't survive without them. Rule number two: *don't use unnecessary modifiers.*

Use of Who, What, Where, When, Why, and How. Questions should begin with words people know and can interpret easily. Respondents don't usually appreciate variety. Their job is to respond as best they can. They don't want colorful language or variety in wording or variety in kinds of questions.

It may be dull for the question writer, but it's wonderful for the respondents when questions start with familiar words. The respondent can quickly grasp the nature of what is required and begin to formulate an answer. Journalists know they will be successful with any story if they can answer the "five W's and the H." The answers to who, what, where, when, why, and how serve to describe a situation or event totally. Let's take a look at each one.

"Who" at the beginning of a question immediately tells the respondent the question is about a person or position. "Who is in charge of fire drills?" There is no doubt in the respondent's mind as to the nature of the answer. Most questions that begin with "who" are Level One Cognitive. They don't have to be, but normally they are. Test-wise respondents know this, so they are primed to give a quick reply. Disguising the *who-ness* of a question is often a trick. If you ask, "What famous restaurateur is a favorite of jet-setters in New York City?" you have started with a "what" when you really are asking "who." The respondent must stop looking for a thing and start looking for a person.

This seems a trivial point to most question writers. Why should respondents care? Consciously, they probably don't, but the practice is irritating. Irritation detracts from anyone's ability to respond.

"What" is the most popular beginning for a question. When you start a question with "what," you are looking for a thing or a process. "What happens when the frizmet hits the gammits?" The respondent, on seeing "what," automatically starts looking for a thing or a procedure. It's good to use "what" whenever it's appropriate.

(By the way, you can use "what" for a majority of the questions you write. That's OK. The respondents aren't interested in variety. They aren't there to be entertained. They want to do their best on your test. That is all.)

"Where" is another Level One beginning. Respondents will seek to respond with a place or location. For example, you could ask, "Where is Yellowstone Park?"

"Why" tells respondents their answers will contain reasons. They immediately begin to formulate responses at Level Two. "Why" almost always indicates some sort of application of knowledge or skills: "Why do the swallows return to Capistrano?"

"When" is also used for Level Two questions. It's often used for Level One, but respondents are likely to respond better if they are in a Level Two mode: "When should a duffer use a pitching wedge?"

"How" is process oriented. Because of this, it can easily be used at any level. Once again, respondents are in tune with it, so they stay loose until they know what is required. A couple of examples will show how "how" can differ: "How is the mediation of disputes in business different from *normal* negotiations between labor and management?" This question will be at Level Three for many respondents. "How does a robin insert food into its chicks' mouths?" This is Level One; they simply remember and tell you.

To summarize, the first word in the question cues respondents about the nature of their answers. The six most common beginning words provide a useful way to start more than 90 percent of all the questions you will ask on your tests. They are easy for respondents to interpret, and they don't trick them.

Rule number three: *use the key words* who, what, where, when, why, *or how to begin questions.*

Use of Standard Form. "A jaywalker is more likely to get a ticket in Dallas than in Chicago. Why is that?" This question is confusing. It would be better if it read, "Why are jaywalkers more likely to get tickets in Dallas than in Chicago?" It puts the word *why* in front. Always try to avoid convoluted questions.

"What, for the lack of trying, is the result of failure in a team sport?" Here we have a couple of problems. The prepositional phrase mucks up the meaning and the word *what* is misused. It's easier to see these things when the question is rewritten in better form: "How does lack of trying affect a team player's confidence?"

The point is that, if we are going to test people as objectively and as well as we can, we should do our best not to let our questions get in the way of their answers. One way to accomplish this is to use standard form. No surprises.

The form is fairly easy to describe. Usually there is a key word (*who, what,* and so forth), followed by a verb or verb phrase, followed by an object or clause, followed by a question mark. "Who killed Cock Robin?" *Who* is the key word. *Killed* is the verb. *Cock Robin* is the object.

"Why did dinosaurs vanish from the earth?" *Why* is the key word. *Did vanish* is the verb. *Dinosaurs* is the object. *From the earth* is a prepositional phrase modifying the verb. Now look at some more complex examples:

1. "What will happen to a curve if the point of tangency is moved two-thirds of the way from one point of incidence to the other?" *What* is the key word. *Will happen* is the verb. The word *if* introduces a dependent clause that serves as the object.
2. "What horse in the Kentucky Derby is the favorite?" The word *horse* tells us what the key word, *what,* is. It's the what so it should be included as part of the key word. The key words are *what horse.* The verb is *is.* The object is *the favorite. In the Kentucky Derby* is a prepositional phrase that provides important information about the object.

Even when the thinking involved is a bit complex, you should still be able to express your question in standard form. It may require some thought, but it can be done. By the way, remember to take information out of the question and provide it as a lead-in to the question whenever you can.

This is a skill that will stand you in good stead as a question writer. Practice. Improve your skill. Peruse the following short-answer questions. If necessary, rewrite each in standard form. Write the key word(s), verb, and object in the spaces provided. Delete material that should be taken out of the question.

1. What is the difference between a lunar eclipse and a solar eclipse?

　　　Rewrite if required: _____

　　　_____

　　　_____

　　　Key word(s): _____

　　　Verb: _____

　　　Object: _____

2. The basic servomechanism in the rudder assembly is activated by what post in the control box?

　　　Rewrite if required: _____

　　　_____

　　　_____

　　　Key word(s): _____

　　　Verb: _____

　　　Object: _____

3. How does the grey wolf, the state animal of Minnesota, differ in physical appearance from the coyote common in the western states (for example, Montana and Idaho)?

    Rewrite if required:_____

    _____

    _____

    Key word(s):_____

    Verb: _____

    Object:_____

4. While vacationing in Warm Springs, FDR suffered a massive stroke that cost him his life during what year of his fourth administration?

    Rewrite if required:_____

    _____

    _____

    Key word(s):_____

    Verb: _____

    Object:_____

5. Are the characters in *Wind in the Willows* caricatures of real people at the time it was written, or are they reflections of universal prototypical personalities, or are they simply creations of the author's imagination that happen to compare favorably with models developed by modern social scientists to explain deviant behavior? Justify your answer.

    Rewrite if required:_____

    _____

    _____

    Key word(s):_____

    Verb: _____

    Object:_____

Here are my answers to the practice questions:

1. What is the difference between a lunar eclipse and a solar eclipse?

    Rewrite if required: *Not required for this question.*

    Key word(s): *What . . . difference*

    Verb: *is*

    Object: *lunar eclipse* and *solar eclipse*

2. The basic servomechanism in the rudder assembly is activated by what post in the control box?

> Rewrite if required: *What post in the control box activates the rudder assembly?* (Note: the word *which* is often substituted for *what*.)
>
> Key word(s): *What post*
>
> Verb: *activates*
>
> Object: *assembly*

3. How does the grey wolf, the state animal of Minnesota, differ in physical appearance from the coyote common in the western states (for example, Montana and Idaho)?

> Rewrite if required: *What are the physical differences between the grey wolf and the coyote?*
>
> Key word(s): *What . . . differences*
>
> Verb: *are*
>
> Object: *wolf* and *coyote*

4. While vacationing in Warm Springs, FDR suffered a massive stroke that cost him his life during what year of his fourth administration?

> Rewrite if required: *When did FDR die?*
>
> Key word(s): *When*
>
> Verb: *did die*
>
> Object: *FDR*

This is the appropriate question if the test maker wanted the date, although the original question implied that the years of FDR's fourth administration were required. Most likely, the item writer had not tested the question by anticipating types of responses or hadn't completely defined the knowledge the question was intended to measure.

5. Are the characters in *Wind in the Willows* caricatures of real people at the time it was written, or are they reflections of universal prototypical personalities, or are they simply creations of the author's imagination that happen to compare favorably with models developed by modern social scientists to explain deviant behavior? Justify your answer.

> Rewrite if required: *How did the author of* Wind in the Willows *develop the characters?*
>
> Key word(s): *How . . . author*
>
> Verb: *did develop*
>
> Object: *characters*

The author of question 5, hoping to restrict the scope of the answers, included the answers in the question. It is hard to decide what she was trying to measure. Perhaps her question should have been, "Who was the author of *Wind in the Willows* trying to portray?" Or maybe, "How are the characters in *Wind in the Willows* related to historical personalities?" Whatever she was attempting, she failed. The respondents were denied an opportunity to show their stuff.

The reason for using standard form is to allow the respondents the best possible opportunity. Tests are for respondents. This point is crucial. Too many test makers think of a test in terms of their own desires for expression or to exert control. This is a common and regrettable tendency. Tests are devices that allow respondents chances to demonstrate competence. That's it. *Any test that tends to support or enhance the test maker at the respondents' expense is a travesty.*

A test should be designed solely to accommodate the respondents. If it does not, it is suspect. That doesn't mean test makers shouldn't have organizational or social reasons for providing a test. Far from it. Those are the reasons for tests. But once a test has been justified, it should become a means of expression for respondents.

Rule number four: *use standard form.*

Ease of Response. Many authors would, at this point, say something like KISS (keep it simple, stupid) and let it go at that. Somehow that doesn't seem like enough to me. What is simple? As a demonstration, try answering this question: "What are the ecological ramifications of the hole in the ozone layer at the South Pole?" You don't have enough information, do you? Try this one: "What effect does the mission statement of an organization have on the average employee of that organization?" You're going to tell me you still don't have enough information.

OK, try: "What justifies the use of questions to generate responses on a test?" Can you answer the question? Of course you can, but your answer probably won't be much better than your answers for the other two questions would have been. That is because questions like these are based on what the questioner wants to ask rather than on what the respondent wants to say.

To get a better feel for this idea, think about yourself the last time you took a test. No doubt there were some things you wanted from that experience. First, you wanted to do well, to respond in a way that satisfied you. Second, you wanted to be able to understand the questions and why they were used. Third, you probably wanted to complete the thing as quickly and painlessly as possible. Those three *wants* may not be in the best order for you personally and they aren't the only possibilities. These three basic respondent concerns, though, all have implications for the way the questions on a test are asked.

People want to understand the questions they are asked. At the onset of America's confrontation with Iraq, journalists tended to ask every famous person for his or her opinion. But how could a rock star respond well to a question about a complex international issue? Even a simple-sounding question such as, "How likely do you think it is that the United States will have to go to war with Iraq?" is without merit unless the rock star majored in international politics in college.

Understanding depends on good communication. There are ways to ensure this. One is to avoid using complex or lengthy verbiage, as was mentioned previously. A second way is to avoid confusing respondents. Some test makers try to trick respondents into saying something they might not if they understood. Let's revisit one of the questions: "How does the mission statement of an organization affect the average employee of that organization?" It's too wordy, but even if that problem were addressed, respondents would still be stuck. They wouldn't know how to answer.

Perhaps this point will be easier to understand from another perspective. The manager of an order-entry department wants to find out how well her people know the product line. She decides to prepare a simple quiz to find out. She decides to ask about three important areas: the basic products that provide 80 percent of the company's revenue, the products that support those in the basic group, and the products being brought out to expand market share.

Here is the quiz she developed:

1. Suppose that a new customer representing a large manufacturer asks you to recommend products. What three products would you recommend?
2. One of your current customers, with whom you have a good relationship, complains about the performance of one of our products. How would you respond?
3. How can you get customers to provide information about new products?

How will her employees respond to these questions? My guess is, they won't be able to identify her intentions well enough to respond adequately. The results are, predictably, going to be poor. Our manager will probably be very upset with her people. She may decide to give them extensive training in product knowledge and applications. Chances are, her training won't help her employees answer the same questions if they are ever asked again. The manager has clouded the real purpose of her quiz so well that her employees will probably never be able to answer to the best of their abilities.

What should she have asked? How about:

1. List the six basic products that provide 80 percent of our revenues. What is the purpose of each one?

2. Name four products that support the basic products. What basic product or product(s) does each one support?
3. Name three new products the company is putting on the market. What new or expanded services will they provide for our customers?

The new questions aren't very glamorous, but the manager will get what she wants—a fairly accurate estimate of how well her people know the product line.

The idea is to make the mandate as clear as possible. What should respondents be saying? The more they know about the nature of the question, the more likely they are to respond well. This makes sense, but test makers are often guilty of writing items that are unnecessarily difficult to answer. Try to avoid confusion. Be as clear in your request as you can be.

Rule number five: *make it easy to respond.*

Trick Questions. So far we've looked at some pretty poor practices. None of them, however, is as bad as the development of trick questions. I don't mean questions that accidentally trick respondents. That happens. It's usually a case of missed communication. I mean questions that are deliberately developed to trick respondents. Those are the worst sin a test maker can indulge in. Writers of trick questions should be hung by their toenails until they scream in agony.

Trick question writers are thieves who take away respondents' opportunity to do their best. Let's look at a few examples:

1. A homemaker orders a new washing machine from a local department store. The store manager agrees to deliver it and install it free of charge. The delivery men appear to be unsure of what they are doing. What should the homemaker do as soon as the washer is installed?

The correct answer here was, "Sign for the delivery and make sure the warranty information is correct." Most respondents would say something like, "Inspect the machine." That's what they were cued to say in the third sentence of the item.

Tricks are often perpetrated through cues. The question above also contains two *red herrings,* items of information included only to mislead. Delivery and installation aren't pertinent enough to warrant inclusion. What could have been a simple question has been made into a complex exercise.

Look at another example of misleading through cuing:

2. Some people say Carrie Nation was morally corrupt. The same insinuation has been made about Dr. Martin Luther King. What was instrumental in the Senate moving to impeach Richard Nixon?

This questioner is deliberately trying to get any respondent who isn't completely sure of the answer to answer incorrectly. In the meantime, the test maker has managed to sully the reputations of three people. Trick question writers sometimes have questionable ethics. Respondents who have been tricked may feel test makers have no ethics at all.

The following question is classic:

3. At what point in the installation process do you alert your supervisor to the fact that you have made an error?

The context is damning. It is a restatement of the infamous, "When did you stop beating your wife?" No matter how the pigeon responds, he or she could be in trouble.

I'm intrigued by a new wrinkle in this type of question. It's an attempt to garner an implicit admission of guilt. Take this question for example:

4. What, in your experience, is the most dangerous?
   a. Using pot.
   b. Using cocaine.
   c. Using heroin.

Simply by selecting an answer, the respondent has admitted to using an illegal substance. Here is another example from a national survey.

5. What is the best way to prevent nonsmokers from having to breathe tobacco fumes?

By responding, the people surveyed appear to have agreed that nonsmokers are at risk.

Another trick occurs when the questioner tries to soften the impact of a response by painting a pretty border around an ugly subject, such as in this example:

6. Good health and a hearty appetite indicate a good outlook on life. How would you classify your current weight?
   a. I'm underweight.
   b. I'm just about right in weight.
   c. I'm overweight.

The introductory statement puts the overweight person in a dilemma. Choosing response c is made even more difficult by the lack of a middle position. You are either overweight or you are not. Of course, the question can be tricky in other ways. For example:

1. How do you feel about your weight?
    a. I'm concerned I might not weigh enough.
    b. I'm not concerned about my weight.
    c. I'm concerned I might weigh too much.

All of these examples fail because the question writer hasn't supplied a context. In the last two examples, the item writer could have supplied a table showing how much people of certain ages, sexes, and heights should weigh. The question then becomes:

1. Where does your current weight place you on the chart?
    a. Underweight.
    b. OK.
    c. Overweight.

The question may still be difficult for a sensitive person to answer, but its purpose is clear.

Some authors have a tendency to try to fool the respondents into choosing the wrong answer. This is a very bad habit. Tests are for respondents. Tests are an opportunity for them to show their stuff. Tricking respondents is a no-no.

So why do we do it? Why do we continue to try to trick respondents, even when we know we shouldn't? The subject is controversial. Some people would disagree with me that it's an abomination. Others would argue that respondents learn valuable lessons from the experience (never trust a test maker?). However you think about it, the tendency exists. Almost universally, test makers find themselves writing trick questions from time to time. Some delight in it. Their basic goal is to be able to say to a respondent, "Gotcha!" It is a very bad practice. Don't do it.

Rule number six: *no trick questions.*

In summary, there are six rules. If you abide by them you will find writing questions a relatively straightforward, satisfying task. Without adornment they are:

1. Questions should not contain new information.
2. Don't use unnecessary modifiers.
3. Use the key words *who, what, where, when, why,* or *how* to begin questions.
4. Use standard form.
5. Make it easy to respond.
6. No trick questions.

These rules apply universally. Whether you're producing a pop quiz or a nationally standardized certification examination, you are well advised to keep them in mind.

Selecting Types of Items

Items come in several forms. Simplistically, it can be said that they are all just different ways to request performance. The nature of the performance to be tested suggests the type of item to be used. It makes sense, for example, to test a person's ability to write a test item by asking him or her to write a test item. On the other hand, if you wish to know if a person can swim twenty-five meters, you would not ask him or her to write about it.

A test item is a request for performance—nothing else. It does *not* teach. It does *not* provide special experience. It does *not* do anything except attempt to measure a person's knowledge or skill. That is all, but that's a lot.

Good items provide good fair opportunities. Poor items don't. But the basic reason for the items is simple. One of the most common errors test makers make is to overcomplicate the mission of an item and try to make it function in more than its assigned role. When we do that, we may screw up the test for the respondents.

A good test maker knows what the answer is before he or she begins to write the item. This seems obvious, but it is not always the case. There are, in fact, item writers who take pride in not knowing the answer before they begin. They believe this lack forces them to write better items. This is a questionable practice.

You will have developed a performance hierarchy, done a job analysis, or in some other way decided what you want respondents to display. You will know the skill or skills to be tested.

This point has been made in several ways so far in this book and it will probably be made again. As a test maker, you have a responsibility to project the nature of the respondents' answers. You can't anticipate every possible response, but you will know their nature. You must know enough to be able to separate the good ones from those that aren't so good.

This is true even if you're asking someone for an opinion. You may not know what the opinion will be, but you can know its general nature. As you study the kinds of items in this book, keep these ideas in mind.

In Chapter Two, I mentioned six kinds of items. There was a detailed discussion of the supply-type items: essay, short answer, and fill-in. The discussion here, therefore, is devoted to the selection items: multiple choice, matching, and scaled.

The item you will probably use the most is multiple choice. Let's begin with it, and then address the others as modifications of the basic form, which they are.

Before I continue, though, I must pay homage to a grand tutor, Dorothy Adkins Woods. In 1960 she wrote a neat little book called *Test Construction*, which I used as a basis for many of the rules you find in this book. If you wish to see them in her words, you should be able to find the book in the library of any university where teachers are trained. Many others have written books about tests and test construction. Those authors, too, deserve credit, but because my early years were dominated by Ms. Woods, I will cite her work most frequently.

Writing Good Items

A good test item has two basic characteristics: (1) it elegantly provides people with an opportunity to show off, to succeed and (2) its form and substance are transparent to respondents. These two things are appropriate no matter what kind of item it is or what its purpose might be. The success or failure of the test depends on them.

> **transparent**
> Easily understood;
> very clear.

Good items have additional salient qualities. They are easy to read and interpret. They sample the content as expected. They are compatible with the test taker's thinking.

Construction of test items, therefore, is not something to be taken lightly. Most tests are important to those who will take them. That makes them doubly important to you, the item writer. In essence, the test takers' opportunity for success is dependent on your ability to provide an adequate arena in which they can perform.

So let's take a close look at what good multiple-choice items are and how you can construct them.

Multiple Choice

Most test items, including multiple choice, have two major parts: a stimulus and a response area. The stimulus is what test takers must respond to. It always includes a stem and may also include graphic material that test takers must use to answer the item. The stem is the part of the item that presents the problem, describes a situation, or asks the question. The response area presents respondents with opportunities to answer. For essay or short-answer items, the response area is a space in which respondents write what they want to say. For multiple-choice items, it is a series of alternatives from which they select the one they like best.

Stem. The stem is the key to success. If respondents understand what is required, they can respond to the best of their ability. If not, they must make their best guess. As discussed earlier, guessing does not lead to success.

There are two kinds of stems: questions and open-ended statements. Questions are much preferred because, when asked a question, respondents' minds immediately begin to seek an answer. When faced with an open-ended statement, respondents must reformulate the stem in their minds (make it into a question) before they can begin to seek the answer. Therefore, *use questions in the stem.* Avoid open-ended statements.

Alternatives. The correct alternative should echo the respondents' thinking. When a question is asked, respondents immediately seek the answer in their minds. When they look at the alternatives, they should see that answer written out for them. Any incorrect alternatives should be plausible. They should sound right. A person who doesn't know the answer will be forced to guess.

Item Writing. Your task when writing items is to:

1. Select an area to be tested and make sure you understand what it implies.
2. Study the objective or material that defines the area. Know the content *and* context and select a criterion to be tested.
3. Develop a defining statement about the criterion.
4. Form a question about a specific single idea, concept, or task within the scope of the criterion.
5. Provide the answer to the question as concisely and accurately as you can.
6. Develop two, three, or four more alternatives that would seem as plausible as the correct answer to an unskilled person.
7. Review the resulting item for obvious problems with flow, style, or consistency. Make revisions as appropriate.

Here is an example of how the process works. It comes from a recent attempt to develop a certification exam for facility managers.

1. Select an area to be tested and make sure you understand what it implies.

Assume you have studied the needs assessment data. As you did so, you learned that "negotiate facility contracts" is an important content area. The criteria for the statement include:

- Functional business goals are supported.
- Functional needs and expectations are addressed.
- The results of the negotiation satisfy the needs of both parties and others.

2. Study the objective or material that defines the area. Know the content and context and select a criterion to be tested.

You know what's in the objective because that's where you got the idea. You seek confirmation by reviewing the material. Then you study the criteria. You must select a specific criterion for your item. It should be one you feel will support the reasons for the test, that is, provide an opportunity for respondents and discriminate between those who can and those who can't.

The criteria associated with the requirement to negotiate real estate contracts are:

- The benefits of the recommended alternatives are stated and agreed on.
- The ways the recommended alternative satisfies the requirement are:

    a. Cost.
    b. Time.
    c. Productivity enhancement.
    d. Environment and so forth.

- The tradeoffs from the other alternatives are explicit and understood.
- Contractual issues are confirmed and clarified, and agreement is documented:

    a. Terms.
    b. Deliverables.
    c. Schedule.
    d. Liability insurance, bonding, and so forth.
    e. Contract termination.
    f. Agreement with drawings and specifications.

- Agreements can be explained.
- Criteria for compliance can be discussed and agreed to and agreement documented.
- Value engineering can be done (International Facility Managers Association, 1993).

Wow! You could develop a hefty test from this one set of criteria. Which criterion should you choose? Perhaps you will choose more than one. Perhaps you will use them all. Those decisions, of course, depend on how you respond to the two mandates. One or more good items can be generated from any good criterion. This set provides ample opportunity.

Which one will give the respondents a good opportunity? Which one will separate the competent respondents from the incompetent? For the sake of this exercise, I've selected one criterion. (Keep in mind that any of them would probably do the job.) The criterion I selected states, "Criteria for compliance can be discussed and agreed to and agreement documented." One element of this statement concerns how each party in a negotiation feels about the results.

3. Develop a defining statement about the criterion.

The idea is to pin down your thinking by defining what you mean. As you think about it, you know negotiations usually work out best when both parties are happy with the results. You write, "Negotiations should come to a win/win conclusion."

Before you proceed, you should double-check to make sure your defining statement actually reflects the intent of the referents. If it doesn't, write a new defining statement. This is an important check. It prevents you from wasting time and energy writing items you might have to reject later because they don't test the content and criteria.

The material doesn't provide a direct reference to a win-win solution to a negotiation. The criteria are referenced to outcomes rather than process. No specific process is mentioned in the criteria. Therefore, we must reject the defining statement. Let's see if we can come up with another one. How about, "Negotiations with contractors should end in agreement about what is to be done, who will do it, and when it will be done." The new statement conforms to the criteria very well, touching on several of the statements.

4. Form a question about a specific single idea, concept, or task within the area.

Although our statement seems simple, it assumes much. What are the possible outcomes? How will people be assigned? Will time lines be drawn? These are only three of the obvious questions. Other assumptions and implications are inherent to the defining statement. As you study it, think about them and their relative importance. The task is to select just one and write a question about it.

It's important to realize that not every question in a topic area will be directly connected to the criteria. Often you can provide insight about results by asking about process. For example, the following question about process directly impacts the kinds of results that will come from a negotiation: "What information should a facility manager share with a contractor during contract negotiations?" This question impacts all elements of negotiations and their results.

5. Provide the answer to the question as concisely and accurately as you can.

Be careful. The temptation is to write an essay here. Keep it simple. Try this: "What information should a facility manager share with a contractor during contract negotiations?" The answer is, "Information that has a direct bearing on the intended outcomes."

An important element comes into play here: flexibility. The answer you have may require modification to fit the set of alternatives when the item is completed. Don't be concerned at this point about how it looks or sounds. You can better deal with these issues when the item is complete in draft form.

6. *Develop two, three, or four more alternatives that would seem as plausible as the correct answer to an unskilled person.* (*Note:* For this example, I've chosen to use four alternatives.)

There are many possibilities. Three selections should be fairly easy to construct. Visualize a continuum of answers going from one extreme to another. In this case it would be an information continuum.

All Information   No Information
_____

The correct answer lies somewhere near the left end of the continuum. One obvious alternative is, "No information that might give the contractor an advantage" or perhaps, "Only information the contractor can acquire through other means" or, "Information that leads the contractor to the result you have in mind."

Now the item looks like this:

1. What information should a facility manager share with a contractor during contract negotiations?
   a. Information that has a direct bearing on the intended outcomes.
   b. Information that does not give the contractor an advantage.
   c. Information the contractor can acquire through other means.
   d. Information that leads the contractor to the result you have in mind.

Notice that the absolutes have disappeared. Other modifications are in order to make the item as good and fair as it can be.

7. *Review the resulting item for obvious problems with flow, style, or consistency, and make revisions as appropriate.*

Read the item you have developed. Make changes that help both the stem and alternatives work better. Concentrate on making the alternatives say what you intend. After some reworking, the item in the example looks like this (note the changes in italic):

1. What information *must* a facility manager share with a contractor during contract negotiations?
   a. Information *with* a direct bearing on the intended outcomes.
   b. Information that *avoids* giving the contractor an advantage.
   c. Information the contractor has *access to through others.*
   d. *As much as possible. The more he knows, the better.*

Alternative d changed completely. It may still require work because the style change draws attention to it. But for now it reflects a widely held opinion about negotiations, particularly outside labor disputes.

The seven steps are always appropriate. You may be tempted to skip one or two as you become more skilled as an item writer. Please don't. The steps provide assurance of quality and elegance for the exam.

This chapter is devoted to helping you write the best items you can. Here are some helpful hints about style, use of conventions, and process.

Specific Determiners. Woods (1960) talks about specific determiners as the single most common error an item writer makes. She has a very good point. Specific determiners are clues to the correct (or incorrect) choice in a multiple-choice item. Quite often, unskilled test makers provide so many specific determiners in a test that test-wise respondents can score well without any skill in the content being tested. Look at this item:

> **specific determiners**
> Clues to the correct or the incorrect choice in a multiple-choice item.

1. What size hook is best for dry flies in the months of August and September in the Yellowstone area?
   a. Number 12 for all river and small stream conditions.
   b. Number 14 or number 16, depending on water clarity.
   c. Number 10 because streamers are always best for that water.
   d. Number 14.

What's the correct answer? Choice a is no good because it contains the absolute *all.* Choice b is the only compound answer, so it is either the best choice or the poorest. Choice c sets a condition for the response that goes against the stem. Even if you don't know a streamer is *not* a dry fly, you would still come to this conclusion. It also has the absolute *always.* Choice d is the only choice without an explanation. It lacks parallel structure so it almost has to be incorrect. Choice b must be correct.

Specific determiners can turn a test into a farce. Let's look at my interpretation of the most common rules.

Lack of Parallel Structure. If one alternative is compound, all of them should be. If two have subject, verb, and object, the others should, too, because any alternative that varies will stand out. The structure of alternatives within items should be straightforward and consistent. Look at the four alternatives from our fly fishing item.

   a. Number 12 for all river and small stream conditions.
   b. Number 14 or number 16, depending on water clarity.
   c. Number 10 because streamers are always best for that water.
   d. Number 14.

Now give them all the same structure.

a. Number 12 because the water is usually moving.
b. Number 16 because Montana water is very clear.
c. Number 10 because streamers are always best for that water.
d. Number 14 because of the size of insects at that time of year.

Better? Now all are verb phrases, but there are still problems with the item. Let's look at another specific determiner.

Particular Words. Woods (1960) warns against the use of absolutes such as *always* and *never.* Her emphasis, though, is on other word clues that may not be as easy to recognize. Many times these terms are technical or content-sensitive. In the sample item, the phrase *Montana water* refers to a specific quality of water found in that area. The phrase gives away the answer.

Most content areas are rife with such words. Often the item writer feels pressed to use such words in context in the correct response. Sometimes it's incumbent on the writer to do so. When confronted with this choice, take as objective a stance as possible. Is the term or phrase really helpful to the respondent? If not, delete it. If so, make the other alternatives seem to contain similar terms.

Our example is easy to correct. Simply delete the word *always* in c and substitute *the* for Montana in b: "Because streamers are best for that water" and "because the water is very clear."

Relative Length. The length of the correct response is often different from the other alternatives. Usually it's longer—sometimes a lot longer. Choose the correct response:

a. Rope in hand.
b. Pitons belted.
c. Ice axe sheathed.
d. Day pack slung low against the hips.

Almost anyone would choose d without reading the question. Let's try again.

a. Corrugated steel.
b. Brass.
c. Anodized aluminum.
d. Tempered steel.

Because *brass* is shorter than the others, it begs to be chosen. If you had to guess, you'd probably choose it, and, given the way most people write items, you'd probably be correct.

This particular way of providing clues is the one most likely to trip up the experienced item writer. We all have a tendency to make sure the correct response can't be criticized. Therefore, we tend to add modifiers and conditions to make sure it won't be questioned. Let's look at another revision of our fishing question:

1. What size hook is best for dry flies in the months of August and September in the Yellowstone area?
   a. Number 12 because the water is usually moving.
   b. Number 16 because even moving water is very clear at that time of year near Yellowstone.
   c. Number 10 because streamers are best for the water.
   d. Number 14 because it's the size of most insects.

Our writer has put two clues in alternative b. It has been modified to make sure the meaning is clear, so it is much longer than the other alternatives. It also has a word, *Yellowstone*, that refers directly to the stem. Because none of the other alternatives refer to the stem, *Yellowstone* is a specific determiner of the type we are talking about. This type of inadvertent clue is sometimes called a *clang*. The test taker matches it to the stem and chooses the alternative that contains it almost automatically.

Notice also the change to alternative d. It has been shortened and is now relatively the same length as a and c. Change b back to the way it was and the item looks like this:

1. What size hook is best for dry flies in the months of August and September in the Yellowstone area?
   a. Number 12 because the water is usually moving.
   b. Number 16 because the water is very clear.
   c. Number 10 because streamers are best for the water.
   d. Number 14 because it's the size of most insects.

If we keep working on it, we may get a good item out of this. Another important revision is to put the sizes (numbers) in ascending or descending order to avoid tricking the respondent.

1. What size hook is best for dry flies in the months of August and September in the Yellowstone area?
   a. Number 10 because streamers are best for the water.
   b. Number 12 because the water is usually moving.
   c. Number 14 because it's the size of most insects.
   d. Number 16 because the water is very clear.

Vague Pronouns. You will almost always write the correct answer first. It's a natural tendency and that's OK, but watch out. You may write pronouns in the other alternatives that refer to terms you defined in the correct one. Our fishing example provides a good illustration. Suppose you wrote the item, then the correct response, and finally the other alternatives. It might look like this:

1. What size hook is best for dry flies in the months of August and September in the Yellowstone area?
   a. Number 16 because the water is very clear.
   b. Number 12 because it is usually moving.
   c. Number 10 because streamers are best for it.
   d. Number 14 because it's the size of most insects.

What happened? The pronoun *it* has been used for the word *water* in alternatives b and c. This seems OK until we scramble the alternatives into ascending order, as we did before:

a. Number 10 because streamers are best for it.
b. Number 12 because it is usually moving.
c. Number 14 because it's the size of most insects.
d. Number 16 because the water is very clear.

The antecedent for the pronoun *it* in a and b is in alternative d. The reference becomes vague. Is the antecedent the hook size, streamer, or what? Respondent confusion will extend to alternative c where the pronoun *it* is used correctly. It has an antecedent (number 14) but, because in a and b the pronoun stands for water, respondents will tend to give it the same meaning in c.

Avoid using a pronoun in an alternative unless the antecedent is in the alternative. Be particularly sensitive to the pronoun *they.* It's notorious for being used vaguely.

Opposites. Opposites can be sneaky. What happens is the item writer writes the best answer. Then, naturally, he or she puts down the opposite as an alternative. When respondents see this on a test they believe one of the two has to be correct. They forget about the other alternatives and concentrate on the opposites. In essence the item becomes a true/false item.

Technical Terms. I touched on this previously. Be wary of technical terms. If the correct response has them, the others should too.

Overlapping Alternatives. Overlapping alternatives appear most often in Level One Cognitive items. Overlaps tend to make more than one alternative correct. For example, suppose respondents are asked to choose the optimum number of people to be included in a nominal group session. The alternatives are

a. 3 to 7.
b. 5 to 9.
c. 7 to 11.
d. 9 to 13.

The correct answer is b, but because a and c both include part of the range in b, people who choose a or c have a valid argument that their answers are also correct. By the way, there is another problem with these alternatives. The extreme answers are far less likely to be correct than the others. A person who has to guess should guess either b or c because, most of the time, the item writer working with numeric alternatives will tend to keep the correct answer near the middle of the range of answers presented as alternatives. In either ascending or descending order, this is likely to put the answer in either b or c.

Synonymous Distractors. When we are in a hurry or having trouble coming up with plausible but incorrect alternatives, we have a tendency to write the same wrong answer more than one way. The respondents who recognize this can then eliminate the synonymous alternatives, if only one alternative can be correct.

What Woods (1960) pointed out is, be careful how you use the language. Watch out for clues. They will sneak into your work, even when you are vigilant. This is a very good reason for using a developmental test. Ask a test-wise friend to take the test in draft form with the goal of passing it even though he or she doesn't know the content. If he or she can do so, you have given too many clues. You've inserted specific determiners.

Another way to avoid giving clues and other language troubles is to be familiar with the following basic rules for writing items. (Copy them and keep them by your side as you write your next test.)

♦ ♦ ♦

Rules to Remember

Here are a few guidelines that should help you as you write items. They are simply guidelines to use as you will, but *the first three are critical.* These three should always be in your mind. If you follow the guidelines faithfully, your items will work well. If you don't, you will probably have trouble.

One (and Most Important): Never Trick the Respondents. Your respondents are trusting you to treat them fairly. If they feel tricked or cheated by a test item, their resentment will be powerful. A single trick question can generate more bad publicity than an entire advertising campaign. You will be tempted. Don't do it. Even a seemingly innocent thing like, "Who makes Armstrong tile?" can ruin a respondent's mindset and cost him or her points. Trick items are a big *no-no.*

Two: Don't Assume a Superior Stance or Attitude. You are dealing with peers— others who want what you can give them. Avoid talking down to them. Avoid language conventions that distance you from them. Some of those conventions are mentioned below.

Three: Remember That You Are Testing the Respondents' Ability to Show Competence. This is not a test of their ability to read or interpret your wonderful prose. Make your prose truly wonderful. Keep it simple.

Four: Use Second-Person Singular Whenever You Can. Ask, "What should you do?" instead of, "What should the manager do?" Say, "You are working with a client," instead of, "A consultant is working with a client."

Five: Avoid the Imperial We. There are times when the use of the word *we* implies the writer's superiority. Make sure the respondent feels included when you use *we.*

Six: Try to Limit Each Sentence and Question to Twelve Words or Fewer. This makes them easier to read. You aren't testing reading skills.

Seven: Do Not Use Negatives Unless You Can't Avoid Them. When you do, underline or italicize them so the respondents will be sure to see them.

Eight: Use a Question in the Stem Whenever Possible. Open-ended statements are permissible, but the respondents react to them differently than they do to questions. This change of mind-set often trips a respondent up. Open-ended statements can usually be rewritten as simple questions, which makes the items much easier to deal with.

Nine: Do Not Say, "Which of the Following . . ." A simple "What . . ." communicates better. The respondents know the possible answers are listed below. To tell them so is redundant and, if you think about it, an insult to their intelligence.

Ten: Use Standard Question Format and Conventions. It's true that you *can* introduce variety, but it makes the respondents' task more difficult. It forces them to decode the question before they can work on answering it.

Eleven: Avoid Unnecessary Prepositional Phrases. Phrasing like, "The artisan, with whom the client has contracted," complicates what could be a simple, straightforward question.

Twelve: Do Not Teach in the Stem. It's natural to try to give the respondents information, but keep it to a minimum. Supply only what they should have. Consider this example:

1. Modern furniture makers have perfected techniques for aging wood and finishes to make their products very difficult to distinguish from antiques. How should you protect your client from these products?

You could ask the same question by saying, "How can you help your client avoid purchasing counterfeit antiques?"

Thirteen: Avoid Asking Trivial Questions. If respondents can look information up in a catalogue or an easily secured document, they shouldn't have to memorize it.

Fourteen: If Possible, Limit Each Alternative to a Single Line.

Fifteen: Each Alternative Should Have About the Same Number of Words. Long or short alternatives draw attention. Many item writers tend to put more detail into the correct response, thereby alerting the test taker to the fact that it is correct.

Sixteen: Avoid Repeating the Same Phrase in Every Response. Instead, incorporate phrases into the stem.

Seventeen: Make Each Alternative a Natural Response to the Question. If each is a semantically correct response, fewer clues will be given as to the answer.

Eighteen: Place a Period at the End of Each Alternative. Do this even when they aren't complete sentences. The period tells the respondents to stop. It prevents them from mixing alternatives together or becoming confused.

Nineteen: Every Alternative Should Be as Plausible as You Can Make It. The idea is to make the test easy for people who know the work and difficult for those who don't. To the uninitiated, the test should be a total mystery.

Twenty: For Level Three Items, Try to Make Every Alternative at Least Partially Correct. This forces the respondents to choose the *best* answer for the question posed.

Try to be consistently aware of the level you intend your items to sample. Usually, this will be Level Two or Level Three. Don't let yourself slip back into Level One.

Level One items are very poor predictors of success in a process or a profession. They test respondents' ability to remember facts, make comparisons, or discriminate among remembered data. Although these skills are important, they usually don't require testing. Level One skills are enablers. They enable people to perform at the higher levels. An apprentice in a trade or craft can be said to be able to perform at Level One.

Level Two items test ability to apply a principle or process. Application can be described in many ways. Generally, it's using knowledge and skill to accomplish a task. Application items are the best kind to use to discriminate between those who can perform and those who cannot. They are, therefore, preferred for performance examinations. Level Two is personified by the journeyman.

Level Three items move beyond the ordinary into what may be. Although most people must be able to solve problems to do well in their work, the kind of problem solving called for by Level Three items is usually innovative or creative in nature. These items are often called *developmental* because respondents are asked to develop unique or insightful ideas about the content. All the alternatives in a Level Three item will often be correct. Respondents are asked to select the best correct answer, depending on the circumstances described. The master craftsman is at Level Three.

◆ ◆ ◆

If you keep these rules and the discussion in previous chapters in mind, you will be ready to write good fair multiple-choice items. It isn't a particularly difficult task. In fact, it can be fun and satisfying. You'll place yourself in your respondents' minds and provide them an opportunity to show their stuff.

In time you will want to expand on the multiple-choice concept. You'll find yourself with content or skill areas that don't fit the classic format well. Matching items are often a good solution to such a problem.

Matching Items

A matching item is really five to seven multiple-choice items combined. The classic example is a Level One Cognitive check on relationships of some sort. It usually looks like this.

1. Choose the kind of saw from Column B that is best for each job in Column A. Write the letter of your choice in the appropriate blank.

   Column A

   __ 1. Cut thin steel.

   __ 2. Make interior cuts.

   __ 3. Make angle cuts.

   __ 4. Cut sharp curves.

   __ 5. Cut along the grain.

   __ 6. Cut against the grain.

   __ 7. Cut firewood.

   Column B

   a. Rip.

   b. Compass.

   c. Coping.

   d. Dovetail.

   e. Crosscut.

   f. Back.

   g. Hack.

   h. Bow.

   i. Keyhole.

   (1. g, 2. i, 3. f, 4. c, 5. a, 6. e, 7. h)

You can see this is an extension of the concept behind multiple-choice items. Each task in Column A could be the stem of an item with four or five of the answers in Column B as alternatives.

The sample exhibits other characteristics of matching items. It tests Level One. Respondents are expected to remember what saw is best for each use. This is usually the case. Its wording is terse, with short phrases that take little space. The directions are clear and specific. Matching items require better directions than other types of items.

Note there are two responses that don't have a home. This makes it more difficult for respondents to connect the right answers to the parts they don't know through elimination. Suppose, for example, that a respondent doesn't know what kind of saw to use to cut firewood, but knows the others. That leaves the person with three choices: throw, compass, and bow. Guessing won't help much.

I find it convenient to call the terms, phrases, or statements in the first column *stimulators* and the answers in the second column *responses.*

There are some special rules for writing matching items:

1. The number of stimulators and responses should *not* be balanced. There should be more of one or the other to prevent people from discovering a correct response through the process of elimination.
2. There should be no more than seven stimulators. This conforms to the rule of "five plus or minus two." Respondents should not be presented with the task of trying to organize the test while they are taking it.

3. The columns should be homogeneous. They should all belong to the same class of things and conform to the same literal style. Don't mix apples and warthogs.

The matching item is gaining a larger following. This is principally because good item writers can use it for Level Two or even Level Three tasks. One method for doing this is illustrated by this item.

1. Choose the phrase from Column B that best fits each term in Column A. Write the letter of your choice in the appropriate blank. Use care. Several of the answers in Column B apply to more than one term. Choose the best response for each.

Column A	*Column B*
__ 1. True/false.	a. Best used to test a single concept.
__ 2. Fill-in.	b. Most commonly misused item type.
__ 3. Essay.	c. Best for psychomotor tasks.
__ 4. Short answer.	d. The most flexible type of item.
__ 5. Multiple choice.	e. Best for the cognitive domain.
__ 6. Matching.	f. Only good for direct recall.
	g. Best for the affective domain.
	h. Best for Level Three.
	i. Best for Level Two.
	j. Best for Level One.

(1. b, 2. f, 3. h., 4. g, 5. e, 6. j)

Another, perhaps even more effective, technique is to have fewer responses than there are stimulators and inform respondents they can use each response as many times as is appropriate, as in this example.

1. Assume you are going to test each of the skills in Column A. What sort of item would probably be best for each application? Choose the item type from Column B that best fits each application in Column A. Write the letter of your choice in the appropriate blank. You may use a response as many times as you wish.

Column A   *Column B*

___ 1. Ability to throw a football.   a. Multiple choice.

___ 2. Skill in writing job descriptions.   b. Matching.

___ 3. Skill in solving linear equations.   c. Essay.

___ 4. Ability to interpret a foreign language.   d. Short answer.

___ 5. Ability to select the best pronoun for a use.

___ 6. Skill in setting a rhyme sequence in poetry.

___ 7. Ability to identify irrational numbers.

(1. d, 2. c, 3. d, 4. c, 5. a, 6. b, 7. a)

Interesting, isn't it? The respondents will know more than one of the responses is correct for each application. They are put in the position of choosing the one that is best. It's at least Level Two and may be Level Three, depending on whether the respondents have discussed the applications before they take the test.

> **scale**
> A system of grouping or classifying in a series of steps or degrees according to a standard or relative size, amount, rank, and so forth.

Another kind of choice item is the scale item.

Scale Items

Scale items are most often used in opinionnaires and surveys. Such usage has increased to the point that skill in developing them has become very important. The scales from which the item receives its name can be one of three types:

1. Scales derived from continua, for example, hot to cold.
2. Scales developed to describe a sequence, for example, take a stance, set posture, adjust grip, address the ball, swing.
3. Scales devised to show rankings, for example, top, middle, bottom.

Using the term *ranking* here recalls (for some readers) tests on which respondents are asked to rank alternatives. This is a ploy used to force respondents to supply a continuum. It has limited application because it can easily be unfair. Responses can have the ranking correct except for one part and lose credit for the whole item. Look at an example:

1. Rank the following causes of cancer according to the number of deaths attributed to each per annum. Write the number of the rank for each in the blank provided.

    __ Smoking.
    __ Too much fat and cholesterol.
    __ Anxiety; fear.
    __ Alcohol and other drugs.
    __ Genetic tendencies (parents died of cancer).

    Suppose you know the ranking of four of the causes, but not the fifth. The whole item will be counted wrong, which is not fair.

    Let's return to our discussion of scales and discuss each in turn.

Continua. Continua are the most common type of scale. They are fairly easy to write, but you must be careful to ensure they don't introduce confusion for respondents. Again, examples are in order:

Instructions: for each item below decide how important the activity is to you and your family. Circle the letter that most closely matches your feelings on the matter in question.

1. How important is partisan politics to the political health of the United States of America?
    a. It's very important.
    b. It's important.
    c. I'm not sure whether it's important or not.
    d. It's unimportant.
    e. It's not at all important.

    This is a typical scale item using a scale with an odd number of choices (Likert Scale). With such a scale respondents have the opportunity to register a *no opinion* by choosing the central position. The same item could be written with an even number of choices, as follows.

1. How important is partisan politics to the political health of the United States of America?
    a. It's very important.
    b. It's important.
    c. It's unimportant.
    d. It's not at all important.

    This scale forces respondents to either be for it or against it, which is an unfair manipulation of respondents. They may honestly *not* have an opinion. If so, they are put in the position of supporting or denying an idea they aren't sure of. This is a favorite trick of people who are trying to prove a point. Allow me to illustrate with a totally hypothetical case.

1. How would you rate the quality of life in your neighborhood?
    a. Excellent.
    b. Good.
    c. Poor.
    d. Terrible.

Most people who have no well-defined opinion about their neighborhood will tend to choose b or c (depending on the propaganda they've been subjected to). Let's suppose they tend to choose b. The results could look like this. The percentage of people who chose each response were

Excellent = 12 percent

Good = 47 percent

Poor = 33 percent

Terrible = 8 percent

Clearly, 59 percent of the people think their neighborhoods are OK. Now I'll rewrite the question to include a middle position.

2. How would you rate the quality of life in your neighborhood?
    a. Excellent.
    b. Good.
    c. Neither good nor poor.
    d. Poor.
    e. Terrible.

How will changing the scale affect the results for our hypothetical question? In many cases the tendency is toward the middle, so the results might look like this:

Excellent = 12 percent

Good = 24 percent

Neither = 39 percent

Poor = 17 percent

Terrible = 8 percent

The conclusions of most readers will be very different. Respondents seem to have gone from a favorable opinion about the neighborhoods to one where they are not nearly so sure.

Surveyors and others who use such scales don't like this kind of response. It makes it difficult for them to make claims, so they force respondents to choose. But that doesn't make the practice legitimate. Please don't do it. When you develop scaled items, use an odd number of responses.

Another common fault is to load one side or the other. This often happens with unsophisticated item writers. Three choices will be positive and two negative. Or there may be four negative and one positive, like in this sample.

1. How do you feel about the practice of chewing tobacco?
   a. It is despicably unhealthy.
   b. It's very unhealthy.
   c. It could make chewers sick.
   d. Chewers tend not to feel well.
   e. It's OK in circumspect moderation.

Tobacco chewers don't have a chance with this question. This sort of loading is patently unethical. It gives the test maker an opportunity to make a point and support it with supposedly objective evidence. Sometimes, such loading can be unintentional. Check this item:

1. How do you feel about the programs offered by the local chapter of our association?
   a. All are good.
   b. Most of them are good.
   c. Some of them are good.
   d. Most of them are poor.
   e. All of them are poor.

The writer meant for the middle choice to be neutral, but it isn't. He or she has used the word *good,* so the connotation is good.

Sequence. Scales developed to describe a sequence can be very useful. In this case you don't have to be concerned about balance.

1. When do most golfers make sure they are aiming a shot correctly?
   a. When they take their stance.
   b. As they address the ball.
   c. During the swing.
   d. When the club head strikes the ball.

There is some disagreement as to whether this is truly a scale or not. After all, it can't be described by numbers. Or can it? The activities come first, second, third, and fourth, or they can be at time intervals. Either way, a scale is in use, even though it may not be as obvious as with a continuum.

Perhaps the most frequent use of scales is in items with ranges as alternatives:

1. How many colonies came together to form the United States of America?
   a. 7.
   b. 13.
   c. 22.
   d. 48.

There are two rules associated with this type of scale:

1. Arrange the points on the scale in either ascending or descending order or, for sequential items, in chronological order.
2. Keep the intervals as nearly the same as possible.

The example above is in descending order, but the intervals are different. The tendency in such cases, for test-wise respondents, is to cast aside extreme alternatives. In this case the number 48 is clearly much different from the others. That makes the chance of guessing correctly significantly better. Look at these samples:

1. What number is irrational?
   a. 0.
   b. 3/9.
   c. 7/13.
   d. 1.
2. What number is *not* defined?
   a. 0.
   b. 3/9.
   c. 7/13.
   d. 1.
3. What number is unity?
   a. 0.
   b. 3/9.
   c. 7/13.
   d. 1.
4. What number is *not* in lowest terms?
   a. 0.
   b. 3/9.
   c. 7/13.
   d. 1.

I just made a boo-boo—one made often by test makers. If respondents know the answers to three of the items, they will be able to answer the other one too. This set could also be rewritten as a matching item. Of course, to avoid allowing the respondents to use the process of elimination, the matching item would have more responses than stimulators.

Scales don't have to be written in numbers and often aren't.

1. When do most store managers have the most trouble dealing with shoplifters?
   a. Opening time.
   b. Midmorning.
   c. Around lunch.
   d. Afternoon.
   e. Evening.
   f. Closing time.

Rankings. Scales with rankings for alternatives are often used in surveys. They can be equally useful in performance tests. Typically they use numbers or number substitutes to indicate the rank. However, as the example below shows, that isn't necessary:

1. How do most sportswriters today rate the boxer Joe Louis?
   a. He was the best ever.
   b. In the top three.
   c. In the top ten.

The best use of ranking scales is probably to inquire about respondents' sense of urgency or importance—to test their attitudes—as seen in the next example.

1. Here are three important attitudes employees can have about an organization. They can have trust in:

   • The quality of its goods and services.
   • Management's ability to manage well.
   • Their security and tenure as employees.

   How would you rank the importance of their trust in management?
   a. Most important of the three.
   b. Second most important.
   c. Third most important.

Ranking items are difficult to write well. If you feel you must use them, keep in mind that each answer should stand alone. Respondents should only deal with one set of variables per item. In the previous example, they are only concerned about the second set of variables, those dealing with management. If you want them to focus on each of the variables, you should ask three separate questions.

A final word about ranking items. Don't confuse them with sequences. If you ask someone to tell you what comes first, second, and so forth, you've asked for a sequence, not a ranking.

In summary, as an item writer your task is to write items to produce a viable test. It's an important task—one that becomes more important as tests are used in more and more sophisticated applications. Use the advice and process described here to produce good fair tests that will be fun for your respondents to take and satisfying for you when the results are in.

Trust your own judgment. You have this task because you are good at what you do. Rely on your own instincts when faced with tough choices.

Give yourself *frequent* breaks. You must shift gears continually as you go from item to item. If you don't take a break now and then, your ability to reassess and start over with each item will fade.

Remain determined to write at Level Two. You'll find when you do, items will almost always be appropriate and acceptable to your respondents, your clients, and yourself.

Step 9: Review and Qualify the Items

Once you have items, you don't necessarily have a test. The items must be organized, reviewed, and matched with the criteria they allegedly test.

Organization

Organizing the items is usually not a problem. Most test makers set the criteria in plain sight and use them as an outline while writing the items. That not only provides organization for the items. It also qualifies the items as they are written. Here are a few suggestions for organizing the test to make it a better instrument.

Make the Test Friendly, a Tool for Respondents. First, make sure presentation, format, and style are friendly to the respondents. Keep your instructions clear and concise. Provide space. Don't cut items in half at a page break. Present the test as a useful tool for the respondents. Be sure the language and style are easy to use.

Avoid Surprises. Second, set the pattern of the test quickly and adhere to it as much as you can. Suppose, for example, you want to use a short-answer item followed by three or four multiple-choice items. Try to repeat the pattern throughout. If you deviate, explain why to the respondents.

Let the Respondents Warm Up. Third, let them warm up. Don't put the most complex or difficult items first. Start with items they can address fairly easily and work up to the more difficult ones.

Consider Respondent Fatigue. Fourth, think about fatigue. If the test is long, arrange for breaks while it's in progress. Don't put the most complex items near the end. You want people to address the toughest challenges while they're relatively fresh.

These four guides can help the organization of your test give respondents a fair chance to do their best.

Item Review

No matter how much of a hurry you're in or how sure you are of your work, review the items. Don't risk respondents not understanding or misunderstanding.

One example of a hurried approach was when a nationwide testing organization prepared to administer a certification exam. In selecting the items to be used in the test, their computer misnumbered three of them. The numbers went something like 32, 35, 34, 36, 37, 38, and so forth. What were respondents to do? Should they record their answers on the answer sheet next to the correct number or in the order presented? This minor error caused problems for more than seven hundred respondents.

Perhaps the most important reason for the review is to see your work with a fresh mind. Sentences or questions that seemed to make sense when you wrote them can be seen to have flaws. Typos are common. People leave out commas while typing. Words are misspelled. Murphy's Law (if anything can go wrong, it will) applies to tests as much as to any other things we do. With tests, though, the consequences are more serious. If respondents find obvious errors, they can simply tell you about them, and no harm is done. But what if they don't recognize the error? Look at this item:

1. What part of the average manager's work is most likely to be substantially modified by a time program?
   a. Use of the telephone.
   b. Interactions with others.

c. The daily routine.

d. Personnel decisions.

e. Paperwork.

Most respondents won't realize the item has an error in it. Do you see it? The item writer left out the words *just in*. Without them respondents could believe the program referred to is a time management program or, perhaps, one sponsored by *Time* magazine. The item has been rendered useless through an error in transcription. The problem could easily have been avoided by a review.

Reviews aren't easy. When you read your own work, you tend to overlook errors. You see what you expect to see rather than what is actually there. For that reason, it makes sense to have someone else review the items for you. Your reviewer doesn't have to be an expert in the subject matter. He or she will not be looking for problems with content. Those were taken care of in earlier reviews.

It's an advantage if your reviewer has some expertise in test construction and can check style and format, but those aren't the critical areas. The important things are readability and interpretation. Can respondents read the items? More important, will they understand what you are asking?

If you have to review the items yourself, do it in an atmosphere and at a time when you can concentrate on the task. Be sure you're alert and ready. There is one rule you should keep in mind while reviewing. It's a rule you should share with anyone who reviews the items for you: if in doubt, throw it out. If you aren't sure about an item, discard it. Don't try to revise on the spot. To do so will detract from your review of the remainder of the test.

Discard the bad items until the review is complete. Then you can look at each one with the intent of fixing it or replacing it. You'll find that many of the items can simply be thrown away. The justification for the bad items diminishes once the test has reached this stage.

Align with Criteria

When the test has been organized and reviewed, make one or more pass through it. This time make sure the items test what you intend. For the most part they will. After all, you constructed them from the criteria. You've organized them and reviewed them. So they should be appropriate for the purpose of the test. But make sure.

Look at each item. Make sure you know the skill being tested. Then find the criterion the item measures. It sounds simple, but there can be problems. For example, look at this item:

1. Where, on the line, is the best place to begin the initial search for the problem?
   a. At the first checkpoint where the trouble could originate.
   b. Near the center between the first point where the trouble could be found and the last place on the line where it could be.
   c. At the last place on the line where the trouble could be.
   d. At the place where the reporting operator thinks the trouble is centered.

Now look again at the criterion the item was meant to measure.

A. Given a breakdown on the assembly line, the supervisor will implement the process in the troubleshooting manual.

Does the item actually measure the criterion? The criterion says to use the manual. Does the item test that? No. Is that OK? Yes, if the respondents have a copy of the manual to use while they take the test. Otherwise, it doesn't measure the criterion.

Qualification of each item may seem inappropriate or silly. However, the benefits are illustrated by the example. Until qualification, the decision to use the item was not questioned. The questioning can prove very valuable.

Step 10: Pilot the Test

To skip the pilot test is to court trouble. Up to this point the test is mostly in the mind of the test maker. True, you have asked others to review items. You have checked your content. But you haven't really checked the test itself.

Ideally, the pilot would be a dress rehearsal. It should involve the target audience. It should be conducted with materials as much like those that will be used later as possible. It should be given in the same environment. In short, it should be as much like future uses as possible.

The only difference will be in how the results are used. The results of the pilot are used to make a final decision about whether the test can be used. The results of the pilot dictate the final modifications that will be made.

For subsequent applications, the results of the test should be unchallenged. That is, the respondents won't be expected to appeal their scores. Of course, appeals will be allowed. They simply won't be expected. The pilot makes these conditions possible.

The steps for a pilot are straightforward:

1. Set the time and place.
2. Produce the test in as close to final form as is feasible.
3. Select people to participate as respondents, administrators, and evaluators.
4. Administer the test under conditions as close to those to be encountered later as possible.
5. Evaluate the results.
6. Use information from the results to modify the test and ready it for use.

Time and Place

Setting the time and place for the pilot make it real. Once it has been scheduled, you are committed. If possible, the pilot should be formally scheduled. It should be on your calendar officially. Later you can make sure it's on the calendars of all the people who will be involved. By scheduling the pilot you make it possible.

Produce the Test for the Pilot

Many tests are produced in booklet form with special printing. They are accompanied by answer sheets specially prepared for machine scoring. Support materials such as drawings or manuals are printed. Going to these lengths for a pilot is usually not justified. They are too expensive and time consuming for a one-time application. Therefore, you will usually use draft materials. This is OK as long as the respondents are aware of the nature of the test (pilot) and their roles. Make sure everything that will be used for the test is also used for the pilot. All elements must be in place, or the pilot won't be valid.

Select Pilot Participants

The respondents chosen for the pilot should represent as true a sample of the target audience as possible. The most valid group would be a random sample of the intended audience. I like to be able to treat the pilot as a regular application of the test. Therefore, I try to provide the same benefits for the pilot test respondents as for any others. Their scores should count. If this isn't possible, you may find it appropriate to provide some other kind of incentive. People who do a pilot out of the goodness of their hearts won't have the same attitude about the purpose of the test as later respondents. Therefore they will tend not to provide a valid test of the test.

If the pilot is to be used to set cut-scores, you will also want a group of people who are experts and a third group of people who are qualified in every way except that they don't have the skills to be tested.

Finally, be sure to include support personnel, administrators, jurors, evaluators, and others. The pilot provides a way to see if these people are prepared to provide the support they are supposed to. If a function is wanted, be sure the people who will provide that function can do it well.

Administer the Test

Do it. Have respondents go through the test as others will later. Do not add special assignments or requirements like having them edit the materials or check spelling.

Evaluate the Results

First, run the results as you ordinarily would. If the test is to be machine scored, machine score it. Run your statistics and item analyses. Then look at the outcomes. Make sure each item has worked as it should. This will be discussed in detail in Chapter Eleven, so I won't go into it now. But, in essence, you would do—on the pilot—what you would do for any application. The major difference is that you should spend *more* time. Examine the data critically. Look for places and ways to make the test better.

Use the Information to Make the Test Better

That is the purpose of a pilot. Make the test better. Real respondents have just given you an initial reading on how well they could do with your test. Did they do as well as they should have? Were they treated well? Is the test good and fair? If it isn't, fix it.

Now let's deal with the real world. Many of the tests you build will be one-shot affairs. You construct the test. The respondents respond. Evaluation takes place. And it's done. So what's with this pilot stuff? Well, it's still important. You have to be concerned with whether your test is good and fair. You won't know until real respondents have a chance to tell you. Ergo, you should have a pilot, even for a one-shot affair.

However, you won't be able to do a full-fledged pilot test most of the time. You'll have to make do with something else. The minimum you should do is have at least three people (preferably a target audience) take the test in as realistic a setting as possible.

Let's suppose you are a college professor. You've put together a final exam for a course you intend to teach once. How can you run a pilot on the test? The key is in timing. The test should be developed before the term begins, before classes start. Then it can be used as a pretest for the course. This event can serve two functions: (1) it really is a pretest, and you and your students can derive the benefits therefrom and (2) it is also a pilot of the final exam. You can use the results to make your test better. Of course, the students starting a class aren't the target audience. They haven't taken the course yet. But they qualify in every other way. Their responses can be valuable for revising the test, making it better.

"But," you say, "the students will know what's on the final. They'll know what to concentrate on to get a good score at the end of the term." Isn't that what you want them to do? If the exam is a good reflection of the criteria (objectives) for the course, they will study the right stuff—be aided in mastering the content you want them to master.

Even if you can only get one person to take a pilot test, do it. I have a friend whose long-suffering spouse performs this function. The spouse has often found problems or inconsistencies that proved very valuable. (The spouse loves to do it because my friend buys dinner afterward.) Of course, you can't run statistics on a single score. So you can't run item analysis or cut-score studies or whatever. But you can get an idea of how easy the items are to interpret, whether they test the criteria as hoped, and how long it takes someone to complete the work. This information is valuable enough to mandate the effort.

If you don't have a cooperative spouse, use a colleague or friend. Do *not* settle for a naïve volunteer. This would be expecting an informed critique from someone who should fail the test in a real application. It's like asking a ballerina to demonstrate wrestling holds. The person is not likely to be very helpful.

Step 11: Set Cut-Scores or Other Parameters

> **cut-scores**
> Predetermined scores used to determine whether a respondent passes.

Step 11 appears to be optional. It should not be. What it says, in effect, is that you should formalize your expectations. Two questions should be answered. What will the successful respondent do? How will you discriminate those who fail from those who pass?

If you don't make these decisions at this time, you risk falling into an awful trap. The trap is norm referenced. If you delay making decisions about who should pass and who should fail, you allow yourself to be influenced by the scores when the test is administered. Suppose, for example, you are designing a test for managers. It's a performance test. Qualification and the pilot test indicate a person must score 85 to pass. Then you give the test and the scores look like this:

A. 87	B. 86	C. 72	D. 81	E. 84
F. 96	G. 92	H. 87	I. 84	J. 87
K. 54	L. 85	M. 86	N. 90	O. 86
P. 85	Q. 89	R. 69	S. 86	T. 80

What about the people who scored 84? It doesn't seem fair to fail them. They only missed the standard by one point. But if you decide to lower your standard to include those people, you have just made a decision based on what others scored. Your decision is to compare people with one another rather than with the standard. You've referenced the test to a *norm*.

Using normed data to decide what the cut-score should be is legitimate. It's the basis for the most acceptable practice. But, once the standard is set, *do not change it* for a single application of the test. Modification of qualification scores should only be done when they are being set.

In Chapter Eleven there is a detailed discussion of how to set cut-scores. The point here is to be sure to set them *before the test is used*. In fact, the respondents should know how well they have to do to pass before they take the test.

Test makers often make the mistake of assuming respondents know how well they have to do to pass. This can be very punishing for the respondents. Having accomplished Step 11, you will know what successful candidates will score. You should tell them ahead of time. That way they will know not to quit too soon or, even more important, not to continue after they have accomplished the goal.

Consider a test for swimmers. Say they have to swim a certain distance using a particular kind of stroke in a minimum amount of time. If they know these criteria before they begin, they will be much more comfortable with the test. In fact, swimmers who are aware of their limitations may even refrain from trying because they know they can't accomplish the task.

Whether self-qualification is a goal or not, the fact remains that telling respondents ahead of time is a very good idea. It's a key to fairness.

Think about a multiple-choice test for supervisors. It has 142 items. The items are application and developmental in nature (Levels Two and Three). The test covers skills in interviewing, directing, planning, using personnel, and managing the process. Now think about yourself taking this test. If you don't know how well you will have to score to pass it, how will you feel about the challenge. Scared? Maybe you should be. Even people who are expert in the content should expect to misinterpret or simply not be able to answer some of the items. How many mistakes of this type can the test taker afford to make? It's a question that should not have to be asked. The test maker can easily state what the passing score will be *even if the test is norm referenced.* You could be told you have to answer 117 items correctly (or whatever the cut-score is). You could be told you have to score as well as or better than 70 percent of the other respondents.

Summary

The test has been planned, designed, and developed. The next obvious steps are to produce it, use it, and evaluate its effectiveness. We discuss these steps in the following chapters.

CHAPTER NINE

PRODUCING AND ADMINISTERING THE TEST

It is time to talk about format. Formatting isn't a step by itself simply because it happens throughout the process. Most test makers begin to think about format the moment they know a test is in order. They visualize what it will look like. Format was important again at the design stage. Now, as you produce the test, you can turn your thoughts about format into reality. It makes sense to produce the test well.

Let's begin with some common formatting conventions, what they are, and how they contribute to the test. An important aspect of formatting is how it controls flow and focus—how respondents progress through the test and how easy it is for them to see and understand what you want them to do. Then we'll cover producing and administering your test.

Too many times test format is determined by what I call artificial concerns. For example, if you reduce the type size on a test, you can put more items on one page. This makes the test less bulky, makes it easier to score, and saves paper. But it often causes the test taker problems with reading and understanding. The same is true for extending margins using close spacing conventions and for using long, complex sentences. Look at Figure 9.1.

I suppose we should feel sorry for Harry, but I'm more concerned about the poor guy trying to answer the question. It's a fairly straightforward essay item, but it has been made difficult by the way it's presented. Figure 9.2 shows the same item after a bit of reformatting and editing.

FIGURE 9.1. SAMPLE MIDTERM EXAM.

Midterm Exam
Ed. Psych. 617
Upstate University

Read the question carefully. Consider the dominant and subordinate conditions for each character in the situation, develop a preliminary role designation for each in reference to the situation, and describe how the first and second characters mentioned in each situation might modify their behavior to accommodate the primary drives of the others in the situation.
   Use the space provided to record your responses.

1. Harry and Joe have volunteered to join the marines, they have signed the papers, have taken the oath, and are leaving the recruitment center to return home and prepare for inductions, which will take place in three days. Harry shoves Joe as they exit, causing him to lose his balance and stagger against the door frame. Harry says, "Clumsy, aren't you? How'd you get the marines to accept you? Bribe the sergeant?" He laughs and shoves past Joe. Joe punches Harry in the stomach who falls to the floor obviously unable to breathe. Joe looks at him, shrugs, and continues out the door without looking back.

_____

_____

_____

_____

_____

_____

Which of the items would you be better able to answer? Even without knowing the content, you might want to try the second rendition (Figure 9.2, p. 220).

The example is a bit outlandish. Or is it? Haven't you encountered tests that have been much like Figure 9.1? They aren't much fun. In fact, such tests severely limit respondents, who must spend valuable time and energy simply trying to decode the items.

Formatting Conventions

Formatting doesn't just happen. It should be carefully planned. Consider how you want respondents to perceive the test. Put yourself in their place and develop as friendly an environment as you can. It's good to think about the presentation of

FIGURE 9.2. SAMPLE REFORMATTED MIDTERM EXAM.

Midterm Exam
Ed. Psych. 617
Upstate University

Read the item carefully. Consider the dominant and subordinate conditions for each character in the situation. Develop a preliminary role designation for each in reference to the situation. Describe how the first and second characters mentioned might modify their behavior to accommodate the primary drives of the others in the situation.

Use the space provided to record your responses.

1. Harry and Joe have volunteered to join the marines. They have signed the papers, have taken the oath, and are leaving the recruitment center. Harry shoves Joe as they exit, causing him to lose his balance and stagger against the door frame.

   Harry says, "Clumsy, aren't you? How'd you get in the marines? Bribe the sergeant?" He laughs and shoves past Joe.

   Joe punches Harry in the stomach. Harry falls to the floor, obviously unable to breathe. Joe looks at him, shrugs, and continues out the door without looking back.

   Write your response in this space:

a test as an environment. In a way it is. The respondents will be spending a bit of their lives with the test. They will be interacting with it. The conditions they encounter will, in effect, be their environment for a short period of time.

If you think of the test this way, it's easier to understand the importance of the conventions described here. These conventions can be assigned to three basic arenas: (1) use of space, including white space; (2) flow and focus; and (3) presentation.

Use of Space

Whether the medium is a piece of paper or the state of Arizona, its use can either help or hinder respondents. The ideal situation is when the use of space is transparent, that is, test takers don't notice it. Basically, good use of space depends on four conventions:

1. Have enough space available to do the job.
2. Use the space for the job at hand with as little interference as possible.
3. Use space as respondents expect it to be used.
4. When presented with a choice, choose to help respondents.

Have Enough Space Available to Do the Job. Despite cries to the contrary, paper is not only cheap—it's a renewable resource. I'm not in favor of wasting paper. I recycle with a glad heart. What I'm saying is, "Don't sacrifice respondents to save paper." To do so is to subvert your basic purpose. If you must add a page or two to your test to give respondents sufficient space, do it without regret. The test takers come first in all considerations and conventions.

This mandate pertains to all sorts of space. If the test is a survival test in the desert, be sure enough of the desert is available to make it a good test. (I don't know whether you'll want all of Arizona, but that's your decision.)

I'm reminded of a test I took in the army. It was the final exam for a nine-week course in radar repair. It required respondents to use schematics to trace the flow of electricity through a very complex system. The book the schematics were in was eleven inches long and twenty-four inches wide. It had about two hundred pages. We took the test in an auditorium equipped with seats that had those little-bitty arm rests that swing up into position. They have a writing space about a foot wide and eighteen inches long. We had to balance the schematics on our laps and try to turn pages with our left hands (which were also keeping the schematics from falling to the floor) while we wrote out complex equations and answers with our right hands. Some of the guys were left-handed and there weren't any left-handed desks in the room. Two of my classmates actually quit in disgust and left the room without completing the test.

That was heavy. They gave up a good job because of the test conditions. They opted to return to the infantry because they weren't given enough space to take the final exam. Sad, but true.

Give your respondents enough space, whether the space is on a piece of paper, in the testing facility, or outside. Here are three guidelines.

1. Provide enough space in the testing location for respondents to avoid feeling crowded by others. In the United States, this amounts to a buffer zone of about six feet between respondents (Partridge, 1968).
2. Provide enough space at each testing station for freedom of movement. People at desks should be able to swing their arms without hitting an obstruction. If the test requires a table for work, there should be enough space for test materials plus enough to ensure that individuals don't encroach on the space of others.

3. If the test is on paper, there should be enough white space between items to provide good separation. In addition, there should be space for notes or sketching. As a rule of thumb, provide at least one-inch margins all around and double-space between items.

Use the Space for the Job at Hand with as Little Interference as Possible. Space can be an asset or a liability. If it's an asset, no one notices. If it's a liability, everyone suffers. On a test, space is more critical than for other tasks. Consider the paper-and-pencil test. When there is enough space, respondents are able to see the narrative more easily. Look at the line of print below. Most people can read it in a single glance.

Toads and frogs are close relatives.

Now look at this one.

My little toe hurts because the nail was allowed to grow long too often.

If you can read it in one glance, you're a superior reader. It doesn't have hard words or unusual construction. It's simply too long to read at one glance. Look at it again.

My little toe hurts because the nail was allowed
to grow long too often.

The sentence is the same. Only the use of space has changed. The reason it's easier to read the second time has to do with physical things, such as ability to focus, extent of peripheral vision, ease of head turning, and so forth. The fact is that for most people, short lines are much friendlier than long ones. This is true even for long sentences that continue for two or three lines.

Use Space as Respondents Expect It to Be Used. Respondents come to the test with expectations. If they have taken a test like the one you propose, they expect your test to look like the one they took before. Give them what they expect when you can.

Now and then you may want to get fancy. You may want to put the test on a computer. You may want to print it on colored paper. You may want to add a special logo or type font. OK, but justify these things before you do them. If the respondents don't expect them, such things can literally destroy the value of the test. Take the idea of using a computer, for example.

Computers are good things. This book was written on a computer. The advantages are substantial. But what about a test? If the respondents are accustomed to taking tests on computers, fine. If not, such an administration could cause severe problems for them and could even invalidate your results. Use of a computer requires a set of skills above and beyond the skills required to take a paper-and-pencil test. The respondents have to scroll to the selected answer. They have to press keys to select. They have to turn pages electronically. If these tasks are unfamiliar, they distract respondents from what you are trying to test. Add to this the fear that some people have of computers, and you have a potential for disaster for the respondents.

If you must test by computer, give the respondents a couple of breaks. First, let them practice before they take the test. Give them a series of practice items formatted like the ones they will see on the test. Second, make sure someone is available to help them if they inadvertently press the wrong key or get stuck. Take these precautions each time you administer a computer test until respondents voluntarily state they no longer want them. This leads us to the final convention about space.

When Presented with a Choice, Choose to Help the Respondents. A client had to make a hard choice. There were four thousand applications from people who wanted to take their certification exam. The test sites could only comfortably accommodate three thousand. They bit the bullet. Rather than inconvenience their respondents, they limited the number to three thousand. They had to turn down one thousand people who would have paid a total of $50,000 for the opportunity. They did the right thing.

You, too, may have to make such a choice. When it happens, put yourself in the respondents' moccasins. They have to live in the environment, endure the conditions you provide. Provide enough space for them to do their best.

Formatting a Paper-and-Pencil Test

In general, formatting a paper-and-pencil test means making a series of related decisions about how the test will look. These decisions are most often about things such as:

- Type style (font and size).
- Size of margins on the page.
- Spacing between items on the page.
- Spacing within items.
- Use of broken lines between items.

- Consistent use of instructions for items and item sets.
- Single versus two-column format.
- Consistent use of capitalization and punctuation.
- Underlining of negatives in items.
- Ordering and spacing strategies for alternatives, such as:
    Numeric responses for choices in ascending or descending order.
    Responses containing decimal points aligned on the decimal point.
    Extra spacing around fractions.

The way a test is formatted can help or hinder respondents. The formatting allows the administrative stuff to be transparent. It helps keep the test takers at task. How the test flows and how it focuses respondent activities are formatting issues.

We talk about format often, but do we really know what it is? If you're like me, when format is mentioned, you see words printed on paper. That visualization is inadequate. Perhaps it would help if you think of it as the presentation. Formatting determines how the test is presented to the test takers.

Remember the swimming test in Chapter One? What would the format be for that test? Visualize the swimming test. There is a pool. The swimmers are near the edge, ready to begin. How will the coach present the test? She'll begin by explaining what the test is and how it will be conducted. She'll show them the form she will use to score the test. She'll explain how they can earn a passing score, what to do if they have a problem, and what to expect whether they pass or fail. She will have thought out what they can do to get another chance to succeed if they fail.

Although all the things the coach does are not part of the format, they all depend on it. Look at the swimming test in more detail. One of the items is a fifty-meter freestyle swim. The swimmers assemble at one end of the pool. They take their places. The pool has eight lanes. The coach decides to use lanes 1, 3, 5, and 7, leaving empty lanes between swimmers. She has done this to reduce the competitive nature of the test, to encourage each swimmer to swim his or her best no matter what the others are doing. Before starting the swimmers, the coach explains that they will be judged on how well they start, their form at the start, how they enter the water, their ability to swim, the kind of turn they use, how well they turn, their overall speed, and their finish. She doesn't advise them on how to do any of these things, just that these are skills that will be measured. She explains how the swim will be started, how it will be timed, and who will measure their performance. She tells them to do their best and not worry about what to do when they finish. One of the other members of the team will be on hand to help them from the pool. She has towels and other equipment easily available.

The coach makes sure each swimmer understands the task completely before they begin. In effect, she has developed and put in use a nice format for the test.

Flow and Focus

Flow and focus are the keys to good formatting. Webster (1987) says a format is, "The shape, size, and general make up" or "general plan of organization or arrangement." That's the general idea. But there is more.

Every testing process has flow and focus, whether it is a paper-and-pencil test or the test of a specific hard-skills performance. The format does two things: it provides the flow for the test and focuses participants on what they must do to succeed. The flow is how the test will be done. What happens first, second, third, and so on, until the end. The focus should be on the tasks to be performed by the test takers—how they will respond. In the swimming test example, the flow was how they would take their places, where they would perform, and how the test would proceed. The focus was on their form and the time they took to complete the test.

Flow. Flow is controlled by instructions, procedures, and culmination. It determines how test takers will begin, how they will take the test, and how they will complete it. If the flow of a test is good, respondents will accept the test easily. The test will feel comfortable, right.

> **flow**
>
> How test takers will begin, how they will take the test, and how they will complete it.

The instructions are critical. You must do all you can to make sure test takers know what to do and when to do it. It is usually much better to overinstruct than to risk a respondent having to guess about what to do. One way to help respondents is to give them relevant information about how the test items are sequenced (in difficulty) and weighted (for scoring). If all items are equal in point value, if items become more difficult within skill sets, if "guessing and going" is recommended (for timed tests) or skipping and returning to items is better (for untimed tests), respondents should know so they can develop a test-taking strategy that works for them. It's a good idea to announce the end at the beginning, that is, let respondents know if there is a time limit, if the test will be over when each test taker has completed three trials, or if respondents can have as long as they like to finish and may leave quietly when they are through. Every test maker should be very sensitive about instructions. Without good instructions, the best test in the world would be useless.

The procedure is what they do in what order. This may seem obvious. The problem is that the test maker often doesn't consider the basic impact a procedure has on test takers. Consider a common practice. Suppose a test maker decides to use three kinds of items in a test. There will be three short-answer items, twenty-five multiple-choice items, and four matching items. The test maker decides to mix the items up to provide variety for the test takers. The test will start with five multiple-choice items, followed by a short-answer item, five multiple choice, another short answer, one matching, four multiple choice, and so on through the test. What the test maker has done is cause the respondents to reorient themselves a dozen times during the test when they could have done it with three orientations. What the test maker thought would add variety and a bit of relief has added distraction and confusion.

The best way to make the test as positive an experience as possible is to make sure it's a good fair test.

The culmination is simply the end. Normally it's sufficient to say so and let it happen. Just be sure the test ends in a way that encourages rather than discourages. Conventional thinking says the easiest items, for example, should come at the beginning and the most difficult at the end. Check the reasoning. Should we give respondents the simplest tasks when they are fresh and full of energy and save the complex items for when they have expended that energy? How fair is that? Perhaps the best way to end a test is at a level consistent with the rest. If you feel you must arrange the difficulty, try to begin with a few easy items to get them warmed up. Then give them the most challenging work. End with something less threatening. If you do arrange the difficulty of the test, tell the respondents ahead of time so there won't be any surprises.

Focus. Focus depends on how the test is set up and how different aspects are emphasized. Usually its basic considerations are how points will be awarded and how test takers can be successful. Some may argue the focus should be on the content, on the skills to be tested. But how do you do that? By awarding points.

> **focus**
> How points will be awarded and how test takers can be successful.

Look at the sample test in Figure 9.3. The way the test is presented, all the questions have the same impact. Let's add a line to the instructions. "Items 1, 7, 8, and 9 are worth 5 points each. Items 2, 3, 4, and 6 are worth 8 points each. Item 5 is worth 15 points." The nature of the test has changed significantly.

By the way, I don't recommend such a change. It gives the test a bias that can easily make it unfair for some respondents. My feeling is that all items should carry the same weight. If the test is a good one, the scores will reflect relative ability no matter how the weight is distributed. In this case, keep it simple.

Back to the example. Changing the way the items are scored changes the focus. The respondents discover that item 5 is more important than the others. Most of them will concentrate on it. Some may sacrifice one or more of the other items to make sure they do well on item 5.

There are many ways to arrange the focus of a test. You can use more than one item to test a single concept or performance. You can use a different kind of

FIGURE 9.3. EXAMPLE OF TEST ITEM SELECTION.

Directions: Read each question carefully. Consider the implications and decide what kind of item to use to test the content described. State the type of item you would use. Briefly explain why your choice will provide a good fair test of the content. Write your answers on a separate sheet of paper. Be sure to number the answers so I can find them easily.

1. How would you test the ability of army recruits to fire a semiautomatic handheld weapon?

2. How would you test complex reasoning skills of people who wish to enroll in NASA's astronaut program?

3. How would you test the ability of facility managers to operate a facility to meet the needs of occupants?

4. How would you test the ability of graduate students to do basic research?

5. How would you test the ability of a group of people to form good working relationships with others in a team?

6. How would you test the ability of managers to conduct interviews of people applying for a job?

7. How would you test the basic mathematics skills of children under five years old?

8. How would you test order-entry clerks' skill in handling customer complaints?

9. How would you test whether high school students know the proper safeguards to use in woodworking shop class?

item to do the same thing. You can change the requirements for an acceptable answer. However you do it, you will be adjusting how points are awarded. If you keep this simple idea in mind, focusing a test will be easier.

Tests should be focused. Any learning activity will have objectives. Seldom will all the objectives for an experience be equal. Some will be more important than others, so they should receive more emphasis on the test. They should be the focus of the test.

The same kind of reasoning pertains for all kinds of tests. An achievement test for sixth graders will concentrate on reading, writing, and arithmetic. An accomplishment test will assess basic skills more than subordinate or auxiliary skills. A survey developer will be more interested in some opinions than in others. The focus of the test can be modified by the points given for the answers.

Sometimes awarding points is done informally. For example, a manager may ask all entry-level people to take a comprehensive test of their skills in the job. When they take the test, they believe each section receives the same number of points. When the manager scores the tests, however, some sections are given more consideration than others. Suppose the test has five sections: telephone skills, order-form completion, selling, human relations, and knowledge of company policies. All sections appear to have the same number of points. But the manager is most concerned about sales, so the score on that section is given top priority. The manager has informally raised the number of points for selling.

I have seen situations in which scoring poorly on one small section of a test would have long-term ill effects on a worker's chances of receiving satisfactory evaluations or promotions. Yet that section didn't look any different from others to test takers. Only later did they learn they had been done in.

All test takers should know in advance what will be tested. The manager should tell the order-entry people about the importance of selling before they take the test. That's the focus, and they should know about it.

Presenting Hard-Skills Performance Tests

The format for a hard-skills performance test is usually dictated by the arena in which the skills are normally used. To test basketball players' ability to shoot free throws, the coach places the players in position, gives them a ball, and asks them to give it a try. The format he uses has to be consistent with the purpose. So he may go a step further. He has other players line up where they would normally be and asks substitutes and others to cheer or boo. His presentation of the test is as close to a game situation as he can make it.

> **hard-skills performance test**
> A test that concentrates on psychomotor skills and on the manipulation of materials and objects to accomplish a specifiable goal or to produce a particular product.

That's the ideal, of course: to make the test as much like the real world as possible. Usually this isn't practical. You must test to see if the skills are in place before people are allowed to use them in the real world.

Presentation depends on your ability to communicate, to enable test takers to understand the purpose of the test—its value for them. The mechanical aspects of test presentation are discussed above. The final concern is basically one of style, specifically, how you tell people what is happening and why.

Presenting Paper-and-Pencil Tests

Many conventions are recommended for good writing. It makes sense to have a good stylebook at hand and to use it. There are four conventions I want to emphasize:

1. Make your writing easy to follow. Use a style that makes the presentation transparent to the reader.
2. Use language that's easy for your readers to interpret.
3. Be brief.
4. Be yourself.

Writing is easy to follow if it is what the reader expects. *Remember: most readers expect to see writing like they've seen before.* They expect sentences, paragraphs, and other conventions of *ordinary* verbal presentation. Lots of underlining, bold, italics, quotation marks, exclamation points, and so on detract from good communication. Use those things when they would ordinarily be used in standard texts. Special fonts or all capital letters cause test takers to have to read material more than once. They emphasize important points, but they take precious time away from respondents. Most respondents resent them. The first rule is *don't stray from standard presentation techniques.*

Another thing to remember is *use a friendly style.* Most test makers adopt a writing style that is cold and precise. They make the test seem to be a formidable challenge whether it really is or not. I prefer a style that makes the test seem friendly, even if it is a formidable challenge. Which question would you rather answer?

1. Given the circumstances surrounding most litigation today, plaintiffs have a decided advantage in opening arguments. What can a defense attorney do to ameliorate this tendency in a case where the opening arguments will set the stage for what will follow? Base your answer on accepted precedents.
2. In the opening arguments, how can you prevent a plaintiff from putting you on the defensive?

The second question gives respondents much more latitude in their answers. It assumes they are aware of the basic conventions. More important, the language makes it more personal—friendlier.

Consider this book for a moment. It's fairly easy to read. Does that make the content less important? No. It simply makes it easier to comprehend and digest. So it should be with your tests. Make them easy to read and understand. Easy reading is more important for tests than for any other writing except, perhaps, for writing about emergency procedures and things like that.

Two considerations will help you immediately. First, be friendly. To make your writing friendly, don't be afraid to use first or second person. Write as if you are having a conversation with your readers. You'll be more direct and more likely to anticipate their questions or concerns.

Above all, be readable. I believe tests should be written at the sixth-grade level or lower. Even people with Ph.D.'s appreciate material that does *not* get in their way. Your stylebook will suggest ways to keep material readable. I use computer software that tells me what reading level I have used. The reading level for this paragraph is 8.8. A ninth grader could read it easily.

Finally, help respondents read your material. This is most easily accomplished by the way material is arranged on a page. Again, your stylebook can help. Double-space between paragraphs, but don't double-space between lines in a paragraph. Editors ask you to double-space so they can write in the spaces, but it does not make the materials easier to read. The opposite is true. Because people are used to close spacing in most material (books, magazine articles, papers, memos, and so on) they are most comfortable with close spacing on tests.

Indent paragraphs. That is what people expect so, if you don't, they may not recognize them as paragraphs. Their ability to identify a new topic is impaired.

Begin alternatives with a capital letter and end them with a period even if they aren't complete sentences. The capital says this is the beginning of the thought. The period tells the reader he or she has come to the end of the alternative. Look at this item:

1. What is the best warning of the danger of a thunderstorm?
   a. hair begins to stand away from the body
   b. lightning and thunder less than two seconds apart
   c. loudness of the thunder
   d. deep darkness under the clouds
   e. driving rain

Notice how much easier it is to separate and understand the alternatives in this rewritten item:

1. What is the best warning of the danger of a thunderstorm?
   a. Hair begins to stand away from the body.
   b. Lightning and thunder less than two seconds apart.
   c. Loudness of the thunder.
   d. Deep darkness under the clouds.
   e. Driving rain.

Avoid repetition in the alternatives. Again, look at an example:

2. Why should interior designers schedule periodic meetings with their clients?
   a. In order to avoid liability in case of some legal problem.
   b. In order to keep the client happy, make them believe they are part of the process.

   c. In order to develop new ideas and innovations as the project unfolds.

   d. In order to make sure the client knows what is happening and why.

Simply removing the words *in order* from each alternative makes the item easier to read and understand:

2. Why should interior designers schedule periodic meetings with their clients?
   a. To avoid liability in case of some legal problem.
   b. To keep the client happy, make them believe they are part of the process.
   c. To develop new ideas and innovations as the project unfolds.
   d. To make sure the client knows what is happening and why.

It's not dramatic, but it is important. By the way, the phrase, *in order to*, should always be replaced by *to*.

Style issues revolve around making the stem as clear and concise as possible and keeping the alternatives consistent and appropriate to the question of the stem. We've talked a lot about how to ask questions and set up the stem, but what about the alternatives?

Basically, the alternatives should be parallel. Each should answer the question in about the same way as the others. They should be about the same length, and if one is a complete sentence, they all should be. If possible, each alternative should be one line or less. If one of the alternatives is compound or complex, the others should mirror it.

Most of these issues can be clarified through using common sense and trying to see the item from the position of respondents. Much of what we do, we do to help ourselves. We try to make a test easier to score. Remember the teacher who always had twenty-five or fifty items on her tests? We try to make it easier to print. Or, perhaps, we try to save paper by crowding it. Many times we use a certain style to call attention to ourselves deliberately—to show off.

None of these things is particularly helpful to respondents. They want the best opportunity they can get. If our style gets in the way, we've short-circuited our own purpose.

This is a good time to bring up the use of humor. Normally humor does not work well because it detracts from respondents' ability to concentrate on the task at hand. However, some writers have been able to use it well. Remember, though, that humor can be very divisive for some respondents. They feel as though they are the butt of the joke. It is not funny. My advice is to avoid it, unless, of course, you are good at it and the respondents expect you to use it.

Finally, *be brief.* Your respondents aren't on hand to applaud your ability to use English or Hebrew, or whatever language you're using. Their concern is doing well on the test. Brevity allows them to concentrate on the task at hand. Of course, there is a caveat. Be sure you don't leave something important out. The temptation is to shorten or omit instructions to obtain brevity. That is a big no-no. Being brief is writing so everything respondents should have to do their best is mentioned, but nothing detracts from efficient use of the test.

Many of the style issues previously discussed support the idea of brevity. For example, if you shorten your sentences (are brief), you automatically reduce the fog level and increase the readability of the material. Short sentences are easier to read.

> **fog level**
> Readability.

Years ago I asked a course developer to write a test. When I returned his first effort to him, my main comment (found on several pages) was, "Be brief." So he went through the test reducing the number of words in each statement by substituting more technical terms for phrases. For example, he had this question on the original test.

1. Given the capacity of a modern multiple virtual storage computer to select and store bit streams rapidly, what is the advantage of using an on-line programming software like CICS?

In response to my comment, "Be brief," he wrote:

1. Assume the architecture is an MVS environment. Why use CICS?

Well, he was brief. Unfortunately, his new question was a wonderful example of a *snow job*. He lost sight of the respondents. Sometimes brevity is *not* a desirable attribute. Usually, though, it is. In attempting to be brief, he discarded his ability to communicate effectively.

Which brings me to a last bit of advice. An important thing is to *be yourself*. Most of the time the tests you write will be yours. That is, the respondents will know you have produced them. Your normal style reflects how you think. It allows you to communicate at your best. Therefore, the tests you produce should be consistent with your usual way of writing. If you are Will Rogers, write like Will Rogers. If you are not, do not.

You will find it fairly simple to use the guidelines I've provided. You may wish to come up with others that suit your style. That's fine. Just remember your audience. Any test should be an opportunity for them, not you.

In summary, formatting is usually more important than it seems. This is particularly true of the formatting for tests. Often test makers rely on formats they have seen without much thought about how those conventions will affect the respondents. Most good formatting observes three sets of conventions. It controls:

1. Use of space.
2. Flow and focus.
3. Presentation.

To *use space well* you must be concerned about all sorts of space. The space on the paper is important, but you should also think about the physical space around each respondent.

Flow and focus define formats. The flow is how the test will happen. What will be first, second, and so on? Focus allows respondents to concentrate on the task at hand. It's tied closely to the way points are awarded.

The *presentation* is what most people visualize when they think of *format*. It includes use of language, style, arrangement on a page, and anything else pertinent to respondents' understanding the test.

Step 12: Produce the Test

Producing a test is not as simple as it may seem. Formatting, administration, and respondent environment are some of the considerations that should be taken into account. Similarly, how a test is used with the people who are supposed to benefit most, the respondents, can support or detract from its usefulness. Care must be taken. Consideration must be given to this important task.

This is a step that can jump up and bite you. Most tests are easy to produce. It's normally a process of simply reproducing the materials, but it must be planned and done well. Your test will not have the same type of formatting as most written materials. The items will be presented in a certain way. You must make sure whoever produces the test can do it as you want it done. Go over the process with your producer. Be especially particular about illustrations, examples, and forms. Make sure the print quality will be the best possible.

Check the answer sheet, if you have one, to make sure it's easy to use. Respondents should be able to respond with little or no instruction about the process. It should be transparent. If the respondents have to learn how to use the test once they've begun, it detracts from their efforts on the test itself.

You or your manager may want to produce the test in the most cost-efficient way possible. It's almost an automatic response. Be careful. Cutting costs may entail a severe reduction in quality. Think about it this way. You've put some effort into this thing. You've spent time and money to develop a good fair test. Why threaten that work with poor quality production?

I am certainly not recommending a four-star production complete with binders and four-color illustrations. Bells and whistles could easily detract the respondents from their primary task, which is to pass the test.

The key is to think of elegance. Elegance is "tasteful richness of design." It is "scientific precision, neatness, and simplicity" (Webster, 1987). An elegant test presents itself to respondents. They recognize it and understand its purpose as soon as they see it. More important, they aren't intimidated by it. They see it for what it is—an opportunity for them.

Aim for these things as you produce your test or cause it to be produced. When you administer the test, your respondents will thank you, and your results will be enhanced.

Step 13: Administer the Test

Test administration has five critical elements:

1. Scheduling and setup.
2. Appropriate facility.
3. Presentation and instructions.
4. Proctoring.
5. Debriefing.

Scheduling and Setup

Scheduling and setup require control of three variables: availability of the test, selection of an appropriate facility, and respondent acceptance.

The test must be available. That seems obvious. Often, it's not. You must make sure your revisions are in place. You must be sure the answer sheets, support materials, and special equipment are ready. You must be sure there is enough of everything.

If you are negligent about these things, you can almost guarantee something will go wrong. Being ready doesn't take a lot of effort. It's a matter of simply making sure what should be in place is in place as you have envisioned it.

Ask yourself three questions:

1. Are there enough copies for everyone?
2. Are there enough support materials, and are they of good quality? (e.g., Are there enough number 2 pencils for each respondent to have at least two? Are they sharp?)
3. Does everything work? If your test requires a videotape or special equipment, are these things tested and working?

Appropriate Facility

I once took a test in a room with twenty-four desks. Unfortunately, there were about forty respondents. Another time a test was scheduled in a large auditorium to accommodate six of us. Both of these examples seem absurd, but they happened. Similar problems can crop up for you.

Look at the facility before you use it. Is it the right size? Are the desks or tables appropriate for the task? Is lighting OK? How about air quality? Do room features detract from the work to be done?

Is It the Right Size? What is too big or too small? There is a rule of thumb you can use to judge the size of the room. Adults in the United States generally feel crowded in a test situation if their neighbors aren't at least three feet away. I recommend six feet of separation. The reason for this is cultural. You should have little or no concern about people cheating on the test. The main reason for separation is the relative comfort of the respondents. They require more room while taking a test than at other times because they are more sensitive to the presence of others.

A room thirty feet square can accommodate twenty-five test takers. Naturally if the test materials or equipment occupy more space than is normal for a person at work, take that into consideration.

Are the Desks or Tables Appropriate for the Task? All of us have been in situations where we had a small desk or arm pad to balance a test booklet, an answer sheet, and whatever else while we tried to concentrate on the items. It can require a contortionist. Don't do it to your test takers. Consider the elements of the test.

Assemble the materials, sit down at a work surface, and try it out. Discover how much space is required by actually placing the materials on a desk or table. Turn the pages. Write on the answer sheet. If you can do these things without having to shift things or rearrange them, your setup is probably OK. If possible, try the materials in the facility and with the furniture that will be used during the test. And make sure the surfaces of the work areas are appropriate. Are they too slick, or sticky, or marred by carvings left by former occupants?

Is the Lighting OK? Engineers have developed rules for the number of lumens required by most people to do several different tasks. They can recommend whether you should have incandescent or fluorescent light. You probably won't be able to find a device to measure lumens. You probably won't be able to specify the kinds of fixtures or style of lighting. What you can do is control the amount of light available and the glare.

Sit down at the work surface your respondents will be using. Spread the materials out as the respondents probably will. Discover for yourself whether the light is sufficient. Be picky about glare. It's the most common problem for people working at any task in a closed space. Windows can be a big problem, particularly when the sun shines brightly.

One final caution. Use materials that are friendly to the users' eyes. Slick glossy paper may feel nice, but it's the most common cause of glare. Use a matte finish for your materials. Do not use special colors. Black print on white paper is OK.

How About Air Quality? Air quality in some buildings is so poor these days it makes canaries sick. Poor air directly affects respondent productivity and thinking. If the facility proposed for your test has bad air, do everything you can to find another. Open the windows if you can. This is effective even on cold winter days. Teachers in Minnesota often open their windows in the winter. The kids may complain about the cold, but their work almost always improves.

Two aspects of air quality can bother test takers. The first is obvious. The air should be good for breathing. It should circulate. It should be clean. It should contain oxygen and nitrogen in the proper percentages.

The second is how it smells and tastes. Some facilities smell funny. They may have mildew. They could smell of the product produced in the facility. They could be invaded by outside smells. Tobacco smoke is a common example of a distracting smell, particularly for people who are sensitive to it. Give your respondents frequent breaks. Let smokers have a place where they can enjoy themselves in relative peace.

You may want to freshen the room before and during the test. Use a recommended spray (avoid perfume, which annoys many of us). Test takers are often tense. Tense people sometimes exude a disagreeable smell. Spray the room during the breaks. This can become important for a test that takes more than three hours.

Do Room Features Detract from the Work to Be Done? There is a room in a small college I know that has giant macrame hangings on the walls. They are magnificent. I could spend hours looking at them and the intricacy of the work. Unfortunately, so can people taking a test in that room. Distractions such as noise, visual effects, and other anomalies should be accounted for if they can't be eliminated. Suppose, for instance, the floor is ceramic tile and, therefore, people walking on it make clicking noises. Or maybe jet planes pass over from time to time. Simply telling the respondents what these things are will usually be enough. The respondents will be able to ignore them.

There are distractions that can't be ignored. I once used a facility on the third floor of an old building in downtown Chicago. The city decided that day to tear up the street below. The sound of jackhammers pounded at us all morning. I rescheduled the test. Such things happen. The best advice I can give you is to deal with them as you encounter them. Plan as thoroughly as you can. Then surprises will be much easier to overcome.

Presentation and Instructions

There is a convention for presenting a test and giving the instructions. It has evolved over a couple of hundred years. You can use it with confidence for most tests. Here's how it goes:

1. Place the materials the respondents will be using on the desks (or whatever) before they come into the room. Be ready for them. Don't waste their time with administrative tasks such as passing out materials.
2. Put basic information on a chalkboard or flip chart at the front of the room where the respondents can see it without difficulty. Normally you will include:
    - An identifier for the test—its name and reason for existing. An example might be, "XXXXX Corporation Certification Exam for Middle Management."
    - Your name and the names of other administrators or proctors.
    - Special rules such as treatment of the answer sheet.
    - Administrative details such as the location of a break room for smokers and the rest rooms.
3. Greet the respondents as they enter. If you know their names, greet them by name. If you don't, you can introduce yourself unless it causes a traffic jam at the door.
4. When the respondents come in, introduce yourself formally. Give your name, reason for being there, and the function you will be performing. Introduce anyone else in the room such as helpers or observers. Be sure everyone is accounted for.
5. Go over the instructions for the test quickly but comprehensively. You will be tempted to rush. Don't! Those instructions are important. If there are elements that may cause problems, go over them carefully. Be sure to mention time constraints. Tell them about breaks, when they will occur, and the constraints that apply.
6. Provide guidelines about how to act. If you don't want respondents to converse during the test or breaks, tell them. Be as specific as you can. Try to be friendly about it. *Too many times the proctor or administrator of a test takes it much too seriously.* This seriousness can make the respondents nervous. Be sure to tell them what to do with their materials if they have to leave the room.

7. Go over the mechanics of the process. Tell them how they will know to begin, how to use the answer sheet (if appropriate), and what to do when they've completed the test. Be sure they understand how to ask questions or get help and the kind of help they can expect to receive.

8. Once they've begun, be as circumspect as possible. *Do not tour the room looking over their shoulders.* If you're worried about people cheating on the test, stay worried. Detect malefactors another way.

9. When the respondents have completed the test, have them give the materials to you or a helper. Immediately check to make sure they haven't forgotten something like putting their name or identifying number on the answer sheet. If there is an answer sheet, scan it with the respondent present and point out any missing answers. Do this even if several of them finish at the same time.

You shouldn't have any problems if you use these nine steps. You may not use all nine for every test. For example, if you're asking people to take a test as part of a regularly scheduled class you can be much less formal. However, if you leave a step out or modify it, do so consciously. Review the steps before every test. Then you can make informed decisions about how you want the test to proceed.

Proctoring

The basic purpose of having a test administrator or proctor in the room is to prevent the test from being compromised. Proctors can help with administration, but their basic function is to prevent cheating. Respondents know that. If they come into a test expecting a simple straightforward exam and see a proctor, they could react negatively. Such a reaction could affect the results.

There are two main considerations. First, do you have to have a proctor? Usually the answer to this question is no. A proctor is only appropriate for one of three reasons. One is if you are not able to administer the test yourself, the proctor will do it for you. Very seldom can a test go unsupervised. There are too many chances for problems. Another reason is that a proctor may be required is to help the test administrator with a large group. If you have more than twenty people taking the test at once, you may want someone to help. Finally, you may want a proctor if the test could be compromised. National standardized exams have to be supervised. Ninety percent of respondents will usually be honest. The other 10 percent can be a real headache. Proctors in such situations are a definite help.

The second main consideration is, Can proctoring be avoided? If the respondents are seated ten feet apart, they couldn't interact enough to cause a problem. Many rooms are equipped with television cameras for one reason or another. You can point the cameras out to the respondents. Because they won't know whether the cameras are active or not, they'll have to assume they are in operation. You can give alternating respondents different versions of the test. The point is, even if the test is sensitive, there are steps you can take to avoid proctoring.

Debriefing

Most uninformed test administrators don't bother to say or do anything when a test is completed. This is often a mistake. Respondents want reassurance after they've taken a test. They want to know their efforts won't go unrewarded no matter how poorly they scored. Usually the debriefing can be done quickly with little fuss. A few words to each respondent as he or she turns in the materials is enough.

Sometimes you will want to debrief more formally. If so, the best course is to schedule a time and place where you can get together with the respondents to go over the test and inform them of their results.

Debriefing is often done through the mail. Respondents receive a letter telling them how well they scored and what that means. If you debrief formally, be sure to do more than simply tell people how well they scored. Add comments of appreciation and praise their efforts. It costs you very little to do, but the effect on the respondents can be substantial. Their perception of the test is much more likely to be lasting and positive. Future relationships will be enhanced.

Summary

As you produce your test, think about format. Will it do what you planned to do—what your design requires? Don't forget that format is, in essence, an environment issue. You're actually making sure respondents can focus on the test without distraction. You're making the construction and presentation of the test as transparent as you can.

Test production and administration are largely mechanical. It makes sense, then, to ensure this process is as elegant as possible. Here is an arena where you can save time and effort simply by considering the process and keeping it efficient. Administration has the added opportunity for comforting respondents both mentally and physically. Take advantage of the opportunity as completely as possible. Comfortable test takers respond, as a rule, much better than those who have to endure intrusive conditions.

The next step is to collect the results (answers) and to make some sense of what they may mean to you and to the respondents. This is the point at which you can articulate whether respondents have done well or not and whether your goals for the test have been achieved.

CHAPTER TEN

EVALUATING AND REPORTING THE RESULTS

You have administered the test and have scores, but you don't know what they mean. Perhaps you do know. The results may be fairly easy to interpret. If that is the case, *do no more.* If you can interpret the scores simply by looking at them or performing a simple process, do it and be done with it. This is the case for most tests. But here's what to do if that is not the case.

Step 14: Evaluate the Results

You have set the standard(s). You know the criteria for deciding whether a respondent has done well or not. So make the decision and go on with your life. Too many times we spend excess time debating scores. If your test-development process produced a good fair test, then evaluation should be straightforward.

I make this point strongly because to adjust test scores often causes us to fall into the normed test trap again. You might be drawn to a score that is one point below the standard. You might be tempted to pass that respondent. On the other hand, you might be tempted to fail a respondent whose score is just barely above the cut-score. Do not succumb to these temptations. The respondents may plead their cases and, sometimes they will be able to prove they've been treated unfairly. In such cases, you can adjust their scores. But maintain your standards. Otherwise, the standards become compromised and the power of the test is threatened.

Once you have evaluated the test results, the next step is to report them to the individuals in your organization who want to know.

Report Results

Testing is of little use if results aren't shared with someone. Basically, there are four vested groups, four groups you will want to tell about your test: (1) your direct supervisor, the person who is responsible for your accomplishments; (2) the people who pay the bills, perhaps executive management, your clients, or a public of some sort; (3) people who will use the results in some immediate way, whether for decision making, development of remedial materials, or whatever; and (4) the respondents themselves. Perhaps they should have been listed first, as they are the ones with the highest stakes in the success or failure of the test.

The first three groups usually receive basically the same thing, a basic client report. Each group does require increasing amounts of detail, so the report has to address each group separately; however, you don't have to write three separate reports for them.

The basic client report has three sections. Each is aimed specifically at one of the three groups. Different authors call the sections different things, but in general they mean the same thing:

- Executive summary.
- Processes and procedures.
- Data and data analysis.

The titles reflect what each section contains.

Section One: Executive Summary

The executive summary has four purposes. It should:

1. Present the purpose of the test, that is, why it was developed.
2. Describe how the test was administered and any problems encountered.
3. Provide a general description of the results and what they mean.
4. Suggest conclusions and recommendations signaled by the results.

The executive summary should be short and concise. It should be about a page and a half in length. Don't use technical or flowery language or lengthy explanations. Say what should be said (all of it) and stop. Details and explanations will be covered in the remaining two sections. Remember, it's for executives. These people want to know only what happened, why, and what actions may or may not be appropriate because of it. That is all. They don't care how happy respondents were. They don't want to know how wonderful your test is. They want the basic information and your best estimate of its meaning. They want enough information to make an informed decision and no more.

Section Two: Processes and Procedures

This section is for people who will use the results to take action. They have to interpret and understand the results. Therefore they will want to know how the test was administered, what it tested, who responded, and whether there were any problems with it. Consequently this section should have clear explanations of:

- *How the test was designed and developed.* The criteria it tested should be included, as well as an explanation of why it was designed the way it was. You may want to add who developed the items and how the test was developed.
- *The review process (formative evaluation).* How was development controlled, and how were recommendations implemented?
- *Test integrity.* Validity and reliability should be ensured. Summative evaluation results must be included.
- *Administration and scoring.* Describe the environment in which the test was taken, who took the test, and how they reacted. Include how it was scored, who scored it, and any problems with scoring.

Section Three: Data and Data Analysis

If you feel you must have a data dump, this is where you do it. Many times it may be necessary. My own inclination is to provide easy-to-use but comprehensive data summaries. This section is for people who will follow up on an action plan. For example, if remedial instruction must be developed, the developers will rely on this section for information they need in their work. The section will contain:

- The data or data summaries—the results.
- Full disclosure of techniques used to analyze the results, including statistical treatments, reviews, and comments from respondents and reviewers.
- Any information you must have to support the conclusions and recommendations reported in Section One. The rationale and logic used should be explained as fully as possible. There is little value in statements that can't be supported directly. That support must be included in this section.

There you have it. If you want another reporting method or would feel comfortable with another approach, feel free to use it. However, be sure to include the elements previously described. There are two very good reasons to do so. First, whether the people described read and use it or not, the report should be complete, as it could be valuable in the future. Second, your report will be the foundation on which you will base continuing efforts with the test, its descendants, and the consequences and activities that follow it.

Without a report, a test can become a phantasm—something everyone seems to be aware of but no one can put a finger on. Without good documentation, much of the value of any test is lost.

Reporting to Respondents

Your respondents want to know how well they have performed. This information is usually simple to provide. You tell them what their scores were and what that means. The keys are to be definitive and quick.

Try to keep it simple and easy to interpret. For example, if you have administered a multiple-choice performance test, respondents will want to know what their scores were and what the cut-score was. To give them more information is usually not appropriate.

Sometimes it's important to interpret the results for respondents. This is particularly true if the test unearths weaknesses or areas where they should take some kind of action. Attitude tests usually require interpretation. Let's look at these two circumstances separately.

Remediation. Because most of your tests will be performance tests, it makes sense for you to offer people help in improving themselves once the test is complete.

> **remediation**
> The act or process of remedying or overcoming learning disabilities or problems.

Whether respondents pass or not, a good test should delineate areas where they can become more skilled. If they should want to do so, they will probably look to you for help or guidance.

In many situations, a test monitor or administrator will immediately suggest actions for respondents to pursue to improve themselves. A football coach may say, "John, you're doing very well; you've made the team. Now, I want you to concentrate on moving the defensive man up and out." He gave his offensive lineman a test. John passed, was competent. Then the coach told John how to become even better.

You should have a similar attitude. In most cases, your responsibility is to discover what respondents can do and how they can improve.

Standards set for performance tests almost always determine competence. A person who passes is competent in the skill being tested. He or she can be far from exemplary. Your organization would be delighted if all of the people who pass could become exemplary. The reason is the bottom line—profits. Exemplary workers produce far above the standard. Because the standard for most organizations is the point where profits begin, any productivity above standard increases profits extraordinarily well. Profit, in this sense, includes revenue and all else that increases the overall productivity of the organization.

A good fair performance test provides an excellent opportunity for an organization to increase productivity. Each item on the test is tied directly to a criterion. Any respondent who does poorly on an item has, in some way, failed to meet the criterion. If she or he knows this and wants to improve, the improvement will take place and, ergo, productivity for the individual and the organization will increase. Do I make it sound too easy? In about 80 percent of the cases it is that easy.

For some reason (probably cultural), most of us expect to have to correct ignorance. We assume that people who do poorly on tests will have to learn new skills. They will have to be trained to do the things the test indicated they could not do. This is only true about 10 percent of the time. Ten percent! Most of the time people know something about the skill being tested. In 80 percent of the cases they only have to be told why they were wrong. They will correct the problem themselves without much help. In 10 percent of the cases they should receive some kind of structured practice. In the other 10 percent they should require formal training. (The percentages quoted here are my own. However, research done on the subject is in basic agreement. Although different authors have offered different percentages and categories, the consensus is that total ignorance, which prompts the need for training, exists a very small percentage of the time.)

Suppose, for example, I give you a test on how to write good test items. When the test is complete, your score is 83 out of 87. What will you do? If you're like most people, you'll try to discover which items you missed, find out what the correct responses should have been, and make sure you remember them. If you are given the opportunity (adequate information about your performance), you will increase your skills on the spot. There are times when skills aren't easy to acquire, but about 80 percent of the time they are. We want to know what we did wrong. We are told. We say, "OK, I won't do it that way anymore." That's it. Remediation is complete.

What about situations where remediation isn't that easy? The football player mentioned above will have to practice blocking opposing linemen. This is a common result. Respondents learn what they must practice. They may want to work more math problems with two unknowns. They may want to practice scales on the piano. They may want to make more presentations to large groups. They may want to practice writing poetry. As they do these things, they can polish the skills until they are competent. My job and yours is to give them information about what they should practice and then make it possible for them to practice.

Training is prescribed too often. The usual reaction of an administrator is to offer training to people who have failed a test. That's an error about 90 percent of the time. But, when the need for training is properly identified, the return on the investment can be enormous.

Research has been done on interventions and how to develop them. I'm particularly impressed by Judith Hale's article (1993) on them. She tells us what they are, how to use them, and the kinds of results one can expect from them. Enough has been said about these things for our purposes here, but skill in selecting and using interventions can be of great help to you. I urge you to learn more about the topic.

Interpreting Opinions. The results from opinionnaires, value inventories, attitude surveys, and other tests eliciting opinions are often misrepresented in reports. Let's discuss this for a bit.

"There are three kinds of lies: lies, big lies, and statistics." That quote (or one similar to it) is often used by people who have learned not to trust reports based on statistical analyses. They have a point. For example, journalists often report the results of surveys used during important political campaigns. A survey may show that Candidate A has 51 percent of the vote and that Candidate B has 46 percent, whereas 3 percent of the voters are still undecided. The reporter will conclude that Candidate A is ahead. Polling organizations will be the first to say there is always a plus or minus factor of 3 to 5 percent. In other words, the two candidates are virtually tied. Neither has a clear advantage. The reporter has misled his or her audience. Whether journalists do this type of thing on purpose is immaterial. My feeling is that they don't understand statistics well enough to report them accurately.

The same kind of thing can happen with test results. This is particularly true for attitude tests. Some people believe percentages are used to mislead as often as they are to inform. Two influences contribute to misinformation. The first has to do with interpretation of a baseline, the second with interpretation of the results. Let's look at these in turn.

> **baseline**
> The foundation supporting the data.

The *baseline* is the foundation supporting the data. Consider a graph. Normally, information on a graph is referenced to an accepted notion of zero for the idea or product being measured. For example, consider the graph in Figure 10.1 (p. 246), which shows the average times for six races.

Now look at the same information as presented on the graph in Figure 10.2 (p. 246), shown in tenths of a second from the baseline of 16, which seems like a rational choice for a baseline.

The new graph has 16 seconds as the baseline and 17.5 as the end. Now it seems the times are very different from one another, and all of them are less than

FIGURE 10.1. TIME FOR
ONE HUNDRED–YARD DASH IN SECONDS.

Race
1. XXXXXXXXXXXXXXXXXXXXXXXXXXXXXXXXXXXXXXXXXXXXXXXXXXX
2. XXXXXXXXXXXXXXXXXXXXXXXXXXXXXXXXXXXXXXXXXXXXXXXXXXXX
3. XXXXXXXXXXXXXXXXXXXXXXXXXXXXXXXXXXXXXXXXXXXXXXXX
4. XXXXXXXXXXXXXXXXXXXXXXXXXXXXXXXXXXXXXXXXXXXXXXXXXXXXX
5. XXXXXXXXXXXXXXXXXXXXXXXXXXXXXXXXXXXXXXXXXXXXXXXXX
6. XXXXXXXXXXXXXXXXXXXXXXXXXXXXXXXXXXXXXXXXXXXXXXXX

```
 0  1  2  3  4  5  6  7  8  9  10  11  12  13  14  15  16  17  18
                         Time in Seconds
```

FIGURE 10.2. TIME FOR
ONE HUNDRED–YARD DASH IN TENTHS OF SECONDS.

Race
1. XXXXXXXXXXXXX
2. XXXXXXXXXXXXXXXXXXX
3. XXXXXXXXX
4. XXXXXXXXXXXXXXXXXXXXXXXXXXXXXXXX
5. XXXXXXXXXXXXX
6. XXXX

```
16 .1 .2 .3 .4 .5 .6 .7 .8 .9 17 .1 .2 .3 .4 .5
         Time in Tenths of Seconds
```

they should be. We know, because we've seen the analysis done by the coach, that this is misleading. The times were virtually the same. The sophomores were expected to average 16.5 seconds. The times are very close to what was expected, neither above nor below by enough to warrant comment.

It is easy to see how anyone who wishes to sway opinion or make a point can arrange data to support the chosen point of view. Changing the baseline is the most commonly used technique for doing this.

Sometimes changing the baseline makes sense. This is particularly true when a faithful presentation would obscure differences that are really there. Be sure you communicate these considerations if and when you change a baseline. Otherwise, in my opinion, you will have acted unethically.

The quotation earlier is wrong. Statistics don't lie, but liars often use statistics. Let's look at the second way to misuse results to prove a point: misinterpreting the results.

I once read an article supporting Title III funding of special education for children whose IQs range between 70 and 90. The author's contention was that these children should have help because they are so much less gifted than children whose IQs are between 110 and 120. All of those IQs are virtually the same! To be below average, a child would have an IQ of less than 70. To be above average, the child's IQ would have to be higher than 120. The range for average children, at that time, was thought to range from 70 to 120. The educator who wrote the article was advocating special attention for some average children without comparable treatment of others who were also average.

The argument was so strongly put that several states actually implemented it. They were convinced because the differences between the scores were emphasized without an explanation of what the true basis for inference was.

The point is that you must be careful about how you present information. Most people who read it won't be in a position to challenge what you say. They will tend to assume you have spoken well and clearly. If you don't, your evaluation *will* be misleading. Keep this point in mind as we work with reporting attitudinal data. Even if you don't intend to misrepresent, you might.

Inference

You must infer when you present results. Your inference will incorporate your evaluation of the results and what the outcomes probably are. You really can't avoid doing so in most situations, nor should you. Go ahead and make inferences. In most cases you will be the person best qualified to do so. Results from attitudinal measures must be interpreted. If you don't interpret them, you force your reader to do it. Which would you prefer? A better question is, What is best for the well-being of your organization and your respondents?

> **attitudinal**
> Having to do with a manner of acting, feeling, or thinking that shows one's disposition or opinion.

You can ensure that your inferences are appropriate through the use of simple statistical analyses. In most cases, this can be done quickly and easily with the mean (average) and a standard error. If you want more information (such as a formal analysis of variance or multiple regression analysis), you can defer to someone who can do the work more efficiently and effectively than you can. Most large organizations have these people on staff. The skills are common for people who have advanced degrees in industrial engineering, organizational psychology, or computer science. Most mainframe computer systems have software in place to perform the drudgery.

However, ninety-nine times out of one hundred, you won't require help. You'll be able to develop the information you want through use of a mean and standard error (or standard deviation). I have an inexpensive handheld calculator that provides those statistics quickly and reliably. You should have one too. There are at least a dozen models on the market.

The basic process can be modified to work with almost any data. You enter the data into your calculator and find the mean (average). On most calculators you punch the number for the data and enter it by pressing a key marked $+(\sigma)$. You do this for each score, and when you've entered them all, you press a key marked *mean* or X. The calculator will give you the average. Then you press a key marked *s, sd,* or $(\rho)n-1$. The number you get will be the standard error. That's all there is to it.

Figure 10.3 shows the scores of the order-entry clerks from Chapter Seven (Figure 7.10, p. 155). Note that you don't have to put the scores in any kind of order. Just get your calculator out, enter all the scores, and then press the key for the mean. You should get 33.095 if you chose to average the first column or 73.476 if you chose the second. Now (you don't have to enter the data again; the calculator has it in memory) press the standard error key. You should get 5.09 for the first column, or 11.30 for the second. Do a quick check. The percentages, 33 and 73, should be the same. It's that easy.

We can tell by looking at the scores that Mellon and Novak are average. But who else is? That's where the standard error comes in. It tells us how far on either side of the mean we will continue to find average scores. For this set of scores that is plus or minus 5.09 (11.3 for the percentages). So anyone who scored more than 38 is above average, and anyone who scored less than 28 is below average.

Now you are ready to infer. Statisticians use the word *significant* to indicate when a score is outside the zone where it would be called *average*. In our example, a score over 38 would be significantly positive and one less than 28 would be significantly negative. Because of this we can infer that people who scored less than 28 are significantly less skilled than those who scored 28 or more. That is, they did not score high enough to be grouped with the people who, we can be fairly sure, passed the test. Also, people who scored 38 or more are significantly more skilled than those who scored less than 38. They could be exemplars—at least in this context.

Now be careful. We've just compared people with other people, rather than with a standard. To say they have passed or failed is improper. However, there is a strong indication that there are significant differences between respondents' abilities as measured by the test.

FIGURE 10.3. LIST OF HYPOTHETICAL SCORES.

Person	Score	Percentage
Albers, J.	27	60
Anthony, G.	42	93
Baldridge, A.	38	84
Dankins, M.	39	87
Everly, O.	22	49
Foster, O.	31	69
Hawthorn, Q.	30	67
Hymne, R.	38	84
Jackson, A.	29	64
Jackson, H.	38	84
Jones, A.	32	71
Jones, R.	35	78
Jones, S.	39	87
Jones, W.	33	73
Kelly, G.	24	53
Mellon, M.	33	73
Novak, T.	33	73
Perkins, R.	36	80
Plonski, R.	34	76
Shranski, Y.	30	67
Williams, R.	32	71

We used these values to establish a cut-score. You can use them to verify evidence already in hand, as was done above. They are very valuable tools. Perhaps their highest value lies in the fact that they allow you to infer with confidence. You will be using statistics to support truth, not to deceive your readers.

Summary

Perhaps the best way to summarize a chapter on reporting results is to provide a sample report, as shown in Figure 10.4 (p. 250). It's not a complete report, as a complete document could easily run fifty pages or more. In this example, Section Three has been omitted. You should be able to infer the elements that have been omitted.

FIGURE 10.4. SAMPLE REPORT TO MANAGEMENT
ON ORDER-ENTRY TEST RESULTS.

Date: 12/12/98

To: Maria Caravelli, VP Operations

From: Odin Westgaard, director of human development

Re: Order-Entry Test

The results so far have been both satisfying and enlightening. You will be pleased to know that there is every reason to think the impact will be very good for OE and for the company.

This report has three sections. First is an overview of the results and what, at this time, I believe they mean. Second, I've summarized the data treatments and developed recommendations based on those summaries. Third is a presentation of the scores of individuals showing how they are distributed. It also contains item analyses and other supporting information. I have not included the third section in this rendition because it is a bit cumbersome. However, it is available for your inspection. Mr. Jarvis's copy includes Section Three.

Section One

The test has two parts. Part One is a performance test that measures how well order-entry people are able to do their jobs. Part Two samples their opinions about the job and how those opinions affect the productivity of XXX Corporation.

Twenty-nine people took the test. This number included all current operators and their supervisors.

Results

Part One. Of the operators and supervisors, twenty-three scored at the cutoff or above. In other words, they showed competence in the job skills sampled. Three people were weak in their ability to interact with the order-entry system, two had trouble dealing with demanding customers, and one was unable to perform well in any job skill area.

Part Two. The test showed significant opinions in three areas. First, respondents like the new order-entry system. Comments indicate it's easier to use than the old system, is much quicker, and (perhaps most important) prevents operators from making dumb mistakes. Second, they feel they are much better at handling customers. This was especially evident when dealing with difficult or irate customers. Third, they believe the training they are currently receiving is poor. People commenting about this complained about the training being boring, not enough practice with the system, and too much reliance on their having to memorize the steps in using the system.

FIGURE 10.4. SAMPLE REPORT TO MANAGEMENT ON ORDER-ENTRY TEST RESULTS, cont'd.

Recommendations

It may be premature to offer recommendations at this time, but the results point toward two areas that could be promising. First, it appears a sophisticated job aid would both speed up order-entry operations and reduce the number of errors committed by operators. Second, the training should probably be reviewed with an eye toward streamlining it and providing more practice with the system and interacting with customers.

Job Aids. At this point this recommendation must be to start at square one to develop a job aid (or series of aids) that would support the entire job. It might be like the tutorials offered by software firms to help people learn to use the software. However, my own feeling is it should be in the form of a shell that could incorporate more specific instruction and, especially, practice. A second area for development would be practice in the interface with customers. Our department, I believe, would need help with this one. We don't have anyone on staff with expertise in this particular area.

Training. Perhaps I'm being simplistic, but I feel the need for training should be rethought. If the job aids mentioned above are produced, it could be that we would cease to need formal training for the function. Supervisors (after having been adequately trained themselves) could provide any instruction needed on the job. I would suggest, if this is the direction we take, that instruction be structured so that every supervisor does it about the same way as the others and no important processes or content are inadvertently omitted.

Section Two

A printout of the test results is reproduced in Appendix A (Figure 10.4A). The results are summarized below. Responses to each question are categorized the same way:

1. No answer or answer completely incorrect.
2. Answer partially correct.
3. Correct answer (conformed to standard practice).
4. Correct answer (showed initiative or ability to improvise correctly).

The letters across the top of the data sheet indicate individual order-entry operators. The totals at the bottom show how well each respondent scored overall. The two columns at the right show the totals and means (averages) for each *item*.

The cut-score designated by the pilot of the test was 52. Six people scored below the cut-score (c, j, m, r, s, and aa). Clearly these people are less skilled than the others.

Of the twenty-nine full-time operators and supervisors shown in Figure 10.4A (p. 252), twenty-three scored at the cutoff or above, demonstrating competence in the job skills sampled. Three people were weak in their ability to interact with the order-entry system, two had trouble dealing with demanding customers, and one was unable to perform well in any job skill area.

FIGURE 10.4. SAMPLE REPORT TO MANAGEMENT ON ORDER-ENTRY TEST RESULTS, cont'd.

FIGURE 10.4A. APPENDIX A: INDIVIDUAL SCORES FOR ORDER-ENTRY CLERKS.

Item	a	b	c	d	e	f	g	h	l	j	k	l	m	n	o	p	q	r	s	t	u	v	w	x	y	z	aa	bb	cc	tot	mean
1.	3	3	1	3	3	3	3	3	3	2	3	4	1	3	3	3	3	3	3	3	4	3	3	3	3	3	1	3	3	82	2.8
2.	3	3	1	3	3	3	3	3	3	1	3	3	3	3	4	3	3	3	2	3	3	3	3	3	3	3	1	3	3	81	2.8
3.	3	3	1	3	3	3	3	4	3	1	3	3	3	3	4	3	3	3	3	3	4	3	3	3	3	3	2	4	3	86	3.0
4.	4	3	1	3	3	3	3	3	3	1	3	3	2	3	3	3	4	3	3	3	4	3	3	3	3	3	1	3	3	83	2.9
5.	3	3	1	3	4	3	3	3	2	2	4	3	2	3	4	3	3	2	3	3	4	3	3	3	3	3	1	4	3	82	2.8
6.	4	3	1	3	4	3	3	4	3	3	4	4	3	3	4	3	3	3	3	3	4	3	3	3	3	4	3	4	3	94	3.2
7.	3	3	1	3	3	3	3	3	3	2	3	2	1	3	3	3	3	2	2	3	4	3	3	3	3	3	1	3	3	78	2.7
8.	3	3	1	3	3	3	3	3	3	1	3	3	1	3	3	3	3	1	2	3	3	3	3	3	2	3	1	3	2	74	2.6
9.	3	4	1	3	4	3	3	3	4	1	4	3	1	3	4	3	3	1	1	3	4	3	3	3	3	3	1	3	3	81	2.8
10.	3	3	1	3	3	2	2	3	3	1	4	3	1	3	3	2	3	1	1	2	3	3	3	3	3	4	1	3	2	72	2.5
11.	3	4	1	3	2	2	2	3	3	1	3	3	1	2	3	2	3	1	1	2	3	2	2	3	3	3	1	3	2	67	2.3
12.	3	3	2	4	4	3	4	3	4	3	3	4	2	3	4	3	3	3	2	3	4	3	3	3	4	2	4	3		98	3.4
13.	1	2	1	2	3	2	2	3	3	1	2	2	1	3	3	2	2	1	1	3	3	2	2	2	3	3	2	3	2	62	2.1
14.	3	3	1	3	3	3	3	3	3	2	3	3	1	3	4	3	3	3	1	3	4	3	3	3	3	3	2	3	3	81	2.8
15.	3	3	1	2	3	3	3	2	3	1	3	4	1	2	3	3	3	1	1	2	3	2	3	3	3	3	1	3	3	71	2.5
16.	3	3	1	3	3	3	3	3	3	1	3	3	1	3	3	3	3	1	1	3	4	3	3	3	3	4	1	3	3	77	2.7
17.	3	3	1	3	2	3	3	3	3	2	3	3	1	3	4	3	3	1	1	3	4	3	3	3	2	4	1	3	2	75	2.6
18.	3	3	1	3	3	3	3	4	3	2	3	4	1	3	3	3	3	1	1	1	4	3	3	3	3	3	1	3	3	83	2.9
19.	3	3	1	4	4	3	4	3	4	1	2	4	1	3	4	4	4	1	1	3	4	3	4	4	3	3	1	3	3	85	2.9
20.	2	2	1	3	3	3	3	3	3	1	1	3	1	3	3	3	3	1	1	3	3	3	3	3	3	3	1	3	3	71	2.5
21.	3	3	1	3	4	3	4	3	3	1	3	4	1	4	4	3	3	1	1	2	4	3	3	3	3	3	1	3	3	80	2.8

```
    64   22   67   73   65   62   30   73   64   35   76   62   61   27   58
       65   65   60   65   31   68   62   61   37   57   60   63   68   67
```

When we look at the content of the items that people had the most difficulty with, we see two recurring themes. First, people tried to hurry past the first three screens in the order-entry system. They therefore tended to forget to enter key data items on those screens. (Perhaps a programmer could streamline the call-up process.) Second, some individuals forgot to call customers by name and used the honorifics "Sir" or "Ma'am" during their conversations.

The report in Figure 10.4 is merely an example. It does not refer to a real test, but it is very similar to actual reports I've used in the past. Read it carefully. As you read, think about what is going on in the mind of the executive to whom it's addressed. How will the report affect his or her thinking? Consequently, how might it impact the future of the group being discussed and the organization as a whole?

Producing a report like this may seem to be a lot of trouble for the benefit derived. I suspect you will resist doing a report for every test you administer. That is the real world. However, you should make it a standard practice to document all of your work. Even the most rudimentary or trivial of tests should be documented for future reference. That's what the final step in this process is about—what can or should you do with the results of a test?

CHAPTER ELEVEN

USING TEST RESULTS

Have you ever taken or given a test that made absolutely no difference to you or to the organization? Frustrating, wasn't it?

Using the fifteen steps almost guarantees it won't happen for you any more. You have designed and developed your test to get results. Because of the work you've done in Steps 1 through 14, those results will be of use to you, to your organization, and to the respondents. All stakeholders can, and should, benefit.

Step 15: Use the Results

The important thing is to follow through. Use the results. You have expended a lot of effort to obtain good, dependable results. If you don't use them, that effort is wasted.

The results will be in one of two forms, either narrative answers to questions or numbers (or letters) representing answers. They will be associated with particular respondents. Your job is to make some sense of them. It usually isn't difficult. Test results usually provide one or more of four kinds of information:

1. Respondents' opinions about something.
2. Estimates of respondent repertoires (cognitive, affective, or psychomotor).
3. Definitions of respondent skill levels.
4. Definitions of respondent attitudes or values.

Opinions

Opinions are useful in many contexts. Perhaps the two most important are decision making and marketing. The decision maker often has several alternatives available, each with its associated risks and positive and negative aspects.

When assessing the viability of an alternative, the decision maker should discover how the people affected will react. Consider, for example, the CEO of a large corporation who must hire disabled workers. There are many things to be taken into consideration. An important consideration is how others in the organization will react to the policy. A well-developed survey will provide the CEO with enough information. He or she will be more likely to make the right decision.

Opinions are crucial to successful marketing efforts. Most market research is aimed at discovering potential consumers' opinions about a product, its uses, and its applications. Before production begins there should be some indication that a process or product will be accepted by consumers. Otherwise, the company is likely to lose money. It's important to consider giving an opinion test in relation to any anticipated offering, whether it's a new model of an automobile or a modification of a course at a university. A successful organization produces what its clients want. The alternative is failure. Finding out what clients want is a critical function for any organization.

Repertoires

Repertoires exist in many forms. We normally think of them in terms of knowledge and cognitive skills, but they are just as important in the affective and psychomotor domains. Consider the skills needed by people to understand deep affection or grief. Think about keyboard skills or other physical manipulation activities. All people have extensive repertoires in all domains (cognitive, affective, and psychomotor). It's often important to discover the nature and extent of those repertoires.

For example, before a company installs a complex communication system, it should find out how difficult it will be to help people develop the skills to use it. Not all people will want to be trained in all the skills. Some will want little training. Some will want a lot. A well-developed test can determine who should have what and how much.

The primary purpose of schools of all types is to develop repertoires. Most of their tests are, therefore, dedicated to identifying the scope and depth of what their charges can do.

Skill Levels

Although defining skill levels is closely associated with estimating repertoires, it is *not* the same. The basic difference is in the nature of the test. Repertoires can be sampled successfully through norm-referenced instruments. Of course, performance tests do a better job, but schools have demonstrated for many years that they can assess students with norm-referenced tests. However, defining skill levels is a different challenge.

This can be illustrated through consideration of what competence is. Unless competence is measured against a set of standard criteria, it can't be pinned down. Ergo, because a norm-referenced test is used to compare people with other people instead of with criteria, it can't be used to define skill levels with any degree of certainty.

Values

The argument is as true for values as it is for skills. We can identify values through norm-referenced tests, but we can't define them. After skills and values have been defined, we can put them to many uses. The uses depend on the desire for information that prompted the test in the first place.

It may seem strange, but often the test maker works a terrific test through the first fourteen steps and forgets what he or she is supposed to do with the results. If you aren't sure what to do with your results, review Step 2. Your efforts to justify the test included specifying the reasons for having it, the benefits. Use of the results is a matter of studying the justification and applying the results toward a solution of the problem(s) documented there.

What to Do with Test Results

You've designed the test and developed it. Respondents have responded. Now what? How should the results be treated? What about cut-scores? How can validity be ensured? Why is transfer important? What is transfer anyway?

You need answers to a lot of questions. This is true whether your test is a nationally standardized certification examination or a pop quiz in third-grade social studies. Let's take a long hard look at results, what they mean, and what to do with them.

Results: What Are They? Just what are results? If you take one perspective, they're just numbers and comments. From another view, they're the product of human endeavor. Either way, without someone making some sense of them, they're less than worthless. They can actually do more harm than good.

Results are not the same as answers, nor are they outcomes. An answer is a response to a question. It can be the solution to a problem. It may or may not be a result. Answers lead to results. "She smiled with great pleasure and said 'yes.' There was great joy in the land when the Prince announced her decision to marry him." The answer was yes. The result was the announcement, the outcome was the marriage (or the joy). Perhaps it's easier to understand the differences if we think of each of these terms in context. *An answer is an activity.* It may be written, oral, or physical (a nod or an activity that's prompted by the question). It happens as a direct response to a stimulus, usually a question of some sort. *A result is the documentation of an answer.* It could be a direct translation. It could be an interpretation. However it's achieved, it is an event. Normally, results are documented in some way. *An outcome is an activity that follows a result.* It is the second antecedent in the sequence: antecedent, performance (action), consequence, antecedent.

Let's explore two sequences. The classic form of a chart for the management of a project has the form: activity, event, activity, event—to a concluding event. A question/answer is an activity. It's followed by the event called a *result*. The result is followed by another activity called an *outcome* (which poses another question or questions). So outcomes also lead to results. The outcome is the next question that can be represented by its answer. The sequence rewritten is: question/answer, result, outcome/question/answer, result, outcome/question/answer—to a concluding result.

Now look at the other sequence: antecedent, performance, consequence. It's the classic sequence posed by philosophers centuries ago. It's embodied in the operation of a test. The question and its answer create the result that prompts the next question. Any activity, no matter how trivial, has some motivation. Antecedents infer conditions that exist before an action or performance can occur. People are born. They live their lives. Then they die. Being born is the antecedent. Living is a performance. Dying is the inescapable consequence. In baseball a pitcher throws the ball, the batter swings, the ball is hit. Those same philosophers quickly point out the consequence of one performance invariably becomes the antecedent for another. The batter hits the ball; a fielder tries to catch it; it's caught.

This old paradigm can be interpreted as a question (the antecedent) that prompts thinking (the performance), which generates an answer (the consequence). Outcomes are derived from results (such as answers). Therefore they are antecedents as the cycle continues. If you think this way, it helps separate the terms and makes them more meaningful as you contemplate your task, which is to make some sense from the results of a test. You will develop outcomes from the results. Those outcomes are the antecedents for a new cycle.

This isn't just misguided wandering about in a philosophical quagmire. It's important. Results are static. In the action, event, action, event sequence, they are an event. They are never an action. In the antecedent, performance, consequence cycle, they are consequences. They don't prompt action (act as antecedents). They aren't action (act as performances). They are the fait accompli. They are consequences.

The crucial point is *unless someone does something with them, results are without value.* Unless you turn your results into some sort of outcome, they are useless. I'm tempted to recommend any kind of action (even a wrong one) because it is so important to act. *Remember:* unless they are acted on, results (and therefore the test) are wasted. This point will be discussed again later in this chapter. First, though, let's agree on what a result is.

Webster (1987) says a *result* is "something that arises as a consequence, issue, or conclusion; *also:* beneficial or tangible effect." I like their use of the word *beneficial.* If a result is not beneficial, it's called something else. Our definitions must include three aspects of test results: (1) they represent a sample of the respondents' repertoire; (2) results are never precise; and (3) results decay at surprisingly rapid rates.

Sample. A test can only sample. Although many tests are considered "comprehensive," the term is misleading. At their best, tests bring to light a small percentage of a person's ability or knowledge. Even in finely focused inquiries, the material omitted will outweigh that submitted by a huge margin. For example, suppose you ask a person to explain his or her name fully: its origin, why it was chosen for him or her, and anything else about it. You can give the person a year to write it all out, critique it, submit it to review, and even add controversial aspects. Still that person will *not* be able to answer the question completely. Something will be left out.

Precision. The accuracy of results is a moot point in this discussion, but precision is not. Precision is in the eye of the beholder. What may seem very precise and complete to one observer may seem general to another. Precision is a phantom.

We counter the lack of precision through the criteria used to develop test items. The more demanding the criteria are, the more precise results are likely to be. Still, keep in mind that even the most demanding criteria will not guarantee complete precision. There are some who say such a goal is ridiculous. It can't be reached. Perhaps not. The point is that precision, if possible at all, is difficult to achieve. That is not to say it should not be attempted. On the contrary, it *must* be attempted. Results without at least an attempt at precision usually aren't very useful.

Decay. Results decay. Their accuracy and precision start to melt away as soon as they are on paper (or whatever). This is particularly true of results in the affective domain, but it holds for any kind of results. Results remain an accurate estimate of a person's ability as long as that person doesn't change in reference to the matter in question. Because change happens whether we desire it or not, decay happens. A respondent's learning can accelerate decay at a tremendous rate.

My own experience is that for adults decay doesn't substantially change the nature of results for at least a week. After that amount of time, I assume inaccuracies have crept in for at least *50 percent* of the sample. My conceptualization is like the decay rate for radioactive materials. Results have a half-life of about one week for adults. There is a caveat. The half-life depends on how sincerely the respondents want to retain what they know.

Learning involves reinforcement. Whenever an idea or skill is reinforced in some way, it is strengthened. If reinforcement does not take place, the learning wanes. Cigarette smokers provide a good example. Smokers have learned to like to smoke. If a smoker goes without a cigarette for a week, the desire is reduced by about half. After two weeks, the residual is reduced again by about half. Most ex-smokers will testify that after a week, quitting became much easier. The learning they had accumulated decayed. But, like radioactive material, knowledge or skills don't completely disappear. Ex-smokers will always be able to resurrect the pleasure they learned from their habit. Even after years of abstinence, a trace of that learning will remain.

So it is with test results. The moral is, *use the results as quickly as possible to maintain their integrity.* The longer you wait, the less faith you can have in their integrity.

So what does this mean? Should we throw up our hands in despair and give up? If we can't depend on the results of a test, the whole exercise seems like a waste of time and energy. Nothing could be farther from the truth. Knowing this about results is an advantage to us and to the respondents to our tests. Consider an analogy.

Strobe photography illustrates the benefits of test results. Suppose a photographer takes a series of pictures of a tennis player hitting a serve. Each picture shows the player's body in a different conformation, the racket in a different position, the ball a different distance from the racket, and so forth. Yet there is no doubt about what every picture represents. Every picture shows a tennis player hitting a serve. Some may show it better than others, but all of them show the same thing. There is no doubt.

So it is with tests. Although results may picture the knowledge and skills of respondents differently, depending on the circumstances, a good fair test will always describe what it is supposed to describe. And it will do so well.

Test results are treasures. They are dividends of huge impact. They bring order from chaos. They provide the only viable insights a person can have about the working and wonder of others. If you take this perspective, test results are the communication device human beings require to understand one another well enough to form a society. Think about how often people test one another formally and informally. Think about our basic reasons for testing one another. Whether our motives are good or not so good, our basic device for finding out about other people is the test. A good fair test can be very important indeed.

Treasure the results. Don't be careless with them or play them down. Give them the respect and interest they deserve. Most important, be sure to present them so they fairly represent the respondents. Present them so that whoever mandated the test will understand what they mean, what they portend.

The rest of this chapter is devoted to displaying results and making sense of them. As you work with these methods, keep in mind the implications of what has been said so far. Treat the results with respect and they will provide the benefits you envisioned as you designed and developed the test.

Decoding Raw Data

raw data Data that has not been interpreted or analyzed.

When respondents finish a test, they leave you with raw data. It's up to you to make some sense of it, to derive information from it. Your job is to judge the adequacy of their efforts and record that decision in a fashion you and they can understand. It can be a daunting task. To attempt it without forethought is often foolhardy.

The nature of results from different types of tests is very different. Supply items require you to read, assess, and decide. Selection items are more mechanical. Still, you must decide. The next three sections examine this task in relation to the two kinds of items: supply and selection.

We have discussed the nature of the responses for these items. The thrust here is to come up with a scheme or process to rate the results. Our goal should be to take raw data and manipulate it in acceptable ways to obtain information. The information derived should serve to fulfill your objectives and those of your respondents.

Supply Items. Supply items yield answers that, by their nature, are undefined. Every participant will provide a different answer, even when he or she is trying to make the same point as everyone else. The same individual will answer differently on different occasions. Depending on their mind-set and motivation, their answers will vary from day to day (or hour to hour). Your job is to read, understand, and assess. To do so objectively is sometimes difficult. To attempt this task without preparation opens the door to major problems.

It's easy to visualize the kinds of things that will have to be done to come up with scores. The answers must be read. They must be compared with some conception of an acceptable answer (a psychological template). They must be rated as to how well they approach the ideal. In a way, the nature of the item type determines how the results will be handled. But if you let yourself be satisfied with that, you could regret it.

Essay tests are common in academia. You would expect professors, therefore, to be accomplished in scoring them. Sorry. Most professors attempt this task with little or no preparation. They trust their extensive knowledge of the subject matter and their experience in weighing the worth of responses to carry them through. Unfortunately, these things alone don't guarantee respondents a fair hearing. There are too many distractions, psychological barriers, and mechanical problems.

Suppose, for example, a professor asks this question on a test:

> Assume an employee of a large corporation has had to deal with several major traumatic events in the past week: a death in the family, threats to his or her marriage, and the purchase of a new home. What effect could these events have on his or her productivity and relations with other employees? Explain your reasoning and suggest a course of action for the employee's immediate supervisor.

The item is fairly straightforward. The responses will be direct and easy to connect with the question. Yet, the professor will have problems. Suppose he has thirty-seven people in his class. If he simply sits down at his desk and begins to read the responses, the chances all thirty-seven respondents will receive the same unbiased treatment are slim. This is true whether the professor is good at the task or not.

Allow me to explain why this task is so difficult. Let's assume the professor has a study at his home where he takes the papers to grade them. It's well insulated, so sounds from outside won't be a problem. He pulls the shade on the window to remove the distractions from outside. He pulls the plug on his telephone. Then he begins to read the papers.

It will take about sixty seconds for the professor's attention to focus on the task. By that time, he will have read two or three paragraphs of the first response he picked up. During the next ten minutes, his mind will drift away from the task about twenty times. Because he's conscientious, each time he will pull his attention back to the task. After ten minutes have elapsed, his mind will drift more often. For some people the rate can be as high as three times per minute. Nonetheless our professor will persevere and complete his reading and critiques. It will probably take him about fifteen minutes per test.

The judgment he renders, the score he awards, and the relative success of the first respondent are precedents. The second paper will be judged in relation to the first. Whether he tries to or not, the professor will not be able to refrain from comparing the second paper to the first. The first paper has become his template, if you will, for judging the second.

> **template**
> A model or a set of parameters for a response.

There are four possibilities. One, the professor can judge the second paper to be inferior to the first. In that case, he will give the second respondent a lower score and proceed to the next paper. Two, he could judge the paper to be about the same and give it a similar score. Three, he can decide the second paper is superior to the first and give it a better score. In the process, he will probably change criteria. The second, better, paper will become his new template. Papers that follow will be compared with it. The fourth possibility is that he will decide the second paper is *not* comparable with the first. He will judge it on its own merit. He will establish it as an alternative template.

After reading thirty-seven papers, there is a good chance the professor will have changed or added templates more than a dozen times. In other words, he will have changed the criteria for judging. Even though the respondents, his students, will probably not complain, they should. He has not treated any of them fairly. The first paper read is treated unfairly because it must stand alone. Subsequent papers are compared with a shifting set of criteria. That is patently unfair. The professor is probably doing all he can to maintain objectivity and treat everyone with care and respect. Even so, he will treat his students unfairly.

Professors have evolved techniques to counter this tendency. Some deliberately seek the paper of the student they consider best and read his or her paper first. That way, the template established is more likely to endure. Ideally, all other papers will be compared with the best one. The major fault with this procedure is the first paper becomes the template, whether it's the best one or not.

Another ploy is to avoid identifying the respondents, thereby giving the appearance of objectivity. Unfortunately, it doesn't work. The same four possibilities will still apply. Obscuring the identity of the students merely makes the templates anonymous. It doesn't make them go away.

A third tactic is to ask someone else, usually a graduate assistant, either to take on the whole task or to assist by providing a second reading of the papers. The reasoning is that the second, less involved, person will bring objectivity to the task. But because the second person has the same tendencies as the first, all that is accomplished is a second opinion. Of course, that is valuable, but it doesn't solve the basic problem.

The problem is objectivity. However, it isn't connected with identities. *It's inherent in the way the templates are (unconsciously) developed.* Sure, some people are easier to like than others. There is, therefore, a tendency to try to help them score well by shading a judgment here and overlooking a problem there. But most of us are aware of this and try to counter that tendency. Sometimes we're too aware of it and end up punishing the people we like.

There is a better way to develop the template. Our professor should do it deliberately *before he reads the first paper.*

Templates. Webster (1987) says templates are "a gauge, pattern, or mold (as a thin plate or board) used as a guide to the form of a piece being made." A psychological template uses the same kind of logic. It's a conceptualization of how something should look or be when it is complete. Templates are common. We use them almost constantly to develop ideas about things and people. When someone asks you, for example, what your dream house looks like, you may have developed a visualization of it you can share with him or her. That visualization serves as a template. If and when you move into a home, you will compare it with the visualization.

Templates are used to develop things. We develop what we intend to do or build in our minds before we actually perform. A diver imagines what her dive will look like to spectators before she performs it. A designer builds a cabinet in his mind before he begins to draw plans for it. A lawyer imagines how a witness will respond to a question before she asks it. All of these are examples of psychological templates. They are conceptualizations of the way something or someone ought to be or perform that will be compared with the actuality or performance.

Simplistically, you could say that without templates human beings would be little more than unimaginative animals. (This is not the place for that discussion, although it's of vital interest to us all.) The point is that templates are important to judging and scoring supply-type items. When you score an essay or short-answer item, you should do so by using a psychological template you have developed of what the response ought to look like and the information it should impart.

By the way, we also use templates to score selection items. Many multiple-choice tests are scored with a piece of paper with holes in it where the correct answers should appear. That's a template in the full sense of Webster's definition.

So professors use templates. What they don't usually do is formalize those templates to ensure that all their students are treated objectively and fairly. It's a shame because templates are easy to develop and normally make the scoring task both easier to do and much faster.

There are many ways a template can be articulated. You could simply make an outline of the important arenas you wish respondents to explore and how the responses should be structured. My own preference is to arrange the template in three sections:

1. Aspects of the item that should be noted.
2. Elements that should be addressed.
3. Problems or circumstances about which respondents should draw conclusions or make recommendations.

Notice that none of these sections details what should be said, how it should be expressed, or wherein correctness lies. To make these decisions for the respondents is to take away the developmental nature of the item. It's important with most essay items to encourage innovation and creativity. Therefore, prescribing what ought to be said counters the intent of the item.

Let's look at the item again to see how a template might be developed:

Assume an employee of a large corporation has had to deal with several major traumatic events in the past week: a death in the family, threats to his or her marriage, and the purchase of a new home. What effect could these events have on his or her productivity and relations with other employees? Explain your reasoning and suggest a course of action for the employee's immediate supervisor.

The template for this item could look like this:

1. Aspects of the item that should be noted: the employee works at a large corporation. The three traumatic events.
2. Elements that should be addressed: productivity and relations with other employees.
3. Problems or circumstances about which respondents should draw conclusions or make recommendations: how personal trauma affects workers. Discuss types of reactions: anger, resentment, and sense of disembodiment. Projection of how these will affect work and relations. Specify a course of action. Course of action must be related to concepts and procedures discussed in class or in the text.

Consider the effect of such a template on the professor's task in scoring the test. Each of the elements of the template could be related to points. Points could be awarded objectively. Environmental distractions or interruptions need not mess up the results, as the professor can resume the task without having to rethink an entire critique.

Some people will wish to be more precise, to have a more specific model. For them a checklist is a valuable tool. Consider the template above recast as a checklist.

Important Facts About Protagonist

1. Is an employee, not a manager.
2. Works for large corporation.
3. Had death in family.
4. Has threats to marriage.
5. Has new home.
6. Other (easily inferred).

Addressed

7. Productivity.
8. Relationships with others.

Explained or Recommended

9. How trauma affects workers.
10. Anger.
11. Resentment.
12. Sense of disembodiment.
13. Effect on work.
14. Effect on relationships.
15. Type of action.
16. Procedure.
17. Decision points.
18. Method of bringing closure.
19. Course materials.

Even though the checklist is detailed, it doesn't preclude innovative responses. The respondents can address each of the elements in their own way. However, their scores will be tied to specific criteria.

There is no provision in the templates above for originality. If a respondent comes up with an elegant solution, the reward will be self-satisfaction and maybe praise from the professor if he or she remembers. That's OK. If you want to reward such things as creativity, go ahead. Keep in mind that it puts some people at a disadvantage. It won't be as fair. Perhaps rewards for originality and elegance should be divorced from test scores.

Although similar to essay results, the answers to short-answer questions are easier to categorize and, therefore, to judge. Still, they are narrative so they can be challenging. This is particularly true when the goal is to sample Level Three skills.

My tendency is to do the same thing I do with essay items. I develop a template, formalize it, and document it as an outline or checklist. The template for each item contains one or more elements. The resulting template looks a lot like the original test. Ordinarily short-answer items contain the criteria for judging embedded in the question. Therefore, I have found it expedient to simply use a copy of the test as a template. I take the liberty of scribbling notes to myself on each item, underlining what to look for and how to judge it, but otherwise I don't change it much.

Selection Items. Here the problem isn't so much with the adequacy of selected responses as it is with how the scores will be handled once the results are documented. The basic problem is in deciding which respondents did acceptably well and which did not.

The idea of a template is still appropriate. Here, though, we usually develop the template ahead of time as a matter of course. We decide which alternatives are correct when we write the items. We arrange them when we produce the test. We develop the scoring guide or key before respondents take the test.

The biggest problem with this sort of judgment is in establishing its validity. Both content and face validity are inherent in the process used to score supply items. They aren't as easy to establish for selection items. You will see how this applies when you read about validity in Chapter Twelve.

Display of Results

Results come in two forms: narrative or alphanumeric. Narrative results are written, acted out, or reported orally. Alphanumeric results are represented by letters of the alphabet or numbers. The responses to supply-type items are usually narrative in nature (even when they're numbers). The answers to selection items are almost always alphanumeric.

In either case, the results are usually manipulated in some way so they can be compared with a standard. This manipulation usually results in a set of numbers. Most amateur testers use percentages of some type to represent scores. More experienced test makers will use so-called *raw data* although they, too, often use percentages. Either way, the results are represented by numbers. Look at the example in Figure 11.1.

Looks familiar doesn't it? You've probably seen many like it. I have seen literally thousands. As soon as I see one, I begin to draw conclusions. It's a tendency I have to be very careful about.

Whether the test was supply or selection, a set of scores has been obtained. These are what we usually think of when we hear the word *results*. It's OK. We know

FIGURE 11.1. HYPOTHETICAL SCORES.

Person	Score	Percentage
Albers, J.	27	60
Anthony, G.	42	93
Baldridge, A.	38	84
Dankins, M.	39	87
Everly, O.	22	49
Foster, O.	31	69
Hawthorn, Q.	30	67
Hymne, R.	38	84
Jackson, A.	29	64
Jackson, H.	38	84
Jones, A.	32	71
Jones, R.	35	78
Jones, S.	39	87
Jones, W.	33	73
Kelly, G.	24	53
Mellon, M.	33	73
Novak, T.	33	73
Perkins, R.	36	80
Plonski, R.	34	76
Shranski, Y.	30	67
Williams, R.	32	71

the scores represent something far more complex. In the example, the respondents could have scored as high as forty-five points (100 percent). Those forty-five points could represent respondents' efforts on three essay items or forty-five multiple-choice items or whatever. The critical aspect is that they are representations.

If you had generated the set of scores above, you would have put together some sort of template and applied it to the responses. It's important that we not lose sight of the source of a set of scores. The respondents won't. They remember what they said. How you and I represent their efforts is secondary to the effort they made. Our representation of their scores must be the best, most fair, thing we do with a test. We are literally symbolizing their thinking. We should do so with all the care and precision we can muster.

I must repeat: it is important to refrain from coming to conclusions about results until we have more information. The previous set of scores could have been generated by a multiple-choice exam for new hires at an insurance company. In such a case, it's easy to imagine that none of the scores would indicate weakness or failure. We'd simply use them to decide what kinds of remediation or learning exercises each respondent might need. On the other hand, those scores could represent the efforts of experienced pilots in mastering the intricacies of a jumbo jet. In this case, all of the scores could indicate critical weakness or failure.

We also don't know how the test was developed or the results from pilot studies. We don't know whether a cut-score was established. We don't know whether it was a performance or norm-referenced test.

Without more information, and a lot of it, the scores in our example are meaningless. To come to any kind of conclusion about them would be a dangerous mistake. Yet we do it. We look at scores and begin to make decisions about them. We look for who did well and who didn't, even though we don't know the criteria for deciding what doing well is. It's a cultural thing, one repeatedly reinforced for all of us through many years of schooling.

I have good news and bad news. The good news is that it's OK. Because the numbers can be assumed to be representative (they can be trusted to be fair representations), noticing trends in the scores makes sense. Go ahead and do it. The bad news is, you must *not* come to a conclusion about the adequacy of any respondent until you have more information. The information you should want is of two sorts:

1. You should know what those scores represent. Where did they come from? How were they generated?
2. You should know their relative values. How do they compare with standards set for them?

As you look at these requirements, you immediately realize why they say multiple-choice exams are easier to score. The scores from any selection test are directly tied to the items from which they were derived. If a person scores thirty-seven on a forty-five-item test, that means he or she responded correctly thirty-seven times. Supply-item tests, on the other hand, can be a puzzle. They don't have to be. If you have awarded scores according to a preconceived plan—an outline or a checklist—those scores, too, will relate directly to the test items.

Scoring supply items isn't as clean and neat as scoring selection items. For example, a single item could generate fifteen points or less. This is not a problem. The process is more complex than for selection-type items, but it's easily handled if you've prepared ahead of time.

Representation. The scores given in Figure 11.1 could have come from a supply-item test or a selection-item test. They could represent a combination, as there could have been both supply items and selection items on the test.

Either way, it's usually helpful to relate the scores to the items. I normally do so with some kind of matrix. For example, the scores in Figure 11.1 could have come from a matrix like the one in Figure 11.2.

In this case, the first six items were short-answer items worth five points each. The rest were multiple-choice items worth one point each. Respondents' names are replaced by letters to enable putting all the scores on one page.

You can relate the respondents' ability directly to the criterion tested by each item. For example, the criterion used to develop item 1 was achieved more often than the criterion for item 6. Perhaps it would be valuable to know whether the difference is important. Another question also arises. What criteria tended to separate those who did relatively well from those who didn't? Assuming the items were valid, the content being tested has had an effect on the scores. It should. Otherwise there would be little need for a test in the first place. Knowing what criteria were most often poorly achieved provides valuable information. You could

FIGURE 11.2. SCORES BY PERSON FOR ITEMS.

Person	1	2	3	4	5	6	7	8	9	10	11	12	13	14	15	16	17	18	19	20	21	Total	Percentage
A	4	2	2	3	1	2	1	1	1	1	1	1		1	1	1	1	1	1		1	27	60
B	5	4	5	5	5	5	1	1		1	1	1		1	1	1	1	1	1	1	1	42	93
C	3	4	5	5	4	4	1	1		1	1	1	1	1	1		1	1	1	1	1	38	84
D	5	4	5	5	4	4		1		1	1	1	1	1	1	1		1	1	1	1	39	87
E	2	1	4	3	1	2		1	1		1	1	1		1		1		1	1		22	49
F	2	3	4	5	2	3	1	1	1		1	1	1		1	1	1		1	1	1	31	69
G	4	3	4	5	1	3	1	1	1	1		1		1		1	1		1	1		30	67
H	4	4	4	5	4	4	1	1		1	1	1	1	1	1	1		1	1	1	1	38	84
I	5	4	4	5	3	4	1	1		1		1	1	1	1	1	1	1	1	1	1	38	84
J	3	3	3	5	3	2		1	1	1		1	1	1		1	1		1	1		29	64
K	4	3	3	5	3	3	1	1	1	1		1	1	1		1		1	1		1	32	71
L	5	4	3	5	4	3	1	1		1	1	1	1	1		1	1	1	1			35	78
M	5	4	4	5	4	4	1	1		1		1	1	1	1	1	1	1	1	1	1	39	87
N	4	3	5	5	3	2		1	1	1	1		1	1	1	1		1	1		1	33	73
O	4	3	3	3	3	1	1	1		1	1			1	1		1					24	53
P	3	3	4	5	4	3		1	1		1	1	1		1	1	1	1	1		1	33	73
Q	3	5	4	5	3	2	1	1	1		1		1	1		1	1	1	1	1		33	73
R	5	4	3	5	4	3	1	1		1	1	1	1		1	1	1	1		1	1	36	80
S	2	4	2	5	4	3	1	1		1	1	1	1	1	1	1	1	1	1	1	1	34	76
T	4	3	3	4	3	3		1	1	1	1			1	1			1	1	1	1	30	67
U	4	3	3	5	3	3	1		1		1	1	1		1	1	1	1		1	1	32	71

devise remedial instruction or other developmental activities to bring those who
did poorly up to the level of competence of those who did well.

Item Analysis

There are things you can do relatively easily to discover how *difficult* the items were
and how well they *discriminate* among the respondents.

Difficulty. The difficulty of items or tests is usually represented by how many people were successful in responding. The overall difficulty of the *test* is indicated by
the average scores of the respondents. In the test represented by the scores in Figures 11.1 and 11.2, the average score was 33.1. On average, the respondents were
able to score slightly more than thirty-three points. For most of us it's easier to interpret scores if they are expressed as percentages. The average, as a percentage,
was .7355 or 73.6 percent. The respondents were correct in their answers more
than 73.5 percent of the time.

Although this information is valuable, it doesn't tell us what criteria were least
well achieved. On most tests, knowing what criteria caused problems is very
important. It becomes, therefore, appropriate to discover the relative difficulty of
each item. The process is the same. You discover the average success of respondents on each *item*.

To find relative item difficulty, it's expedient to change the matrix in Figure
11.2 to emphasize the items for this process, as shown in Figure 11.3.

As you scan down the column headed "percentage," you can see that some
items were more difficult for respondents than others. The larger the percentage,
the easier the item was. Everyone had item number 21 right, 100 percent of the
respondents. You could use one of several schemes to decide which criteria to target. For example, you could simply decide to look at all items on which respondents
scored below average. Average for this set of percentages is 75.2. Knowing this
helps focus your attention on the criteria that could need emphasis of some sort.

Another way to approach the task is to isolate those criteria that were significantly below the others. This can be done by calculating a simple standard deviation (use your scientific calculator). Here the standard deviation is 11.0. By
subtracting the standard deviation from the average, you can isolate those criteria most in need of further study. For this set of scores, that would be all that had
a percentage of 64.2 or less. The items that scored that low were numbers 5, 6,
and 9. Whatever was tested by those items was significantly less well understood
than anything else on the test.

Discrimination. The other handy test for analyzing how well individual items
worked is to determine whether each separated respondents who could from those

who could not. This ability to discriminate provides a basic report card on the items.

The usual way to determine whether items discriminated well is to pick the top scores and compare them with the bottom scores. You can compare the top half with the bottom half or pick a number from each group that seems to represent the group well. My tendency is to do the latter. When the best are compared with the worst, discrimination is cleaner and easier to interpret.

Here's how it works. Isolate the scores of the two groups for each item. Then compare to see what the tendency is. It's not necessary to use statistical treatments, although chi-square works very well. You can usually see any tendency that ought not to be there simply by looking.

In Figure 11.4 (p. 272) I've taken the top six scores from the previous example and compared them with the bottom six. If you use an equal number of people in each group, the arithmetic is easier. You can use raw scores instead of averages.

There are three possibilities for each item. Both groups could have done equally well with it. The top could have done better than the bottom. The bottom could have done better than the top. For an item to be considered a good discriminator,

FIGURE 11.3. SCORES BY ITEM PER PERSON.

Item	A	B	C	D	E	F	G	H	I	J	K	L	M	N	O	P	Q	R	S	T	U	Total	Percentage
1.	4	5	3	5	2	3	4	4	5	3	4	5	5	4	4	3	3	5	2	4	4	81	77.1
2.	2	4	4	4	1	3	3	4	4	3	3	4	4	3	3	3	5	4	4	3	3	71	67.6
3.	2	5	5	5	4	4	4	4	4	3	3	3	4	5	3	4	4	3	2	3	3	79	75.2
4.	3	5	5	5	3	5	5	5	5	5	5	5	5	5	3	5	5	5	5	4	5	97	92.3
5.	1	5	4	4	1	2	1	4	3	3	3	4	4	3	3	4	3	4	4	3	3	67	63.8
6.	2	5	4	4	2	3	3	4	4	2	3	3	4	2	1	3	2	3	3	3	3	63	60.0
7.	1	1	1			1	1	1	1		1	1	1		1			1	1	1	1	15	71.4
8.	1	1	1	1	1	1	1	1	1	1	1	1	1	1		1	1	1	1			18	85.7
9.	1			1	1	1			1	1			1	1	1	1				1	1	12	57.1
10.	1	1	1	1			1	1	1	1	1	1	1	1	1			1	1	1		16	76.2
11.	1	1	1	1		1		1			1		1			1	1	1	1	1	1	14	66.7
12.	1	1	1	1	1	1		1	1	1	1		1		1			1	1	1	1	16	76.2
13.			1	1	1	1	1	1	1	1	1	1	1	1		1		1	1		1	16	76.2
14.	1	1	1	1	1			1	1	1	1	1	1	1		1		1				14	66.7
15.	1	1	1	1		1	1	1	1			1	1	1	1	1	1	1	1	1	1	18	85.7
16.	1	1		1	1	1		1	1		1			1	1	1		1	1	1	1	15	71.4
17.	1	1	1	1		1	1		1	1				1		1	1	1	1		1	14	66.7
18.	1	1	1		1		1	1	1	1	1	1	1	1	1	1	1	1	1	1	1	19	90.5
19.	1	1	1	1		1			1	1		1	1	1	1		1	1		1	1	15	71.4
20.		1	1	1	1	1	1	1	1	1			1	1		1	1	1	1	1	1	17	81.0
21.	1	1	1	1	1	1	1	1	1	1	1	1	1	1	1	1	1	1	1	1	1	21	100.0

FIGURE 11.4. ITEM DISCRIMINATION.

Person	1	2	3	4	5	6	7	8	9	10	11	12	13	14	15	16	17	18	19	20	21	Total	Percentage
B	5	4	5	5	5	5	1	1		1	1	1		1	1	1	1	1	1	1	1	42	93
D	5	4	5	5	4	4		1		1	1	1	1	1	1	1	1		1		1	39	87
M	5	4	4	5	4	4	1	1		1		1	1	1	1		1	1	1	1	1	39	87
C	3	4	5	5	4	4	1	1		1	1	1	1	1	1		1	1	1	1	1	38	84
H	4	4	4	5	4	4	1	1		1	1	1	1	1	1	1		1	1	1	1	38	84
I	5	4	4	5	3	4	1	1		1		1	1	1	1	1	1	1	1	1	1	38	84
G	4	3	4	5	1	3	1	1	1	1			1		1		1	1		1	1	30	67
T	4	3	3	4	3	3			1	1	1	1		1	1		1	1	1	1		30	67
J	3	3	3	5	3	2		1	1	1		1	1	1			1	1		1	1	29	64
A	4	2	2	3	1	2	1	1	1	1	1	1		1	1	1	1	1	1		1	27	60
O	4	3	3	3	3	1	1		1	1				1	1		1				1	24	53
E	2	1	4	3	1	2		1	1		1	1	1		1		1			1	1	22	49

only the second option is acceptable. The top should do better than the bottom. The items should discriminate the top group from the bottom group.

In our example, this is the case for all the items except 9, 18, and 21. On item 9 the low group all got it correct and the top all missed it. On item 18 one of the top group missed it and all the low group got it right. Everybody got item 21 right. We can say that item 21 does *not* discriminate. Nondiscriminators are considered passive. Numbers 9 and 18 discriminate negatively. They actively detract from the test's ability to identify competence.

The obvious next step is to examine the three items, decide why they worked as they did, and either discard them or fix them. Discarding detractors and passive items makes an immediate, noticeable difference in the scores. Figure 11.5 illustrates that impact.

Figure 11.5 shows that people with high scores tended to remain the same or score higher. People with low scores almost all ended up with even lower scores. In effect, removing the bad items allowed the test to discriminate more efficiently. This is made plain by running simple statistics on the adjusted results. The average is slightly higher, 72.9, and the standard deviation is larger than it was, 13.1. This change in the standard deviation shows there is more variance in the scores. You could say with more confidence that respondents A, E, and O are significantly less skilled than the rest of the group.

Be very careful. Having done this you will have set yourself up to make what may be a grave error. Reread the last sentence in the paragraph above. The comparison is made against the rest of the group. It says nothing about competence. The whole group could be incompetent or they could all be competent. The process

FIGURE 11.5. ADJUSTED SCORES.

Person	1	2	3	4	5	6	7	8	9	10	11	12	13	14	15	16	17	18	19	20	21	Total	Percentage
A	4	2	2	3	1	2	1	1	–	1	1	1		1	1	1	1	–	1		–	*25	60
B	5	4	5	5	5	5	1	1	–	1	1	1		1	1	1	1	–	1	1	–	40	95
C	3	4	5	5	4	4	1	1	–	1	1	1	1	1	1		1	–	1	1	–	36	86
D	5	4	5	5	4	4		1	–	1	1	1	1	1	1	1	1	–	1	1	–	38	90
E	2	1	4	3	1	2		1	–			1	1	1		1		–	1		–	*19	45
F	2	3	4	5	2	3	1	1	–		1	1	1		1	1	1	–	1	1	–	29	69
G	4	3	4	5	1	3	1	1	–	1				1		1	1	–		1	–	27	64
H	4	4	4	5	4	4	1	1	–	1	1	1	1	1	1	1		–	1	1	–	36	86
I	5	4	4	5	3	4	1	1	–	1		1	1	1	1	1	1	–	1	1	–	36	86
J	3	3	3	5	3	2		1	–	1		1	1	1			1		–	1	–	26	62
K	4	3	3	5	3	3	1	1	–	1		1	1	1		1		–	1		–	29	69
L	5	4	3	5	4	3	1	1	–	1	1		1	1	1			–	1	1	–	33	79
M	5	4	4	5	4	4	1	1	–	1		1	1	1	1	1	1	–	1	1	–	37	88
N	4	3	5	5	3	2		1	–	1	1		1	1	1	1		–	1		–	30	71
O	4	3	3	3	3	1	1		–	1						1	1		–			*21	50
P	3	3	4	5	4	3		1	–		1	1	1		1		1	–	1	1	–	30	71
Q	3	5	4	5	3	2	1	1	–		1			1	1		1	–	1	1	–	30	71
R	5	4	3	5	4	3	1	1	–	1	1	1	1		1	1	1	–		1	–	34	81
S	2	4	2	5	4	3	1	1	–	1	1	1	1	1	1	1	1	–	1	1	–	32	76
T	4	3	3	4	3	3			–	1	1	1			1	1		–	1	1	–	27	64
U	4	3	3	5	3	3	1		–	1	1	1			1	1	1	–		1	–	29	69

of discovering item difficulty and item discrimination does *not* reflect the relative skills of the respondents. It *does* provide valuable information about the items. It is good to do these things, obviously. But be careful that you don't let them lull you into using norm-referenced decision making if that was not your intention. Your decisions about the adequacy of the respondents should be based on their relative ability to accomplish the standards set for them.

The task at this point is to compare the scores of individuals with the standard for the test. What score should the people above have for you to be able to say they are competent? What is the cut-score?

Relative Values

The basic question most respondents want an answer for is, What is good enough? They want to know whether they have passed the test. They would also like to know whether they passed easily, but the basic question is, Did I make it?

The mechanism for deciding this question is one of determining relative values. It's a matter of finding relationships and defining them well enough to base valid decisions on them. Sports fans often discuss the relative merits of their favorite teams or players. Many of these discussions become arguments without hope of successful solution because the antagonists haven't bothered to define the strengths of their favorites precisely enough for easy comparison.

That's usually OK for sports fans. Whether the Celtics are better than the Lakers or either one is better than the Bulls depends on so many chance variables that there can be no precision. The arguments rage on and everyone has a good time. But with test results, these uncertainties can be dreadful for both the respondents and the clients, the people who have asked you to conduct a test.

The more you can do to establish the relative value of your results, the more likely you are to have a good fair test.

Cut-Scores

I have discussed at some length the inadvisability of relying on norm-referenced data. For most purposes, comparing people to people is neither good nor fair. The alternative (and a good one it is) is to develop a standard or standards against which you can compare results. What you need is a cut-score. Basically there are three ways to set cut-scores:

1. Use your own expertise or that of a trusted authority to set the score arbitrarily.
2. Develop a consensus opinion from a panel of experts.
3. Develop the cut-score through a pilot test. Employ the contrasting groups method.

Shrock and Coscarelli (1989) discuss these in detail in their book *Criterion-Referenced Test Development*.

Set Cut-Scores Arbitrarily. Setting the cut-scores arbitrarily is a good alternative when you're only going to use a test once. To go through a long process to establish a cut-score for a onetime event is silly. Tradition in this country has it that 70 percent is somehow the magic number. Forget that. Base your decision on the best judgment you can muster for the test in question. Consider two examples.

When Colonel Ofiesch (1972) was training bomber pilots, he selected 90 percent as his cut-score. His reasoning was that he had to make as sure as possible that every pilot who took off would also be able to land the plane safely. Competence for that situation required a very high level of skill. Given that, he arbitrarily made the cut-score as rigorous as it could be.

It has been said that, when King John was recruiting men to go on a crusade with him, his only concerns were that they be mobile and want to go. He arbitrarily set his cut-score as low as he could.

Ofiesch had a well-developed test. His cut-score was rigorously defined and rigidly adhered to. King John didn't have much of a test at all. His standard was flexible, to say the least. Still they both used cut-scores, and their standards were arbitrary.

One method for deciding what your cut-score will be that, although arbitrary, is fair and appropriate is to ask a relatively ignorant person to take the test and use that person's score as the cutoff. Anyone who can't score better than an ignorant respondent probably isn't competent with the skills of the test. Of course, you may want to define *competence* as being better than simply "not totally ignorant." If so, you can use your volunteer's score as a basis for making your decision. It gives you a better feel for the scoring potential of subsequent (qualified) test takers.

Use a Consensus Opinion. This process is widely used in academia. The idea is to ask a group of experts to examine the test and form a consensus on how well a competent respondent should be able to do. The process usually requires that the experts study each item, pass judgment on it, and use that series of judgments to suggest a standard for the test as a whole.

There are two requirements for this process: (1) the experts have to be qualified, and (2) they must agree on a single score for the standard. Sometimes these requirements are difficult to achieve. You may be forced to fall back on arbitrarily deciding the issue yourself. However, even then, the group's effort won't have been in vain because you will be able to base your decision on their recommendations.

The group you pick to do this can be of any size. However, the larger the group, the more confidence you can have in their decision. Make sure you can qualify each member of the group as an expert and that the other members agree with your assessment. Thiagarajan and Stolovitch's (1979) suggested optimum number for a decision-making group is appropriate for this task. They recommend five plus or minus two, so from three to seven.

To make your job easier, consider this definition. An *expert* is anyone you could reasonably expect to score significantly higher on the test than someone who is barely competent. Statistically, *significance* means the person will score more than one standard deviation above the eventual cut-score. The experts can be qualified by your anticipation of what they will produce. Assuming you are yourself an expert in the field, this is an appropriate procedure. If you aren't such an expert, solicit the opinion of someone you are sure is.

The process can be formal. You could use a nominal group session or do a modified Delphi study. However, it is usually informal. You gather a group and ask them to form a consensus. Most people chosen for this task are capable and willing to do it. You may have to do it through the mail or on the phone. This shouldn't be a problem. Make sure, though, that each expert polled has an equal say and that each contributes appropriately.

Use a Pilot Study. When the test is important and will be used several times, a formal process is in order. The process I have used with success several times is called the *contrasting groups method.* It's straightforward and easy to administer, and it provides a very reliable standard.

The procedure is to ask two groups of respondents to take the test at the same time in the same environment (to ensure both groups take it under the same conditions). The two groups are at opposite ends of a scale of competence. One group can be called masters. They are people you are sure will do very well on the test. They are capable of exemplary performance.

The other group is people who are relatively ignorant about the skills to be tested. They don't know anything about them. Although they don't fit the definition used by medical doctors in blind tests, we normally call them *controls.*

In theory, the experts should do very well on the test. Their scores should reflect their expertise. The control group should do very poorly. There should be little or no overlap between their scores and those of the experts. Figure 11.6 illustrates how the process works. The scores in the left column were made by experts. Those on the right were registered by the control group.

You can see that some "masters" scored over one standard deviation below the average. One scored twenty-three and two scored twenty-two. This is unexpected. Something was wrong. Maybe those three weren't really experts. Maybe they didn't feel well. Maybe they were confused by some of the items on the test. Whatever the reason, they should not have scored that low. Of course, this happens almost any time a test is given. Some people who should do well just do not. Such results are called *false negatives.* They scored poorly but should not have.

One of the controls scored more than one standard deviation above the average. Maybe he or she was lucky. Maybe that person had more skill than he or she was supposed to. For whatever reason, he or she scored too high. This sort of result also shows up on most efforts of this kind. These are called *false positives.* The person did relatively well but should not have.

Notice the zone between the top of the controls and the bottom of the masters. This zone usually appears on efforts of this kind. It's roughly defined by one standard deviation above average for the controls and one standard deviation below average for the masters. Figure 11.7 (p. 278) shows how it looks for this set of scores. It is called the *zone of acceptance.*

The zone of acceptance defines the area within which you can set your cut-score. If you go above it, you will exclude people who should be included. If you go below it, you will include people you should not. Given those parameters, you should set your cut-score to include as many false negatives as you can while, at the same time, excluding the false positives. In this case, the cut-score was set at twenty-three. The two masters who scored below twenty-three were, therefore, not considered to have passed the test.

FIGURE 11.6. CUT-SCORE DISTRIBUTION.

Score	Masters	Controls
36		
35	X	
34	X	
33	S X	
32	X	
31		
30	XXX	
29	M X	
28	XXXX	
27		
26	XX	
25	S	
24		
23	X	
22	XX	X
21		S
20		XXX
19		XX
18		X
17		X
16		M X
15		
14		XX
13		
12		X
11		S X
10		
9		
8		
7		X
6		

Source: Harwood & Westgaard, 1992.

There is an expedient you can use if you don't have the resources or the time to conduct a full-scale pilot of your test. You can treat the first use of the test as though it were the pilot. Understand that this procedure is *not* as reliable as the contrasting groups technique, but it is better than the arbitrary or consensus approaches.

In essence, you would conduct this process the same way you would conduct a regular contrasting group. However, you would make some assumptions about the respondents. You would assume there are some among them who could qualify as masters and there are some who could be considered ignorant of the skills, who would qualify as controls. These are risky assumptions at best. You would make them with the caveat that experience could justify changes in the cut-score. However, once set, cut-scores have to be adhered to. Otherwise the whole concept is suspect.

With those misgivings, here's how you go about it:

1. Arrange the scores from the test in a distribution similar to those in Figure 11.7.
2. Remove the central third of the scores. (Take out the scores in the middle.)
3. Treat the remaining scores as separate applications of the test and develop a cut-score using the contrasting groups method.

FIGURE 11.7. MODIFIED CUT-SCORE DISTRIBUTION.

Score	Masters	Controls
36		
35	X	
34	X	
33	S X	
32	X	
31		
30	XXX	
29	M X	
28	XXXX	
27		
26	XX	
25 —S—		
24	Zone of Acceptance	
23	X	
22	XX	X
21		S
20		XXX
19		XX
18		X
17		X
16		M X
15		
14		XX
13		
12		X
11		S X
10		
9		
8		
7		X
6		

Let's use a set of scores similar to the one in Figure 11.1 to illustrate the process. Figure 11.8 shows the scores arranged in a single distribution. As is usually the case, the scores tend to pile up in the middle, that is, there are more scores toward the center of the distribution than at either extreme. By the way, if this doesn't happen, there's a very good chance something is messing up the test or the way it was used. In most cases, the people who scored near the center of the distribution are at or near the average. The ones who are most likely, then, to be unusual (or not competent) will score less.

Remember the discussion of the normal curve? This data, like most data of this type, should conform to that model. If such an assumption is appropriate (and it usually is) then about 70 percent of the respondents are at or near the mean

FIGURE 11.8. SCORES ARRANGED AS A SINGLE DISTRIBUTION.

42	/
41	
40	
39	//
38	///
37	
36	/
35	/
34	///
33	///
32	//
31	/
30	/
29	/
28	
27	/
26	
25	
24	/
23	
22	/

(average). In this case, 70 percent of the respondents (there were twenty-two of them) is 15.4, fifteen to keep from slicing people up. That means at least seven of the respondents are not average. The trick is to decide who those people might be. Look at the distribution in Figure 11.8 (p. 279) again. As is usually the case, the scores seem to have natural breaks. Here those breaks occur at 40, 37, 28, 25, and 23. They indicate the person who scored 42, for example, may be significantly above the ones who scored 39. More important, the person who scored 22 is probably significantly below everyone else. How about the one who scored 24 or the one who scored 27? Where should the cut-score be? Where are the seven people?

One of the seven has to be the person who scored 42. Two more are probably those who scored 22 and 24. That leaves four. If we arbitrarily choose the two who scored 39 and those who scored 29 and 27 we can account for all seven. However, if I were the one who scored 29 or one of those who scored 38 I'd be a bit peeved. After all, my score is in the pile in the middle of the distribution.

This dilemma will occur time after time. What you should have is a way to make the cut-score decision without so much guesswork. Let's try a different tack. What would happen if we divided the distribution into four parts? (In statistics, these are called *quartiles*.) We should have four areas we could arbitrarily call high, high average, low average, and low. In this case, there are five people in each of the average quartiles and six in the upper and lower quartiles, as shown in Figure 11.9. Because we're not concerned with the average people (we can safely assume they are competent, that is, passed the test), let's remove the high and low average scores. Now our distribution looks like Figure 11.10 (p. 282).

Now visualize what would happen if we slid the top scores down to meet the bottom scores or vice versa. We would still have a normal-seeming distribution, but with only twelve people instead of the original twenty-two. Let's redraw the distribution and assign new numbers so we can calculate a new mean and standard deviation, as shown in Figure 11.11 (p. 283).

The new mean is 8.5 and the standard error is 3.8. Therefore any score above 12 is significant (for this array), as is any score below 5.

The cut-score *according to this process* should be set above the scores of the two lowest people. Therefore, when we transpose those numbers back to Figure 11.10, the cut-score should be set at 25 or 26. It's fairly evident that only two of the seven people mentioned above are affected (the people who scored 22 and 24). The others are above the line and have, therefore, passed the test.

There is a huge caveat here. This procedure is not defendable. Most statisticians would laugh at it. However, it provides you with a way to set cut-scores that is much better than guessing. It gives you an easy-to-use method based on hard data, and it does so through the implementation of a well-documented, trustworthy model, the normal curve. Attach the caveat when you use it, but go ahead and use it. It works.

FIGURE 11.9. SCORES IN QUARTILES.

42	/	
41		
40		High
39	//	
38	///	
37		
36	/	High Average
35	/	
34	///	
33	///	Low Average
32	//	
31	/	
30	/	
29	/	
28		
27	/	
26		Low
25		
24	/	
23		
22	/	

One additional thought about cut-scores. Once the score has been set, the pass ratio should stay about the same. In our example, 90 percent will pass. That number *seems* arbitrary. But because of the way it was selected, the pass ratio should remain about the same. If it does *not* remain about the same over subsequent administrations and you're sure your candidates are qualified to take the test, you should seriously consider changing the cut-score. Be careful, though. When you do so, you may be fudging.

Fudge and Finagle. *Fudging* is what I call messing with the data after the test has been taken and the scores recorded. It should be against the law. It's certainly unethical. There's a very important exception. It's OK to mess around with the data after it's in if you have made specific (documented) arrangements to do so before it was generated. That's called *finagling.*

FIGURE 11.10. CENTRAL SCORES REMOVED.

42	/
41	
40	
39	//
38	///
37	
36	
35	
34	
33	
32	
31	/
30	/
29	/
28	
27	/
26	
25	
24	/
23	
22	/

In setting the cut-scores for a test, for example, it's perfectly OK to manipulate the data as I have described above if you decided to do so before the test was administered. But let's suppose you decide to set the cut-score through the consensus method. You assemble your experts and get their recommendation. Then you administer the test. When the results are in, you find 80 percent of the respondents have failed to meet the panel's recommended cut-score. Now what?

You're stuck. You must record the failures and, I hope, learn a lesson. Experts often overestimate the abilities of newcomers. They have a natural tendency to set cut-scores too high. If you accept their recommendations without reservation, you are in a position to treat many of your respondents unfairly. They will fail because the standard has been set too high. You can't arbitrarily lower the standard. That would be fudging.

FIGURE 11.11. REVISED DISTRIBUTION OF SCORES.

```
15
14    /
13
12 -------------------------- plus one s
11    //
10    ///
 9    /
 8    /
 7
 6    /
 5 -------------------------- minus one s
 4
 3    /
 2
 1    /
```

Now let's suppose your boss informs you the standard will be set through the expert review method. A panel of gurus will decide what the standard will be. If you fear they will be too strict, you must document the uncertainty and make arrangements before the test is administered. Put it in writing. Say you will conduct a modified contrasting groups method to validate the panel's findings. Then, when the scores are in, you can legitimately display the scores as in Figures 11.7 through 11.10 and adjust the cut-score accordingly. That is called finagling.

The difference is philosophical, but it is very important. If you finagle, you have anticipated a problem and can document your reasons for having to adjust the score *without having seen the results*. Fudging, on the other hand, gives you a license to manipulate the scores without reason or real legitimacy. Never mind that you intend to do the right thing through it. Having done it once, you can justify doing it again. Sooner or later it will get you in trouble. Finagle all you want. But, please, don't fudge.

Summary

Results embody the reason for testing. They are what you and I want to see when the test is completed, but simply looking at them is seldom enough. We must manipulate them so the information they convey can be interpreted and presented.

Results *sample* the knowledge and skills of the respondents. They can't be comprehensive. Although *precision* is difficult to define and accomplish, we must do the best we can to make results as precise as they can be. *Decay* isn't a problem if results are examined and used within a week. After that they seem to follow the pattern of radioactive materials. They seem to have a *half-life* of one week.

Supply items should be scored through the use of a *psychological template*. I recommend either a grading outline or checklist for scoring essay-type items. Short-answer items can be scored through an adaptation of the test questions. Selection items are easier to score. You simply develop an answer sheet and use it.

Results can be narrative or alphanumeric. Either way, it's usually best to symbolize them with numbers—so many points for each answer. The resulting display allows you to develop a rationale for evaluation. Two questions should be answered:

1. What do the scores represent?
2. How do they compare with a selected standard?

Simple *item analysis* is a process used to discover the *difficulty level* and *discriminating power* of each item. Through it you can discover how well the items on the test did what they were supposed to do. Modification of the items before subsequent uses of the test improves their ability to perform as desired and makes a better test possible.

Representation depends on content and intent. The standard can be arbitrarily set or developed through a cut-score technique such as the contrasting groups method. For most purposes, it's *not recommended that you use norm-referenced comparisons, comparison with other test takers.*

It's OK to *finagle*. You can manipulate the results if you have documented plans to do so before the test is given. It is not OK to *fudge*. Messing with the scores after they have been generated, without a previously announced intention to do so, is unethical at best. Do not fudge!

◆ ◆ ◆

The Fifteen Steps

We have covered fifteen steps to good fair tests. It may seem like a lot. After all, most of the tests you will build will be relatively uncomplicated one-shot deals. Why go to so much trouble?

Remember what was said in Chapter One: *the fifteen steps are always accomplished whether you plan them or not.* They happen. My charge to you is to take charge. Make the steps work for you. Know what they are and deliberately use them to build your tests. Use this simple checklist:

❑   1. Identify and qualify potential respondents.
❑   2. Justify the test.
❑   3. Identify performances to be tested.
❑   4. Set criteria for each performance.
❑   5. Select the type of test that best fits the desires of respondents and provides a valid assessment of the criteria.
❑   6. Design test presentation and administration.
❑   7. Design and select the evaluation process.
❑   8. Write the items.
❑   9. Review and qualify the items.
❑ 10. Pilot the test.
❑ 11. Set cut-scores or other parameters.
❑ 12. Produce the test.
❑ 13. Administer the test.
❑ 14. Evaluate the results.
❑ 15. Use the results.

Even if you're in a hurry and rush through the steps, you'll produce a better test than if you had ignored them. This has been borne out through my many years of experience with all kinds of tests.

◆ ◆ ◆

Besides yourself, test developers in your organization may be other in-house people, consultants, or companies who make testing their business. All test developers benefit in similar ways from administration of a test.

When you develop and administer a test yourself, you have aspirations for the test, for the respondents, and for yourself. You want the test to work well for all three. Your priority, if it's like mine, is to have the test work well for you. You can benefit if it does what it's supposed to. Perhaps test development is part of your job. If so, good results mean a job well done. Perhaps you are trying to establish your competence, credibility, or position. If so, good results can be a boost.

It's OK to pursue these kinds of goals because it's a win-win proposition. You win. The respondents win. Think in terms of the bottom line. If a test does what it's supposed to, the results provide a basis for profit. The organization is strengthened by the assurance of competence in the respondents. They will be able to accept new, more productive roles. That translates directly into a better return on investment for the organization—more profit for the same outlay. Similarly, the test developers receive credit for having developed a profitable product. They, in turn, profit for having done so. This is true whether the developer is a single person providing a test for the end of a course or a large consulting company building an instrument for certification of thousands of professionals.

All this potential for success and profit depends on the test administrator. Administered well, a test will be productive. Don't take the administrative task lightly. In many cases it's the keystone on which success depends.

You've completed the fifteen steps. The test was a success. Or was it? Did it meet the expectations of the stakeholders? Did it fulfill the mandate? It's nice to find out. Take a few minutes and evaluate this test. Discover whether it performed as you intended. Evaluate.

- CHAPTER TWELVE

EVALUATING THE TEST

Evaluation, as has been said before, is passing judgment on something. Shrock and Coscarelli (1989) say it is "the process of making judgments regarding the appropriateness of . . . for a specific purpose." For this discussion, it's the process of passing judgment on a test. If you are going to judge people using a test, you have a responsibility to evaluate the test and what it represents. In most cases, if you performed the fifteen steps, evaluation is easy. You compare respondents' scores with the standard to declare whether they have achieved it.

However, you shouldn't overlook evaluation of the test itself. There are still important questions to be asked and answered: Is the test valid? Is it reliable? What about formative evaluation, summative evaluation, or auditing?

The plot has thickened. Be happy about it. It's a good thing. Evaluation is an opportunity (actually, as you will see, it's several opportunities) to discover and promote the positive aspects of your test.

Books have been written about evaluation, what it is, how it's done, and why it's important. Evaluation is a very diverse and often confusing arena. We will concentrate here on five aspects of evaluation that are directly tied to testing:

1. *Validity.* Does the test do what it was designed and developed to do?
2. *Reliability.* Can you trust the test to perform well each time you use it?
3. *Formative evaluation.* What can be done during development to ensure integrity?

4. *Summative evaluation.* How can you specify the strengths and weaknesses of a test?
5. *Audits.* How can you affirm the use of the knowledge and skills tested?

My hope is that by discussing these things in some detail two things will happen. First, you will gain an understanding of what evaluation is and why it's important. Second, you will add several techniques to your professional repertoire.

Validity

For a test to be valid, it must do what it was designed to do. Suppose, for example, you develop a test to see if order-entry clerks can communicate efficiently with customers. They take the test. The results show the clerks are very good at entering data into the order-entry system. Was it a good test? Probably. The results provided valuable information. Was it valid? No. Because it didn't do what it was designed to do.

> **validity**
> The ability of a test to do what it was designed to do.

The distinction is important. Validity is *not* a measure of goodness. A test can be valid and still be a stinker. This happens. Poor test makers can use validity to hide their ineptness. Take another example. John decides to test his custodial people to see if they know and comply with safety regulations. He knows validity is important, so he makes sure the content is good—the right stuff. He makes the test easy for his people to read. He makes the test as much like the job conditions as he can with the resources he has. He makes sure the test is valid. But suppose his questions are poorly written. They are confusing. Some of them are tricks. Most of the test is, therefore, neither good nor fair.

Of course, many experts would say John's test isn't valid. A valid test will perform as expected by both the test maker and the respondents. But the tests he used to show validity worked (with a little help). So he claimed it was valid. His boss accepted that claim. Respondent complaints about the fairness of the test were ignored or thought to be sour grapes.

I bring up John as an example for an important reason. Validity is critical to the success of a test. If a test isn't valid, it's probably a waste of time and energy at best. At most, it could destroy morale and work relationships. So I urge you to ensure validity for your tests. At the same time, though, I ask you not to misuse this tool. Claiming a test is valid when it isn't can lead to big problems.

Why should I admonish you? Because you will probably be the only one in your organization who can validate a test. Very few people understand the concept well enough to apply it. Even fewer know the techniques to use. Ergo, if you are one of those few, you may be in a position to muck with the results for a bit and make a statement like, "This is a valid test," which no one would dispute. Nor should they if you do the right things to the right materials at the right time. As you ensure validity for your tests and results, make an honest effort to do it with the best of intentions. Any tool can be misused. This is a very valuable tool. Use it well and it will reward you handsomely.

The good news is, it's easy. It's so easy you should wonder why more people aren't good at it. I don't know. I only know many of them are not. How easy is it? You can validate a test in about an hour by yourself. Let me show you how.

There are several types of validity. We will look at four of them: content, face, construct, and predictive.

Content Validity

A test has content validity if it tests the specified content in a way consistent with the nature of the content. What that means is that the test should test the criteria.

Suppose you have a performance objective that states:

> The employee will be able to identify areas within the building that don't meet standards for cleanliness and take steps to correct each problem so it will no longer exist. All areas must meet standards. The only exceptions allowed are those the employees either aren't qualified to address or those requiring special aid or equipment.

This is actually two objectives in one. Employees will find problem areas. Employees will correct the problems they find. The conditions are assumed, but they are important. The employees being tested will not be new hires. They know the building they are to inspect. They know how to correct any problems they might find.

The content of a test of this set of skills would relate directly to the criteria stated in the objective. That is all there is to content validity.

You can establish content validity by showing how a test reflects the content it is meant to test. The test of the objective above would assess two things: (1) how well employees find problems and (2) how well they clean them up.

Note that it isn't appropriate at this point to determine how well the test tests. That is a different aspect of validity. What you want for *content* validity is to be able to say the test tests the content specified.

Two problems can arise. First, you must be careful about what you infer or assume. What you assume determines what you will look for. If you assume something without cause, you can mislead yourself. Second, all the content must be considered, whether it's tested or not. In going over the content, you may choose not to test it, but you should review it all during validation because it is not appropriate to judge the whole of something without having seen it all.

Assumptions. Suppose you conduct this test. Before involving respondents, you tour the building and spot three problem areas. You ask the employees to be tested to tour the building with you (one at a time) to see if they will spot the same problems. When an identification is made, you ask the respondent what should be done to correct the problem.

Sounds like a good test doesn't it? It probably is. But think for a moment about the assumptions you made. First, you've assumed the employees will be as vigilant and conscientious when you are absent as they are when you accompany them on the tour. Second, you've assumed a description of the work to be done is sufficient. Third, you've assumed the order in which the tours are conducted won't affect the results (that is, people who tour first or second won't give the others clues about what to look for or say).

As you can see, it's important to check your assumptions. They can make or break the test. *Assumptions are part of the content of the test.* Without checking them, you can't ensure content validity.

Content. In essence, you guarantee coverage of the content by using the fifteen steps of the process. Steps 3 (identify performances to be tested), 4 (establish criteria for each performance), and 6 (design test presentation and administration) practically guarantee *content validity.*

But suppose your boss asks you to do something formal to show content validity. You have two documents that will do this very well. You have a list of criteria you developed in Step 4. They provide direct reference to the content. You also have a matrix you put together in Step 6 that shows what criteria are tested in what ways. Even the most skeptical critic will accept these as pro forma evidence. If questions remain, they will be answered through establishment of the other three kinds of validity.

Face Validity

Face validity is another fairly simple idea. A test should look like a test. Further, respondents should have the impression it's testing what they expected to have tested. A favorite trick of some teachers is to test something that wasn't in the assignments given students. The students will expect to be tested on what they have been studying. If they receive something else, the test is *not* valid. It lacks face validity. The same kind of thing can happen with performance tests in business. Employees expect to be tested on specific skills, usually what they would do on the job. If, instead, the test samples skills they don't normally use, it isn't valid. Such tests do *not* have face validity.

Do you see the distinction? *Content* validity is concerned that the content of the test is actually the same as the content you meant to assess. *Face* validity deals with what people expect, whether it conforms to the criteria listed in Step 4 or not.

When you give a respondent a booklet that contains a series of multiple-choice items, it's fairly obvious the thing is a test. When you add a cover sheet that says it is a test and instructions about how to respond to the items, you have pretty well guaranteed face validity. But don't be too sure. A teacher tells of having given a standardized achievement test to her students one day. They worked through it and handed it in. After they were finished, one of them raised his hand and thanked her for letting them practice. Then he asked when the real test would be given. On the face of it the test was *not* valid. Face validity, any kind of validity, is not ensured until you know the respondents are involved in the right kinds of ways.

Face validity is hardest to achieve with tests conducted without paper and pencil. It's harder for respondents to know they are being tested. Sometimes you have to add elements to a test to make it look more like a test. Often, for example, the test administrator will say something like, "This is a test." Otherwise respondents won't be sure. Their responses may be less well-thought-out or more sloppily constructed. Keep this in mind and you should have little or no trouble establishing face validity.

But whether the test looks like a test or not, face validity depends on respondents knowing it is testing the right stuff. They must feel the test tests relevant criteria.

Checking for face validity is relatively easy. Ask two or three of the people who are in the target audience, the respondents, to comment on it. Ask them to look at the test briefly (flip through the test) and answer two questions: "Is this test what you expected?" and "Does it test skills the way you expected them to be tested?"

Construct Validity

The term *construct* here refers to psychological construct. How do people perceive the test? Is it good? Is it fair? Can they relate to it in a constructive, definitive way? Do they respond as the test maker intended? Do they respond in a way consistent with the nature of the criteria being tested? Many of these questions can be answered by watching respondents as they take the test.

The Trappings of Success. People who are successful on a test are usually easy to spot even before the test is scored. They feel confident. They feel rewarded by their own efforts. They usually finish the test in good time. In short, they exhibit personal traits that mark them as successful test takers.

There is a second group of those who feel as if they passed but aren't sure. Usually, they are worrywarts. But their concerns are often justifiable. They certainly should *not* be ignored. In fact, they should be a focus for you. It's in your best interests to supply these people with information to relieve their anxiety and settle the questions in their minds. This group will also finish the test in good time, but they are apt to go back over it, reviewing their answers and perhaps modifying some of them. Because of this, they are usually well positioned to offer solid advice about the test and how to improve it.

People who fail usually know it. They may protest. Often the protest gives them away. They complain about the test even before it has been scored. Be careful. There is a tendency to listen too closely to such complaints. You may give complainers more credibility than they deserve. If you do so, you will be negating much of the work you have done to this point.

Impact on Respondents. Construct validity has more to do with how the test impacts respondents than with the way it's constructed. Most concerns about physical aspects are considered when establishing face validity. There are, however, presentation aspects in construct validity. Whether respondents understand how the items are presented is a construct issue. Your writing style, fog levels, use of format, and presentation issues affect construct validity.

Basically, a test has construct validity if the *kind of thinking* it generates in respondents conforms to what the test maker had in mind. If the test maker intends for them to solve problems, that is what should happen. If the test maker wanted them to go into a problem-solving mode and they simply recalled and regurgitated answers, the test is *not* valid.

Construct validity is established through use of a developmental test. Developmental tests are important formative evaluation techniques used primarily in Step 9 (review and qualify the items) and Step 10 (pilot the test; revise and rewrite). They are discussed in detail later in this chapter.

Predictive Validity

How do you forecast success for respondents who pass your test? How can you be reasonably sure the test will *predict* a respondent's competence in applying skills on the job?

If a respondent takes a test on a set of skills, you will want to be able to say that person will use those skills to perform a task competently. Suppose a social studies teacher tests students on their ability to identify dangerous trends in social interactions. The teacher will want those students to be able to apply their skills in current or future social situations.

For some skill sets, predictive validity is very difficult. The social studies teacher may not be able to establish it. On the other hand, an instructor teaching employees how to use personal computers can establish it easily.

The process I use to establish predictive validity is the same as the one I use for reliability. In the fifteen-step process, it happens in Step 10. It's described in detail later in this chapter.

There is minor confusion in the ranks of testing and evaluation professionals about predictive validity. The confusion comes from its association with *concurrent* validity. People who prefer to reference their thinking to concurrent validity usually don't feel obligated to consider predictive validity. Others, like myself, who prefer to work with *predictive* validity, don't pay much attention to concurrent validity. Sounds like double talk, doesn't it? Well, in some ways, it is. The two are very similar. The only real difference is their orientation. *Concurrent* validity is not future oriented. Predictive validity is. Both are based on an examination of the differences between the results of respondents who do well on the test and those who do not.

Shrock and Coscarelli (1989) have an excellent discussion of the process for establishing concurrent validity in *Criterion-Referenced Test Development* (pp. 187–194). I heartily recommend it. You will find it is similar to the process described in the next section.

Reliability

When you are fairly sure a test is valid, you can proceed with confidence. For most tests no further work is justified. But if you have a test that will be used several times or for a large population, you may want to assure yourself it will be equally good and fair for everyone. This can be a problem if the respondents are widely scattered, if the test will be used at widely separated time intervals, or if the test represents a high-stakes situation for respondents.

A test is reliable when it measures the same thing consistently. The results are predictable (not for individuals but overall). If a test is reliable, you can safely expect the results to reveal the same kinds of things *every time it is used.*

> **reliability**
> The expectation that a test will reveal the same kinds of things every time it is used.

If you use a test with order-entry clerks at your company this year and again next year, you want both sets of respondents to have the same opportunity. This makes sense. Your problem is finding some way to ensure that it happens. Because time will pass, it's unreasonable to expect people to score the same as they might have a year before. But it isn't unreasonable to expect the same amount and kind of discrimination to take place. For example, if you ask someone who is very good at something to take a test on that thing, that person should score well. On the other hand, someone who is relatively unskilled should not score well. This should be the case whether they take the test in 2001 or 2011. Of course, the caveat applies. The skill set has to remain relatively stable.

Suppose you give a test to new hires in an insurance company. The test is designed to discover how well the people understand actuarial data. Some will score well, some won't. Now suppose you give the same test to another group six months later. Assuming the two groups have about the same background experience, you would expect the scores to be quite similar. If they are, the test has demonstrated reliability.

Assuming reliability can cause problems. This is true even if you obtain the kind of evidence discussed in the paragraph above. If you assume the test is reliable, you (or someone else) will make decisions based on the results. Your decisions may be very important to people who have taken the test. Someone may not be allowed to graduate. Someone may not receive a job or a promotion. Those unfortunates may think the test was *not* reliable. If they have a legitimate complaint, you will be held responsible.

Two circumstances make establishing reliability important:

1. The test is used more than once and/or in more than one location (environment).
2. The results of the test are used to make critical decisions about people or situations.

If these conditions pertain, you want a reliable test. It's relatively easy to establish reliability. Let's examine a process for doing so.

Reliability depends on a test being able to perform in much the same way each time it is used. I have used the process below many times with good success. You may want to use it yourself.

Normally test makers don't do their own statistical analysis. They ask others in their organizations to do it for them using computers and sophisticated software. If, however, you wish to pursue this tactic (or others equally valuable), allow me to recommend a neat little book that leads you through the process without the tedious aspects of a statistics text. The book is called *The Competent Manager's Handbook for Measuring Unit Productivity* (Hale & Westgaard, 1984). It works.

You may wish to get a taste of what I'm talking about right now. If so, here is an example.

Consider a test to determine how quickly a sophomore in high school can run a hundred yards. The test administrator (coach) asks the respondents (runners) to take their positions on the track. The coach tells them to take their marks and get set. She shoots a pistol as the signal to go. At the same instant, assistants at the finish line press the start buttons on their stop watches. The runners run the race. As they cross the finish line, the timers press the buttons again, recording the amount of time each runner took.

The coach tests another set of runners a week later. She conducts the same test in the same way with the same age students with about the same skills. What assurance will she have that the test is reliable, that each group of runners was treated fairly? In this case she can be fairly sure without much further effort. She should consider whether the conditions were the same and whether she used about the same cadence in getting them started. However, there is a large question mark. What if some event at school or in town has caused one or more runners to lose concentration? What if one or more of them are sick? Is the test still reliable? Of course not. It won't show their true ability the second time.

The coach can use a simple statistical treatment to make sure the test is reliable. Let's suppose she has eighteen students the first week and twenty-two the second. The track has eight lanes so the coach divides the runners into relatively equal groups for the test. The first week she has three groups of six. In the second week she has two groups of seven and one of eight. The students draw straws to see which group they will be in and what lane they will run in. (Some lanes are slightly easier to run in than others. The coach has decided, for this test, such small differences won't be unfair.)

For those of you concerned with validity, you should be able to see how the coach has provided content, face, and construct validity through the way she set up the test. In effect the coach is conducting the same test six times. The results (times for each runner) are shown in Figure 12.1 (p. 296).

The coach reasoned each race should be comparable with any other. So she decided to use a chi-square test to see if they were. She found the average time for each race (see Figure 12.2, p. 297). She also recorded the standard deviation, although she didn't feel it was required.

The coach suspected there might be something different about the first race each week. The variances (standard deviations) seemed large to her. Her reference book stated high school sophomores the age and gender of her students should run one hundred yards in about 16.5 seconds. She adopted this number as the expected time in Figure 12.3 (p. 297).

It was obvious to her that the result (the sum of the numbers in the final column) was not significant. (The total would have to have been more than 20.5 to be significant.) Therefore each running of the race was not different from any other. The test was reliable.

Remember, if a test is reliable, it has predictive validity, but it isn't necessarily valid in other ways. Because our coach's test was valid in all ways and also reliable, she should be delighted.

FIGURE 12.1. STUDENT TIMES IN ONE HUNDRED–YARD DASH.

Race	Student	Time
1.	1. Week One	15.6
	2.	14.9
	3.	17.0
	4.	18.2
	5.	16.3
	<u>6.</u>	<u>16.4</u>
2.	7.	16.2
	8.	16.2
	9.	16.6
	10.	18.5
	11.	15.8
	<u>12.</u>	<u>16.4</u>
3.	13.	16.8
	14.	16.0
	15.	16.4
	16.	15.7
	17.	15.9
	<u>18.</u>	<u>16.7</u>
4.	1. Week Two	15.8
	2.	16.1
	3.	16.7
	4.	17.0
	5.	16.4
	6.	18.0
	<u>7.</u>	<u>19.3</u>
5.	8.	15.9
	9.	16.5
	10.	16.3
	11.	16.3
	12.	17.1
	13.	16.8
	<u>14.</u>	<u>16.2</u>
6.	15.	16.3
	16.	15.1
	17.	16.6
	18.	15.6
	19.	16.2
	20.	15.9
	21.	16.8
	<u>22.</u>	<u>16.3</u>

FIGURE 12.2. AVERAGE TIMES FOR ONE HUNDRED–YARD DASH.

	R1	R2	R3	R4	R5	R6
Average	16.4	16.6	16.3	17.0	16.4	16.1
s.d.	1.1	1.0	0.5	1.2	0.4	0.6

FIGURE 12.3. CHI-SQUARE ANALYSIS OF STUDENT TIMES.

Expected	Race Avg.	Dif	Dif^2	Dif^2/Expected
16.5	16.4	0.1	0.01	0.00
16.5	16.6	0.1	0.01	0.00
16.5	16.3	0.2	0.04	0.00
16.5	17.0	0.5	0.25	0.02
16.5	16.4	0.1	0.01	0.00
16.5	16.1	0.04	0.16	0.01
				0.03

The statistical treatment the coach used is called the *Chi-Square Goodness of Fit Test*. It's often used to describe the reliability of a test. You will find a detailed description of how to apply it in Hale and Westgaard (1984). By the way, the coach could use the same treatment to discover which students were significantly slower or faster than the others.

Most tests are presented in print form. Most test makers won't be able to run a test six times to see if it's reliable. However, you can use the same technique for any test even if you only have two sets of scores. The more replications you have, the more certain you can be. However, you can obtain good information from two applications. The challenge is deciding what the expected score should be. If you have a cut-score, you can use it as the expected score. If you think about it, that's exactly what a cut-score is.

Reliability is usually only demonstrated when a test is used more than once. If you won't be using a test more than once, or if you can't justify a reliability study, you can rely on predictive validity. For most of your tests, you probably won't establish either predictive validity or reliability. They take time and resources. Don't worry. If you have used good formative and summative evaluation techniques, you are still in good shape.

Formative Evaluation

Formative evaluation is a fancy way of saying you check as you go along to make sure

<table>
<tr><td>

formative evaluation

An in-process review.

</td><td>

everything is OK. I like to think of it as in-process evaluation. It's a review. Someone examines the materials to check for something or everything. Reviews usually come from: (1) your client, staff, or yourself; (2) experts or others who know the content or testing or both; or

</td></tr>
</table>

(3) potential respondents.

Client or Internal Reviews

Any time you contract to develop a test, whether for an internal client or not, you should make arrangements for reviews by the client. Let your client see your design. Ask him about preferences for formats and administration. And, most important, ask him to review the final draft. The client is paying for the test and has every right to see what's going on. Clients have a responsibility to assure themselves that what they want is what they're getting.

When you review your own material or ask members of your staff to do it, your primary goal should be to locate and correct mechanical and contextual errors. Is the grammar OK? How about the fog level? Will the format help respondents? You may also want to make sure all criteria were covered in the ways anticipated in the design. This sort of review is important. Without it, your test can be a disaster.

A word of caution you've heard before. When you correct your own work, you tend to see what you meant rather than what is really there. You might not see an error because, in your mind, you supply the missing elements. For example, you can easily forget, overlook, or skip by an article, a preposition, or even important terms. It happened in this sentence: "The best writers usually happens in fits and streaks." The author meant to say, "The best work of writers usually happens in fits and streaks." The author, in reviewing the sentence, automatically supplied the missing words *work of.* He was embarrassed when a colleague had to ask what was meant by the sentence.

Expert Reviews

Expert reviews are also important. How else can you make sure the content is represented correctly? How else can you establish content validity? If the test is critical in some way, you may want more than one expert to review it.

Remember this. You must tell expert reviewers what to look for and how you want them to report their findings. Often a test maker will ask a reviewer to look at a test without being specific. The expert will do so and report, "It looks good to me." That's almost as bad as not having it reviewed at all. Don't be shy. Ask the reviewer to supply specific answers to three important questions: Is the content represented correctly? Are the conventions used in formatting and presenting the test appropriate? Does this test test what it's meant to test?

To receive the best information, give the reviewer a step-by-step process for doing the review. Here is an example of instructions for reviewers:

1. Assemble your materials. You should have copies of all test materials, including introductory remarks and answer sheets. You should have something that tells you which answers the test maker thinks are correct.
2. Do a quick overview of the entire document (tape, program, and so forth). Note any elements of style or format that seem strange or difficult to work with. Sample the language. Does it seem straightforward and easy to understand?
3. Read each item twice. The first time, read as you might if you were taking the test. The second time, read as if you were reading it out loud to a respondent. Answer four kinds of questions:
   - Is the item representative of the content? Does it say what it should say in a way consistent with the conventions and nuances of the discipline?
   - Are all answers (on a multiple-choice test) plausible? Could they actually be true? Would a newcomer to the field be as likely to select one as any other? Are they independent or do any of them depend on one or more of the others? Do any alternatives represent two or more different ways of saying the same thing?
   - Will respondents be able to understand what is being asked easily?
   - Is the marked alternative the best answer? Could any of the others be better?
4. After you've examined the items, think of the test as a whole. Write down your impressions. In particular, think about how it will affect respondents, whether it will accomplish its mission, and if it's really appropriate.

If an expert reviews the test using this guide or one similar to it, your chances of receiving a useful critique are very good. Otherwise, you may or may not get what you want.

By the way, you should use the guide yourself when you review a test. It has proven its value many times. It works well.

Respondent Reviews

These can be as important as the other reviews, particularly if your chosen respondents are test-wise. They can review materials in the same way, using the same instructions, but there is a specific process designed to obtain even more useful results from them. It's called a *developmental test*.

A developmental test is a specific formative evaluation technique. It provides three important pieces of information. First, it tells how well potential test takers get along with the materials. Second, it provides specific information about what you can do to make the test work better. Third, it gives you an opportunity to see how well a real respondent can do.

Follow these steps faithfully to secure the best results with a developmental test:

1. Pick respondent(s) who will do the work carefully. They must represent the average respondent. There is a temptation to select people you believe will do well on the test. Avoid doing so. Pick people who may or may not be competent in the skills tested.
2. Supply the respondent(s) with the materials (or a decent draft) they would receive if they were taking the test for real. Do *not* give them the version with the answers on it.
3. Ask respondents to take the test as if it were the real thing, with two important exceptions: if they have a problem understanding anything, they should stop and ask you to explain; and when they answer a question or select an alternative, they should explain, verbally, why they wrote or chose what they did. Tell them to write notes right on the test materials as they think of them.
4. Sit close to them. Have a notebook of some kind and, perhaps, a tape recorder to record their comments. Your job is to note everything, no matter how unimportant it may seem at the time.
5. Implement changes as soon as you can. Some can be made while the test is in progress. If, for example, a term is missing or incorrectly used, you can make changes on the materials the respondents are using.
6. When they have finished the test, interview the respondents. Find out if they thought it was a good fair test. If not, why not? Be careful not to intimidate them or dismiss comments that seem trivial or biased. Recording all of their comments encourages their self-expression. You can sort the comments out later.

This may seem obvious, but don't throw the respondents' materials away. Use them as guides in making your changes.

If the test is especially important, you may want to do this process more than once. It's particularly valuable to do so when the first developmental test results in major changes or a lot of changes. Do it again.

Summative Evaluation

The summative evaluation is the test's first use to determine whether respondents actually have the skills. Reaching that point with a test is what this book is mainly about. Keep the word *summative* in mind. A pilot is a summative evaluation opportunity. It should sum up or provide a summary of what the test is and how it performs. Using the same kind of logic, *a summative test of the test-making process is the pilot study.* It's when you bring in bona fide respondents to try the test out. It's a test of the finished product, a test of the test.

> **summative evaluation**
> A test of the finished product, a test of the test.

A pilot has several functions. One of those is to help make sure the test is reliable—that it will perform as intended whenever it's used. Reliability was discussed earlier in this chapter. When you conduct a pilot of a test and establish reliability, you have, in fact, conducted a summative evaluation of the test.

There are many ways to conduct pilots. Some of them resemble developmental tests with one or two respondents closely monitored by an administrator. Some of them are really reviews during which respondents comment on how well the items work. They can be reviews, tryouts, dress rehearsals, or whatever. The element that makes them summative is that they occur *after* the development process is complete.

Yes, revisions based on the pilot are appropriate, but they aren't the reason for the pilot. The pilot is a formal test run. It's the final check before the test is declared ready for use. Because of this it must be as close to a *normal* application of the test as possible.

However a test is ultimately going to be used, that is how the pilot should be run. If the test is to be self-administered and self-corrected, that is how the pilot should be treated. If the test is for large numbers of respondents in a secure environment, that is how the pilot should be administered.

The pilot study provides the opportunity to do two of the things discussed earlier in this chapter: item analysis and cut-score calculation. If the pilot is a close approximation of the test as it will be used in the future, much valuable information can be obtained. If it is not, these techniques won't be as valuable as they could be.

There is one other attribute of a pilot study that should not be overlooked. It's the best chance you will get to demonstrate how carefully the test was prepared. The report you write describing the results of the pilot may be the only real opportunity you will have to show your executives what the test can do and how good it is. The more management understands about the careful process of test development, the more time will be made available for developing good tests. Don't blow the opportunity through a less than optimal effort.

Audits

<table>
<tr><td>

audit
A way to determine the continuing impact a test has on the organization and on the individuals within it and outside it.

</td><td>

Audits are often confused with summative evaluation. An audit is different. It's an estimate of the *residual* effect of the test. It determines the continuing impact a test has on the organization and on the individuals within it and outside it.

For example, suppose a test is used to establish competence in a workforce. An audit would determine whether results are verified by people trying to do the work in the field. Are the people who passed the test really competent?

</td></tr>
</table>

Transfer

One of the stubborn problems faced by educators and instructors is the problem of transfer. Transfer is a concept that infers people who are educated or trained in a skill will be able to use that skill in an environment different from the classroom or place where it was acquired. Someone, for example, who learns how to boot up a computer in a training session should be able to do it again at his or her own workstation. The idea that he or she *should* be able to do it doesn't guarantee anything. In fact, for many people transfer is very difficult.

Athletes run into transfer problems continually. People who can execute a move or action in practice may not be able to do the same thing in a game or competition. That's why the basketball coach in a previous example had players practice free throws with other people shouting and raising a commotion. His purpose was to simulate a game situation, to provide a better environment to estimate transfer.

The dreaded *word problems* in elementary school mathematics classes are attempts to show children how to transfer math skills to real-life situations.

So what does transfer have to do with evaluation? A large part of the evaluation effort is predicated on discovering whether tested skills will transfer. Will respondents be able to use their skills on the job? That is the question, and it is important. It may be the single most important goal in summative evaluation. It certainly is to your clients. Their concern isn't so much whether people *can* do things but whether those people *will* do those things when their skills make a difference on the job.

Consider this example. A young man won the local spelling bee. He triumphed over three hundred competitors. Yet when he wrote a letter for admission to a college, his spelling was so poor the college rejected his application. There wasn't much transfer of his spelling skills from the test (spelling bee) to a real application.

Part of your job in developing and using tests is to check for transfer. Will respondents be able to use the skills they demonstrate on the test outside the test environment? How can you answer that question?

You can't guarantee such a thing. Too many variables influence human performance. But you do have a responsibility to try. The biggest obstacles to performance on the job have to do with the reward system in place. If people are not going to be rewarded for doing what they have shown they can do, they won't do it. It's frustrating, but it's true. Normally you can't do much about the reward system on the job. Nor can you prevent people from returning to old ways of doing things if those ways were satisfactory in the past.

What you can do is make sure the test tests performance skills. Think of testing in terms of performance. This is where it counts the most. People who have shown they can perform on a test are much more likely to use their skills on the job than those who haven't. Compare two doctors. One of them takes a test that asks him to name the kinds of scalpels used to perform heart surgery. The other is presented with a scalpel and asked to demonstrate how it would be used to make an incision. Which one is more likely to attempt and complete real surgery successfully? Which one do you want to operate on your heart?

My friend who won the spelling bee had memorized thousands of words. Yet when it came time to use those words, he was incompetent. The problem of transfer is illustrated clearly by his performance. The spelling bee was not the best kind of test to sample his ability to spell words correctly in narrative writing. Keep him in mind as you design and develop your tests. Don't allow your tests to project a false impression of respondents' ability to do what they are being tested for.

When you conduct a pilot study of a test, make sure it provides for transfer. Make sure the test you have developed will, as much as it can, forecast respondents' ability to perform on the job. My friend won one spelling bee. He could have won an education, a good job, and, perhaps, a much more satisfying life.

Summary

The emphasis of this chapter has been on five areas within which valuative decisions are made. Those five areas are validity, reliability, formative evaluation, summative evaluation, and audits.

Validity as discussed here has four aspects: content, face, construct, and predictive. All are important, but in most cases your emphasis will be on the first three: the content that was supposed to be tested actually was tested, respondents can accept the test and the way it's presented and respond to it with full confidence, and the test is presented in a way consistent with the mind-set and attitudes of the respondents.

Establishing reliability gives assurance the test will test the same kind of respondents in the same way. A reliable test can be used over and over again with confidence. The assumption is, of course, that it hasn't been compromised by inadequate test security.

Formative evaluation involves the reviews and developmental tests done while a test is still in development. When you ask someone to look at your test and give you an opinion, you ask for formative evaluation. It is evaluation that occurs while development is in process.

Summative evaluation occurs at the end. It sums up the aspects and values of the test in a formal way. It ensures reliability and provides an opportunity to establish cut-scores. The pilot test is often used for summative evaluation.

A performance audit is a downstream activity designed to determine whether people who passed a test are making use of the skills tested. Audits determine, ultimately, whether the skills tested are in use in the organization. The issue of transfer is best addressed through a formal audit. An audit can provide definitive evidence about whether transfer is happening. This by itself justifies the use of performance audits for almost any organization.

Remember, no effort to evaluate is worth much unless it can be shared with people who have a stake in the test. The people to whom you report should want to know how well your test delivered on its promises. The people who will implement changes based on the test results will require a solid foundation on which to base those changes. The people who must do in-depth analysis and development work based on the test results will want anything those results can provide. The respondents want to know how well they did on the test and what that means in several dimensions. A good report makes test results valuable.

There is much more to evaluation. It's something test makers must consider continually. It's a part of each of the fifteen steps because it's how you exercise your judgment about every part of a test and its development. If there is an aspect of testing in which you should develop considerable skill, this is it. A good test evaluator can be a treasured commodity for most organizations. Unfortunately, there aren't many of us around.

If you think about it, evaluation is continuous. We don't stop passing judgment once a set of test results has been interpreted. It's part of who we are and how we operate. Without test results, though, our judgment is often poorly supported. Consider testing as a continuous activity. If you do, a very nice outcome can be attained; you can foster continuous improvement. Today, with our rapidly moving society, continuous improvement is the goal of many organizations. They can't afford to stand still even for a day.

But improvement without guidelines can be counterproductive. If, for example, you expend resources to improve a process with low profit potential, you may not be able to improve other, more lucrative processes. Testing can help define the best place to spend the improvement dollar. It can point out areas in which the potential for improved performance (PIP) is greatest.

A critical part of continuous improvement and of any testing program, no matter how informal, is management. Test management is often done without much thought. As a result the organization can become liable and indulge in unethical practices. Chapter Thirteen provides some thinking about these concerns.

TEST MANAGEMENT: AN ETHICAL PROCESS

Y ou can plan a test well, design it brilliantly, keep your audience in mind, and write wonderful items for it. You can prepare people to take it. You can test it and critique it from every vantage point. But if it isn't managed well, it will fail. I guarantee it. The best test imaginable will be a bust if it's managed poorly.

Because of this, it makes sense to look at test management very carefully. In this chapter, we will find the answers to these questions:

1. What is test administration? What must be administered?
2. How do successful test administrators proceed?
3. What are the ethical implications for test administration?

Test Administration

> **test management**
> All the tasks and activities that take place before, during, and after a test.

As usual it make sense to define the terms first. The *test manager* covers all the tasks and activities that take place before, during, and after a test. The test manager's functions are to facilitate respondents' ability to do the best they can, to secure the information sought by the test maker, and to satisfy organizational requirements. The *test administrator* is responsible for the test event itself, that is, everything done immediately before, during, and after the test to make it a success. The test administrator who is present at the time the test is taken may or may not be the test manager.

Facilitate Respondents' Ability

This has to be the most critical requirement for test administration. This is what Step 13 is all about. The test is for the respondents. Therefore, the administrator must have them continually in mind. Do respondents have enough space? Are furniture and equipment appropriate and well-situated? Is lighting adequate? Are facilities available for breaks? Are respondents with special problems provided for? All these questions and more must be answered in the affirmative. In addition, the administrator must be sure the test is presented properly, instructions are understood, and respondents are given every opportunity to respond as intended by the test developer.

Secure Desired Information

There are myriad reasons for a test. Many different kinds and sorts of information can be sought. The administrator must know what information is sought and the conditions that will best secure that information. For example, a test may be designed to find out whether managers react quickly and well under pressure. Giving them the test in a quiet, restful facility doesn't make sense, but it happens. On the other hand, the test may be to discover whether respondents can develop innovative solutions to complex problems. Most people will do their best with this if they are neither interrupted nor distracted.

Satisfy Organizational Requirements

Remember the two basic reasons for testing:

1. To allow respondents to demonstrate their skills and abilities.
2. To gather information about respondents for an external agency.

The second reason is normally the one that drives the testing situation. Seldom do respondents demand to be tested for their own reasons. Usually an organization of some type supplies the reasons.

Graduate students are responding to a test when they defend their dissertations. The test is a requirement of the university. Students must pass it to be awarded the degree. This is an obvious example, but there are others just as important. Companies may have tests to qualify people for jobs. Instructors are acting for the organization when they prepare and administer tests. The organization requires them to do so.

You might say, "Wait a minute. I don't ask the organization for permission. I provide the test because I think it's appropriate." Right. But whether you tell anyone or not, you are acting for the organization. Otherwise, you have no grounds for testing other than the respondents' requests. When was the last time someone came up to you and asked for a test? It has probably happened, but I suspect it doesn't happen often.

Procedures

It is tempting to say the process is very similar to project management and to advise you to manage a testing situation as you would a project. But it is not, and you should not.

A test has no intrinsic value. Yes, successful respondents feel good about their success, but normally that isn't because of the test. It's because of what the test enables. Tests enable. In and of themselves, they have little, if any, value at all.

This fact prompts special kinds of administrative activities. Administering tests is different from administering almost anything else. To see why this is so, look at the six administrative concerns for testing. To administer a test (even the most trivial) you should

1. Identify organizational motivation.
2. Set the rules.
3. Provide an environment.
4. Support the test.
5. Support respondents.
6. Provide closure.

Identify Organizational Motivation

A test prompts organizational action. So, from the organization's viewpoint (and therefore the administrator's), a test is a beginning of something. It's a device that allows action to begin. A new hire passes a test to become qualified for a job. A group of workers takes a test to provide a baseline for their developmental activities. Students take tests to enable themselves to continue their studies. In most cases, the test guides future action. In and of itself a test has little or no value.

Test administrators must know about motivation to do their jobs adequately. Why does the organization want the test? What social, political, or economic good will it promote? These questions must be answered before the test is administered. Otherwise, the test will serve no useful purpose.

Sometimes motives are easy to identify. For example, consider a test to qualify a worker for a job. The organization would like to estimate the person's competence before allowing him or her to continue. It makes sense and is in the best interests of both the organization and the worker. Both discover whether the worker is able to do the job and, if not, what should be done to help him or her become competent.

Hold on. The organization might have a different motivation. What if it wants to exclude certain types of people? The organization's motive could be to deny older workers an opportunity to work in the organization. It could want to limit the number of women and minorities on the staff. Although these are unsavory motives, they could exist. Assuming the organization is simply trying to ensure competence might be a mistake.

Knowing what the organization wants allows the test administrator to further that motivation and, therefore, to maximize the benefit to respondents. Organizations (as I'm using the term) can be highly complex or relatively simple. They can be comprised of thousands of people or a single individual. Remember the test in which one boy dared the other to make a basketball shot? In that case, the organization presenting the test was the first child. He probably had three motives for presenting the challenge: (1) he wanted to show off, to emphasize the fact that he himself had just made the shot; (2) he wanted the other boy to miss to show his own superiority; and (3) he wanted to enjoy himself at the other boy's expense.

Suppose your job were to administer the young man's test. You would be responsible for maximizing the test's ability to provide what the testing organization wants it to test. How would you do it?

Now assume the first boy's basic motivation is to encourage his friend, to build the other boy's confidence. How would that change how you conducted the test? In the first case, you would make the test as difficult as you could. You might insist the second boy place his body in exactly the same spot, use the same motions, and shoot with the same hand in the same way the first boy did. Adding these and other restrictions could almost guarantee a miss. In the other situation, you could be more forgiving about distance, style, and release. The second boy's chance of success would be significantly enhanced.

As you can see, a change in the motivation of the testing organization can change the nature of the test without changing the test itself. Here is another example of how significant such a change can be.

Several years ago a client company told me about a problem they had. They had a policy that any employee who felt qualified for an opening within the company could apply for the job. Those with tenure were given an advantage over others who had less time with the company or were recent hires. The company's new data-processing center was to be located in a state with hard, bitter winters. Many of the longtime employees in that state worked outside in all kinds of weather. When they heard about the new center, they immediately applied for jobs they felt they could do (even though many of them would be taking large cuts in pay). The company wanted to keep the experienced people in their current positions for two reasons. First, the workers were highly competent. Their error rates were low, they interacted with customers well, and they were excellent "company people." Second, the company wanted to build a professional data-processing staff. They were afraid the long-term workers wouldn't fit in very well. They decided to ask all people applying for the new positions to take a competency test. How would you administer this test? Would your decisions about administration be the same as they would if the company wanted to use as many of its own people as possible, no matter where they came from?

Organizational motivation drives testing. Without it, there can be no real mandate to you or the respondents.

Ask yourself three questions about organizational motivation in administering the test. First, what is the organization's motivation? Second, do you agree that it is appropriate? Third, how can it best be satisfied? All three answers are important. All three will have fundamental effects on your test and on the results.

Organizational Motivation. The answer to the first question requires a bit of investigation on your part. Usually, well-placed questions to the right people will provide the answers. It's often as simple as asking your boss why the company wants the test to be given. He or she could say, "They're going to cut staff and want to retain the best people" or, "Scrap is way up, they want to know if it's due to incompetent performance on the line" or, "We've decided to implement a comprehensive development program. We want to know who wants development and what kind would return the most for our investment." Be careful to ask the right people. If you aren't sure, sample opinions from as many sources as are appropriate. There are times when this investigation requires time and effort. Don't be afraid to pursue it. A mistake can be costly to the organization, to the respondents, and to you personally.

For example, I heard of a trainer who was asked to develop and administer a test of competency for nursing supervisors in a large hospital. The trainer assumed the test was to discover the areas in which current supervisors wanted skill development so training could be provided to help them become better supervisors. Wrong. The hospital administrator actually wanted to identify people he could terminate or reduce in rank. Not knowing this, the trainer developed a test to discover gaps in supervisory skills. It was a good test and the trainer was able to make good recommendations based on the results. Unfortunately, the hospital administrator was *not* pleased. The trainer was the first to get the ax.

Appropriateness. The second question concerns ethical considerations. You must consider it yourself. If you don't agree with the organization's motivation, there are things you can do. It's an important discussion for testing—important enough to deserve its own section. We will leave it for now, but do not ignore it.

Satisfaction of Need. The answer to the third question is reflected in how you perform the other five administrative functions. Your administrative decisions should further the organization's motivation, that is, provide what they want.

Set the Rules

Despite what many think, the rules must be established each time a test is administered, even if the same test is given. Testing is like a game in some ways. If you don't have rules, it becomes dysfunctional. For example, when I was an undergraduate, I took a course called Theory of Equations. The course involved the use of models to develop and solve problems. The final exam for the course presented seven problems to be solved. I assumed the rules permitted me to look up equations in the textbook as I worked on the test. My classmate assumed the opposite. Whether I was correct in my assumption is a moot point. I used the textbook. He didn't. I passed the course easily; he didn't. My classmate was at a distinct disadvantage. The professor was remiss in thinking we knew the rules. (Even more distressing, when informed of the situation, he did not explain the rules or change the scores.)

The rules differ from test to test and from circumstance to circumstance. There is no complete and reliable set of rules. You must develop your own each time a test is administered. There are two basic reasons for this: the characteristics the respondents bring to the activity and the motivation of the organization. Suppose, for example, you have to administer a test to relatively unsophisticated people for a sensitive job (such as a security guard). Suppose, also, your organization is almost paranoid about the security of its facilities. Your rules will be strict, enforced, and unbending.

On the other hand, suppose you are testing potential members for a community chorus. Your sponsoring organization wants as many people as possible. The chorus members will pay their own expenses and dues. Your rules will be as lenient as you can make them, perhaps even to the extent that some relatively untalented singers will be allowed to join the group.

Every test situation requires its own rules. There are three arenas, however, in which rules must be made and enforced:

1. Attitude and comportment.
2. Interactions among respondents and between respondents and the test givers.
3. Test mechanics.

The hints below are for paper-and-pencil tests. They will require some modification for use with other media and/or environments.

Attitude and Comportment. The way people act and conduct their activities can affect whether a test is good and fair. If the test requires quiet concentration, a mumbler in the corner can ruin it for other respondents. You should consider what respondents will have to do to be successful on the test and make rules so that such an atmosphere can be established. This is fairly easy to do. I have three rules in this area that I almost always use:

1. No smoking, food, or beverages in the room where the test is being taken.
2. Acting out by talking or moving around the room is frowned on.
3. However, if people want to leave the room for any reason such as to use the rest room or to have a cigarette, it's OK.

The third rule gives people a chance to compare answers, and so forth. However, in my experience, very few try to do so. They're usually squelched by fellow respondents. This rule is difficult in a timed test, so you may not want to use it.

Respondent Interactions. Normally a test situation is set up so individuals work alone. This being the case, people must be discouraged from talking to one another or communicating in other ways. Not only are we concerned that they may compromise the test but also that such activity will distract others.

Students at universities have been known to go to great lengths to cheat on tests. They put crib notes on various parts of their bodies. They look at the work of others. They use special codes and gestures to communicate. It's amazing. Sometimes they work harder to cheat than they would to pass the test legitimately. When such activities become a disturbance to others, they must be stopped. Telling respondents in advance (making rules about it) will eliminate the problem in most situations.

Test Mechanics. Most tests require some special preparation or setup. This can be critical. If there are test booklets, ensure that they are complete. Provide enough booklets for everyone and maybe a spare or two. Is the test presented as you want it to be? There are many questions like these that should be answered before the test is given. More important, what are the rules? Normally, you must decide how respondents will behave while in the test situation.

- Instruct them about how to interact with test materials.
- Tell them how to register answers.
- Explain important parameters such as time available, use of references, and whether they can access the test givers or special equipment.
- If the test has physiological elements, consider safety precautions and critical parts of the test environment.
- Usually, you should make sure the elements of the test are equally available to all the respondents. Show them where the clock is, how to use the answer sheet, and other aspects of the test that are easy to overlook.

If you consider these precautions and expedients as part of your rule-making responsibility, it's much easier to make sure they are covered. Turn your assumptions into rules and you will be able to legitimatize them. More important, this will give respondents an opportunity to object if they see a rule (or assumption) as being ill-formed or unjustified.

Provide an Environment

This may be a given in some test situations. There are schools and other organizations with space or special facilities dedicated to testing. Even so, it's important for you to guarantee the adequacy of the environment personally. In essence, the environment has three basic aspects: space and ambience; air and light; and respondents and test givers.

Space and Ambience. The facility you use for a test is usually not specially designed for the function. It's a classroom, conference room, plant production area, or other space to be used one time for the test. The rest of the time it is dedicated to other purposes—classes, conferences, production, and so on.

Study the space before the test to make sure it will *add* to the goal: good test results. Respondents will want adequate work space. Make sure they have it. Remember the two soldiers who walked out because the desktops were so inadequate? Most respondents do not physically get up and leave. Many, though, will do so mentally and emotionally.

Give them enough room to think. Make enough space between test takers to provide a barrier. Most folks believe such a barrier is to prevent cheating. That may be so, but a more important reason is to ensure privacy. No respondent likes to feel as if someone else can see what he or she is doing with the test. It's a very private thing. Protect that privacy as much as you can. I recommend a minimum of six feet between respondents in every direction unless they are next to a wall.

Windows are problems. They distract respondents. They cause glare. Reflections and movement outside bother people subliminally. The perfect test site is a room without windows. If this isn't possible, find a way to cover them to reduce their effect.

Colors and textures can also be problems. Bright shiny surfaces are awful. So are dark or brilliant colors like red, orange, dark or royal blue, black, or dark green. Try for neutral shades and textures that are comfortable to the point that they aren't noticed. Chalkboards in a room are OK. Respondents are used to seeing them in similar environments. If they seem to glare, write something on them and erase it. The chalk powder will soften the effect of the surface. Many rooms now have whiteboards that can be written on with colored markers. They can dominate the room. Write instructions on them to break up the expanse of the board.

The floor can also be a problem. Testing environments should be quiet places where people can concentrate. A hard tile will echo with footsteps of even a careful movement. A carpet with a subdued pattern is preferred. If you have to work with tile floors, you can alleviate the problem by mentioning it before the respondents begin. A colleague has a set of carpeted runners she unrolls in the aisles to keep the noise down.

Furniture is critical. Chairs should be ergonomic when possible. If not, make sure they provide good support and don't cause bad posture. If you have a choice between a seat that's too soft and one that's too hard, pick the hard one. Both are bad, but too soft causes back strain that can totally wipe out a respondent. Now picture the work surface. Ideally it should be about three feet long and two feet wide. It should be nonglare and of a color and texture that support the work to be done. It should, in most cases, be flat. If the test has special equipment or materials, make sure the work space can support them comfortably. If the test requires drafting, give the respondents drafting tables.

Find out if any respondents have special needs such as a wheelchair or special equipment well beforehand.

Air and Light. I heard a story, maybe true, maybe not, that illustrates the importance of good air. A test proctor was determined to make the test environment as quiet as possible. He sealed the windows and hung drapes over them. He made sure the doors to the room were close fitting. He was alarmed at the amount of white noise generated by the air conditioner so he shut it off. The test lasted two hours. By the end of that time, fully half of the respondents were barely awake and three had actually passed out. The quality of the air in the room can't be overstressed. Good air leads to good thinking. Good thinking is what we want most. So make sure the air in the room is good, that it flows through the room at a uniform comfortable rate, and that it leaves the room clean and fresh smelling. A certain amount of white noise is acceptable (up to forty decibels). Psychologists will tell you some white noise is beneficial. Too much quiet is too much of a good thing. So if the air conditioner makes a bit of noise, don't be concerned.

Engineers can tell you how much light you should have in your room. There are rules of thumb, but perhaps the best way to judge is to try it out yourself. Assemble the materials on a work surface in the room and work with them for ten or fifteen minutes. Check yourself. Are you squinting (even a little)? Are you holding your head in a particular position? Is glare coming at you from the surface, from the walls, from the windows? Find out before the test begins. It doesn't take much of your time, and the returns for the respondents will justify the effort.

While I was in graduate school, a fellow student and I conducted an informal test. We set up a room for a test as well as we could. Then we asked three groups of people who were of about the same ability to take a simple multiple-choice test in the room. For Group A we used the normal amount of light, the lighting the designer had recommended for the room. For Group B we cut the amount of light in half. For Group C we doubled it. Neither Groups B nor C did very well on the test. They scored significantly lower than Group A did. Lighting does make a difference. If you want good test results, make sure the lighting is adequate and appropriate.

Respondents and Test Givers. The people in the room are a critical part of the environment. Any one of them can make a big difference for the others. For example, suppose you have a person who coughs almost constantly during the test. That person will adversely affect all the others. The same is true of a gum chewer, a foot tapper, or others with similar distracting habits.

Remove them. Perhaps it seems heartless or an imposition, but these people are adversely affecting the ability of others to do their best. Ask them to stop doing what they are doing. Put them in a different room. Ask them to come back when they're feeling better. The important thing is to act without delay. As soon as you feel the distraction will continue, take some kind of action to stop it. Of course, you should be diplomatic about it, but solve the problem before it can become destructive.

I once had a student who, unfortunately, began to sweat when confronted by a test. He was a good student, bright, and a really nice person. But he perspired, and the perspiration smelled bad. What to do? I arranged for him to take his tests in my office alone. When the others were taking the test, he acted as a proctor (something he wasn't nervous about). After a month or two, he was able to take tests without so much fear, so I was able to allow him to take tests with the others. Later he told me he was grateful. He had known he had the problem but, for him, knowing just made it worse. I love stories with happy endings.

One of the most destructive influences in many test situations is generated by test givers. They can be officious, authoritarian, bored, or simply not tuned in to the test. Or they can be supportive and reliable. Look at yourself. Look at the goal, which is good results. Will your actions and demeanor contribute to the goal? There are three little rules of thumb that will help you be a good test giver:

1. Make your appearance appropriate in the eyes of the respondents. Dress well but not ostentatiously. Be pleasant, but make sure you don't appear to favor any one person over any other.
2. Provide good guidance. Articulate the rules so all will understand. Give complete instructions, and do it in such a way that the respondents know they are beneficial.
3. Handle problems quickly and fairly.

Support the Test

Too many times test makers and givers are full of doubt. They worry. Will the test provide the information sought? Will respondents react well? Will my boss like the outcomes? Such questions cause anxiety. Anxiety leads to doubt, and doubt is easy to communicate. Your bearing and language can say, in essence, to the respondents, "I'm not sure this is a good idea, but do it anyway. Maybe things will be OK." Not a good way to put respondents in the best mood.

Imagine you are the publicity agent for a product that will fail if it receives bad press. You know that people won't buy it if they think it's defective. Often the only person they can trust to give them assurance is you. Your boss doesn't know enough about it or what its impact will be. The test developers may know, but they will have difficulty convincing the respondents because they are vested in the test's success. Of course, the test administrator has a vested interest in the test's success, too, but in a different way. You are looking for results. The test developers are looking for evidence that the test worked as it should. Although these viewpoints are closely allied, they aren't the same. You don't care if the test is a good test, or you don't care as long as the results are OK. The test developers do. In fact, many of them will celebrate if the test proves to be good and fair even if the respondents produce poor or incomplete results.

Let me see if I can illustrate the point. Suppose you are to administer a test to discover if a certain group of workers is competent. The test is performance-based. It appears to be valid in every way. The test developers have spent long hours and a lot of effort to produce the best test they can. Now suppose a union steward calls the work group together before the test is administered and tells them, "This thing has been carefully put together to make you guys look bad so management can make some points in contract negotiations next month." If the work group believes the steward, the results are going to be crummy. The test may prove itself to be both good and fair, but you won't be able to trust the results.

This isn't an isolated case, nor is it rare. There are often people who can profit by a test's failure. They may try to negate the power of the results. This is particularly true when the test can establish credibility for successful respondents. The oral examinations conducted in graduate schools have this kind of power. So do final exams for courses of study. There are many examples.

Consider a certification exam for a group of professionals. The test was developed by an association. A rival association knows it will lose credibility and members if the test is accepted by professionals as a valid instrument. What will the rival association do? They will do whatever they can to downplay the test's importance or impugn its results.

Or take a more common example, a survey of attitudes about a political candidate. You can imagine what the candidate's opponent(s) will try to do if he or she is shown to be strong by the survey. You don't have to imagine it; you've read about it in the paper.

Without strong support, any test (whether it is good and fair or not) can fail. The support that counts the most comes from the test manager, you. Once you're convinced of its importance, support is not difficult to provide. This is particularly true if your test is good and fair. The first step is to know as much about the test as you can: its content, the kinds and types of items, how long it will take, the target audience, and so on. Second, identify the people who will benefit most. These people usually fall into three categories: management, the respondents, and the test developers. Third, discover who, if anyone, could be adversely affected if the test succeeds. Fourth, communicate with these vested interests forthrightly and as comprehensively as you can. Tell everyone who is interested what the test is, why it's wanted, and who it will benefit. Finally, make sure the test is administered well.

Support Respondents

Almost everything in this book is predicated on successful respondents. These are the people who benefit most *and* who have the greatest impact on the success of a test and, consequently, on your success.

The people who take the test are, for that moment, the most important people in your work. They have to succeed for you to succeed. There is a tendency, when things go wrong, to blame the respondents. That's wrong. They may blame you, but you can't blame them. After all, you are offering them a service. They are the customers, and the customer is always right.

Support them. Don't defer to them, but be sure that what they legitimately want is available. The best way to do this is to provide them with a good fair test.

Provide Closure

When I was inducted into the Army, the recruits were herded into a large room and given a battery of tests. When the long session was over, the clerks picked up the last sets of answer sheets, checked to make sure they had them all, and departed. They didn't even wave good-bye. My fellow recruits and I were left to stew in our own juices. Not only did we not have any idea of how well we did, but we didn't know when (if ever) we would find out.

The report you write (Chapter Ten) will bring closure for one set of vested parties: management (or your clients). That leaves two other groups: the respondents and the test developers. Closure for respondents involves two actions:

- Disclose the results.
- Discuss implications.

Disclose Results. Whenever possible tell the respondents how well they did as soon as they have completed the test. When you make a test self-scoring, the respondents know immediately how well they scored. If that can't be done, perhaps you can score the test before they leave the room. The old expedient of elementary school teachers, "OK, everyone, change papers," works. Respondents learn, usually from someone they trust, how well they did. Of course, you hear nasty stories about the practice, but usually it's OK.

If you can't give respondents an immediate reading of their accomplishments, give them a time and process for it to happen. Make sure you follow through as expected. Respondents have been known to become violent when they don't find out how well they did. Even worse is when they are promised results and it doesn't happen. Some professors are notorious for not returning papers or tests on time. They are among the most detested people on campus.

Discuss Implications. As soon as respondents receive the results, they will want to know what those results mean. "OK," they say, "where do I go from here?" Tell them. Be very precise and comprehensive, particularly for those who have failed. You can stop apprehension and panic dead if you can help them to understand fully what a failure means and how to work around it. Maybe they can take the test again sometime in the future. Maybe there is remedial work they can do to acquire the needed skills. Maybe there is an alternative path to the one they've chosen. Whatever the expedient may be, don't leave it to them to find out. Provide as much reliable information as you can.

Be specific. Simply saying, "Don't worry about it," (my favorite escape) doesn't work. In fact, it can make things worse. So, as distasteful as it sometimes is, level with the respondents. They took the test. Now, they want to know what it means to them as human beings.

A young man I heard about desired very much to go to Harvard. He failed the entrance exam. The test proctor took him aside and very carefully outlined the alternatives: he could go to a prep school, he could attend a different college (several were named), he could decide it wasn't worth the effort (quit), he could appeal to the dean, or he could try again in a different specialization. The young man decided to try the prep school route. He did well, subsequently gained admission, and is now a very successful professional.

The proctors at many well-known colleges and universities are trained to do these things. One outcome is an unimpeachable reputation for the institution. Another is loyal support from applicants *whether they succeed or not.*

Learn from those proctors. Taking the time and effort to provide counsel to test takers who do poorly can pay big dividends for you and your organization.

Ethical Issues in Test Management

Testing and ethical conduct are closely tied. As a person who provides a good fair test, you are acting ethically. Think about it. By providing a test, you give respondents an opportunity to demonstrate something about themselves. You allow them to make a statement about themselves, which you then honor as they wish. Whether respondents do well or not, you treat them with respect and dignity. You must do so to maintain the integrity of the test. Testing is an ethical thing to do. Take pride in it if you do it well.

The first three chapters of this book could be called "Ethical Considerations in Organizational Settings." I like to think of them as mostly positive. The concepts discussed in those chapters and, for that matter, all through the book are predicated by good ethical thinking and conduct. The precepts and constructs found there can easily be extended to many situations and environments. They aren't reserved to testing.

If you develop and administer tests conscientiously, you are probably an ethical person. Of course, you could be a Jekyll and Hyde type, ethical in the testing situation and otherwise elsewhere. But that doesn't happen often. People I know who are dedicated to the development and use of good fair tests are people I can trust. Similarly, the people who take their tests know they are being treated with dignity and respect.

Tests are good things and people who use them (for the most part) are good people. There are exceptions, though. Although it's distasteful, I feel I must alert you to four of the worst types of unethical behavior.

Most unethical uses of tests are administrative. An administrator can use a test as a *hammer to bring people into line or to establish who's in charge*. Tests can be used *to punish*. They can be used *to frighten respondents*. And they have been used to *brand respondents* one way or another. These activities are unethical. People who do them on purpose should be banished to some cold, lonely place.

Tests as Hammers

Consider the recruits in a military unit. They are tested frequently. Not long ago almost all tests conducted in military training facilities were hammers. Their primary benefits were to bring recruits into line, give them discipline. Whether the new people learned battle tactics or developed skill in using weapons was a secondary consideration. The important thing was to establish unquestioned obedience. Tests were used to hammer recruits into well-honed instruments of war. Perhaps the military is justified in using tests this way, but what about fifth-grade teachers? Are they justified in doing the same thing? They do it. It has probably happened to you personally. For example, teachers have highly structured spelling bees. Ever been in one? Ever know the humiliation the teacher (and your peers) can administer for putting *i* before *e* in the wrong word? Spelling bees are hammers. The ethics of using them are questionable at best.

Perhaps the best example of tests as hammers are tests based primarily on Level One Cognitive, direct recall. People of all ages in all kinds of situations find themselves pounded into memorizing trivia. They are taught to conform. Tests of this type are neither good (they don't sample worthy performance) nor fair (respondents who can memorize easily have an advantage). But such tests are very common in school, on the job, and elsewhere. Recently I was asked to review a test for construction workers. It was almost totally devoted to recall of various tools and procedural steps. Respondents' ability to do the work had little, if anything, to do with success on the test. The test I took to become a wrestling official was composed of hundreds of true/false questions. It was a hammer.

So what does this have to do with ethics? Well, if test developers and administrators are totally ignorant of the impact such tests have on respondents, nothing.

However, I have trouble assuming they (particularly administrators) are that ignorant. They have taken this kind of test themselves. They know the effect such tests have on respondents. In short, they know what they are doing to respondents. At best they are unethical.

Tests as Punishment

I discussed this earlier in Chapter Two without calling it unethical. But what would you call it? To use tests as punishment delivers a double whammy. The respondents are punished, *and* they learn to dislike tests in general. The traditional "pop quiz" is prototypical of punishing tests. Pop quizzes are used to punish students who don't do their homework. They're used to teach kids to be quiet in class (punish unruly pupils). Outside school, these tests are used to put workers "in their place," to punish them for being ambitious or for challenging the authority of a manager. These are abuses. They are unethical when condoned by a knowing test administrator.

Tests That Frighten

Many tests are used to frighten respondents. The threat of a test by a domineering teacher can petrify students. But even more detestable is the practice of interest groups casting a test as a threat to turn respondents against the sponsors of the test. Many organizations have developed tests to qualify workers for specified jobs. Typically, unions point to the practice as a ploy to give the organization an excuse to fire the workers or treat them prejudicially. Perhaps they are justified, but for them to do so without even looking at the test begs the question. If they want to attack organizational practices, they have every right to do so, but basing an attack on the evil implications associated (by them) with a test is not justifiable. They get away with it because they have been able to personify the test, anthropomorphize it, as being an agent of "wicked management." The whole scenario would be laughable if it weren't so successful.

Why can tests be used as a threat? Because that's what they are in the minds of most respondents. We're all afraid of tests. We have been imposed on, belittled, castigated, and branded by test administrators who have managed to make tests the villains. It's ludicrous but it's true. You and I have learned to distrust tests because test administrators have used them to bully and belittle us. Think about it. It's like people being afraid of a whip. Yet the whip doesn't punish; the person using it does. Is that unethical? You bet.

Tests as Branding Irons

On the ranches in the West, calves are rounded up each year and branded to show their ownership. Cowboys (ranch workers) heat iron implements with the owner's brand on them until they are red hot. Then they press the hot branding irons against the hide of a calf. It burns the brand indelibly into the hide. It's a bit painful for the calf, but it's very important. The animal is forever marked as the property of a particular ranch.

Tests are used as branding irons for people. For example, consider the *intelligence* tests given children in elementary school. If kids score well, they are considered "above average" for the rest of their lives, and vice versa. The results will follow them forever. It's very much like using the cowboys' branding iron. Is that fair? Is it ethical?

I know a young woman who took a typing test in the personnel department of a large company. She was verbally abused by the test administrator and, subsequently, did rather poorly on the test. Ten years later, she was denied a promotion to a management position in the same company. Why? It was on record that she could not type well. In spite of the fact that she had carried out her duties very well for ten years, she was forced to leave the company to advance her career.

People leave document trails wherever they go. They earn reputations. Sometimes what is in those archives is valid and valuable, sometimes not. The efficacy and ethics of such practices aren't being discussed here. The focus is on the agent of branding. Branding irons don't brand cattle. Cowboys do. Tests don't brand people either. Test administrators and developers do. You are the one responsible. You and I are the ones who do it. That is why it is a question of ethics.

Allow me to end this short discussion by saying that *testing is always an ethical issue.* Whether the tests we administer are relatively unimportant to respondents or have immense consequences, you and I are the ones who must consider the ethics of their use. Many times we are the only ones who will.

Summary

This final chapter investigated three basic aspects of test management: (1) what it is; (2) how successful test managers proceed; and (3) some of the ethical implications of test management.

Perhaps it's fitting that the final chapter in this book should be about managing the test. Ultimately, the success or failure of a test depends on how it is managed. If the test itself is good and fair, you have a fairly clear path. If it isn't, you must do all you can to make it so.

Of course, you shall have the credit for success. A test is a tool. It can be used well or poorly. Used well it can bring benefits to all concerned. The test developer and manager, in particular, have a great deal to gain. Do the testing well. You won't regret it.

A Final Comment

You may have sensed my joy in writing this book. I like tests. I think they are good things—tools that can serve all of us well. There are several reasons for my feelings. Testing is important to all of us. Doing it well can bring health and vigor to organizations and their people. Knowing tests can and should be good and fair can profit all of us.

APPENDIX

GLOSSARY OF TESTING TERMS

Although the definitions that follow are not definitive, they may be helpful. You can use them to jog your memory about a term or to remember what it means.

Achievement Test. This term confuses many people. It was coined years ago to describe tests given in elementary schools to determine whether children had *achieved* educational goals set by teachers. Normally, achievement tests are still associated with schools.

Affective. One of three psychological domains. (See *domain.*)

All of the Above. A commonly used alternative in multiple-choice items. It provides the test maker with the opportunity to cause respondents to consider all other alternatives as a group. It represents poor practice, in that, if it's the proper choice, respondents need only find two alternatives that are correct to justify using it. If it isn't correct, they need only find one incorrect response to know they should avoid it.

Often this sort of alternative tests a respondent's ability to take tests more than it tests his or her skills in the content.

Use of devices such as *all of the above, none of the above, A and B,* and so forth indicates either that the test maker cannot decide which of a series of correct answers is best or he or she is having trouble writing a fourth or fifth response that works for the item.

Appraise. To test formally. Usually, the term is reserved for measuring the adequacy of a job performance. It's also used to designate the worth of something. Houses, jewelry, automobiles, and so forth are appraised by experts to determine their market value.

Assess. The verb *to assess* is, to an extent, synonymous with *to test*. However, an assessment is always a formal test, the fourth type (see *tests and testing*). The term implies that some sort of measurement has already taken place. Assessment is developing information about a measurement.

Cognitive. One of three psychological domains. (See *domain.*)

Conditions. The environmental aspects of a test. They tend to limit it or the respondents. They are often stated as *givens* in a behavioral (or performance) objective.

Criteria. In this context, criteria are the standards against which responses are compared. They provide the basis for measurement.

Criterion Referenced. This is essential to performance testing. The criteria for any performance are the basis for measuring whether or not the performance has occurred, whether the criteria have been met. Criterion referenced is the alternative to norm referenced (see *norm referenced*).

Cuing. Cues are clues that signal responses. They can be found in use of language, breaks in patterns, or previously asked questions or answers. Good item writers are careful to restrict cuing as much as they can because it damages an item's ability to discriminate as it should.

Cut-Scores. These are predetermined scores used to determine whether a respondent passes. Controversy often occurs because some people may feel a cut-score is too high or too low. However, cut-scores can be set so they are legitimate and fair.

Diagnosis. Diagnosis in measurement is much like diagnosis in medicine. The idea is to determine what learners already know and can do before instruction is attempted. One can take the parallel further and say it's the process used to determine what a learner has yet to learn.

Dichotomous Items. Dichotomous items (such as true/false items) are usually statements the respondents are supposed to classify as one thing or another. The guess factor (50 percent), their tendency to be Level One, and the ambiguity of such items make them a poor choice for most tests.

Difficulty. Refers to the percentage of people who fail to answer an item correctly. Its principal value is in item analysis.

Discrimination. The ability of an item to distinguish between respondents who are competent and those who aren't. Discrimination is an important element of item analysis.

Distractors. Alternatives. Some test makers call all the alternatives distractors, but most use the term to indicate incorrect responses.

Domain. The domains referred to in connection with testing are the three psychological domains:

1. *Cognitive* has to do with thinking and mental imaging. The mind is in control.
2. *Affective* has to do with emotions, values, and attitudes. It is concerned with feelings and values. Judgment and mental manipulation are *not* part of the affective domain.
3. *Psychomotor* concerns are physical. The term means consciously directed movement. Physical work, play, and manipulation are psychomotor activities.

Effective. A test is effective if it's easy to use and if it's a valid measure of the performances targeted.

Efficient. A test is efficient if it deals with people in a fair way psychologically. People are treated as they expect to be treated (that is, in a way that tends to enhance their self-images).

Equivalent Test Forms. These are used when it becomes advisable to provide the same test in two or more forms (to prevent respondents from copying others). Equivalent forms are the result of a process designed to generate more than one test that tests the same thing in the same way without using the same items in the same order. They are most common in certification tests or nationally administered tests.

Essay Item. An essay item requires respondents to supply an answer complete with explanation and rationale. The answers vary in length but are seldom less than a page.

Evaluation. Involves judgment. Someone takes the responsibility to judge the adequacy of whatever is being examined. Usually, such judgments happen as normal events during the course of a day. People attach values to the things they perceive. Whenever such values are rendered as opinions or ideas, evaluation has taken place. We evaluate whether an automobile fits our needs. We evaluate the effectiveness of a play in a football game. But we don't usually call such activities *evaluation.*

Most of us think of evaluation as making a decision about adequacy. And, usually, we are considering someone else when we do so. We evaluate the competence of a worker. We evaluate the success of a learner in achieving training objectives.

The most common usage of the term *evaluation* is in deciding whether the results of a test are appropriate and, if so, how well test takers scored.

Fill-In Item. These items are *not* recommended. A fill-in (sometimes called *completion*) is an item on which the respondents fill in the blanks. It's usually a recall item that tends to punish respondents for areas not being tested, such as bad spelling or grammar.

Frequency Distribution. Scores are often recorded so that an evaluator can see the pattern they exhibit. Usually scores fall into a pattern resembling the normal curve. This is called a normal distribution of scores.

Good Fair Tests. A good test is one that meets expectations of both the test maker and respondents. A fair test is one that allows respondents to display their skills in the best way they can. No tricks. No surprises.

Halo Effect. Term prompted by the Hawthorne studies during the 1950s. People are sometimes influenced in their thinking and/or in decision making by stimuli not necessarily associated with the task at hand. For example, if a test proctor is upbeat, smiling, and helpful to respondents, respondents may score better on the test than if the proctor is dull or abusive.

Hard Skills. These have physical components. Objects or body parts must be manipulated in some way. (See *skills*.)

Incomplete Statement. An item stem that ends in a colon. For example, "The color most closely associated with the Irish is:"

Inventory. An inventory is used to sample opinions and attitudes.

Item Analysis. The process used to assess the validity and usefulness of individual items on a test. It usually consists of an investigation to discover:

- *How well the item discriminates.* People who do not pass should have answered it incorrectly; those who pass should have answered it correctly.
- *How difficult the item is.* The percentage of respondents who had it wrong.

- *Alternative plausibility.* If all distractors (incorrect responses) are plausible, each should be chosen by some respondents.
- *Grammatical and construction errors.*

Item Independence. The characteristic that allows an item to stand alone. Individual items (usually) should not depend on others in any way. Neither should they be cued by other items.

Item Types. There are seven commonly used item types. Each has strengths and weaknesses. They are:

- Essay.
- Short answer.
- Fill-in.
- Dichotomous.
- Multiple choice.
- Matching.
- Rank order.

Kirkpatrick's Levels. These four levels (Kirkpatrick, 1994) differentiate and describe opportunities to measure:

- *Level One:* Measures acceptance; do learners appreciate the learning opportunity?
- *Level Two:* Measures accomplishment; did the learners learn as expected?
- *Level Three:* Measures application; do the learners apply what they learned to the job?
- *Level Four:* Measures impact; did the learning positively affect the organization and/or society?

(*Note:* These levels are not the same as those mentioned in this book, although they are closely related.)

Level. Indicates (in this book) how complex a skill may be. Complexity does *not* connote difficulty. It does refer to the mental, emotional, and physical definition of a skill.

The three levels referred to in this discussion are derived from Bloom's Taxonomy. Level One combines learning based on use of memory, recall, comparison, and so forth. Level Two concentrates on application, use of a concept or skill in solving a problem or performing an action in any of the three domains. Level Three is developmental or creative. It requires discovery or exploration outside a previously defined context.

Mastery. Implies the respondent achieved the desired cut-score. The *90/90 standard* is a mastery term. It states, "Ninety percent or more of the qualified learners were able to achieve 90 percent or better on a criterion-referenced test." The implication is that all qualified respondents pass easily.

Matching Item. A form of the multiple-choice format in which the stem is replaced by a series of stimulators. The given alternatives may then all be applicable to each stimulator. (Normally, once an alternative has been chosen, it is no longer available.)

Measured Results. See *results.*

Multiple-Choice Item. These contain a stem that describes a situation or asks a question, followed by three or more alternative answers from which the respondent is to select his or her choice.

90/90 Standard. See *mastery.*

None of the Above. A commonly used alternative in multiple-choice items used to force respondents to think outside the realm of the choices given. The device is not as objectionable as *all of the above,* but it does present both test makers and respondents with problems not related to the test. Its use is *not* recommended.

Norm Referenced. A norm-referenced test is scored by grading on the curve. Respondent results are compared with others in the group (or a standard group). The comparison is usually made through some representation of the normal curve of expectations. Grades (A, B, C, D, or F) are a common way to express results of the comparison.

Objective Test. Term often associated with tests composed of selection items such as multiple choice where the respondents select answers from those given.

Opinionnaires. See *inventory.*

Performance. A performance is defined by conditions, activity, and criteria. It can take place in any domain or simultaneously in all three. Simplistically, *to perform* is to do something.

Psychomotor. One of three psychological domains. (See *domain.*)

Question. The preferred method for presenting a problem in an item stem. Questions put respondents in the seeking mode. They automatically begin to search for an answer. In a multiple-choice item, the alternatives are more easily separated (mentally) if they are preceded by a question.

Rank-Order Item. This item presents respondents with a list and asks them to put the list in some order. It's useful when testing ability to prioritize tasks or correctly align tasks in a process.

Reliability. For a test, reliability implies that it will perform as expected each time it is used (given comparable respondents and circumstances).

Replication. This is an important aspect of reliability studies. To be replicable, a test must be capable of being repeated with comparable respondents in a similar environment without loss of validity.

Results. The answers and other responses to a test. In a criterion-referenced test they must be measurable, giving rise to the expression *measured results.*

Scales. Some multiple-choice items have the choices arranged in the form of a scale such as "important, somewhat important, may or may not be important, somewhat unimportant, unimportant." This device can be very useful on inventories and opinionnaires because it lends itself to powerful statistical treatments.

Scoring. The act of attaching a label to the results of a test to indicate whether the respondents have achieved what the test maker intended. Scoring is usually based on mastery or is norm referenced. (See *mastery* and *norm referenced.*)

Short-Answer Item. Open questions that, in general, require respondents to supply a single concept, notion, or opinion. Adequate responses may have a single-word answer or may continue for several pages. The usual response length is a single paragraph of two or three sentences. This type of item works well in the psychomotor domain when a respondent is asked to perform a single task.

Skills. These can be in any of the three domains. The assumption is that people develop thinking, feeling, and physical skills. Often a skill is an intimate combination of all three domains. Ergo, a golf swing combines the physical swinging of the club, the mental estimates of its adherence to a known model, and the feelings about its *goodness.*

Soft skills include:

- *Communication techniques,* both oral and written.
- *Interaction activities,* such as meetings, confrontations, and agreements.
- *Thought algorithms and paradigms.*
- *Aesthetic skills and judgment.*

Hard skills include:

- *Procedures and processes* that are rigidly defined, whether mental or physical.
- *Psychomotor skills* of all kinds.
- *Visual, auditory (sensory) discrimination skills,* such as those of a wine taster or meat cutter.

Soft Skills. Skills that do not have physical components. Thinking and feeling. (See *skills.*)

Specific Determiners. Cues that may tip the respondents off to the correct answer. Words such as *all* or *none* are examples. Alternatives containing such terms are almost invariably incorrect.

Stem. The part of an item that asks the question or presents the problem to be solved.

Tests and Testing. A test is a deliberate attempt to acquire information about oneself or others. Basically there are four kinds of tests for people:

1. *Informal, self-imposed tests.* These are usually thought of as exercises of will. Among them might be a choice to start and stay on a diet. We test ourselves often—sometimes frivolously, sometimes with serious intent.
2. *Informal tests of others.* These tests are often used to bait or encourage someone to do something—dares. In some military contexts, these are tests of character or courage. You can see this often on playgrounds. One child will say, "I'll bet you can't do this" and perform some feat of daring. There are also informal tests with serious consequences for adults. For example, a boss might ask an employee to do a difficult assignment.
3. *Inventories.* These are requests for feelings or attitudes. They're often used to critique presentations or courses, but should not be confused with formal tests of acquired skills.
4. *Formal tests.* These have been deliberately designed and developed to obtain *information* from people.

True/False Item. See *dichotomous items.*

Validity. A test is valid if it measures what it's supposed to measure. There are five commonly accepted types of validity:

1. *Face validity.* For a test this implies the test looks like it should to the respondents. It's what they expect. No surprises.
2. *Content validity.* The content is as was advertised. No new areas. No different treatments of the expected.
3. *Construct validity.* The term refers to psychological constructs. Respondents comprehend as they expect to. No mind games. No tricks.
4. *Concurrent.* The test performs as other (valid) measures do. For example, if a child scores well on one placement test, he or she should score equally well on a different one if both are valid.
5. *Predictive.* Implies the scores will be as expected. So, if the 90/90 standard is intended, it will be met.

Weighting. Pre-biasing a test by according individual items or sections more value (higher score potentials) than others. It's an acceptable practice as long as it is done before the test is administered (finagle). Although it happens often, the practice is seldom justified by analysis of outcomes.

BIBLIOGRAPHY

Barnard, C. (1938). *The functions of the executive.* Cambridge, MA: Harvard University Press.

Bigge, M., & Hunt, H. (1963). *Psychological foundations of education.* New York: HarperCollins.

Bloom, B. S. (1976). *Human characteristics and school learning.* New York: McGraw-Hill.

Brethower, D. (1971). *Behavior analysis in business and industry: The total performance system.* Kalamazoo, MI: Behaviordelia.

Brethower, D., & Smalley, K. (1998). *Performance-based instruction: Linking training to business results.* San Francisco and Washington, DC: Jossey-Bass and International Society for Performance Instruction.

Briggs, L. J., & Gagné, R. M. (1977). *Instructional design.* Englewood Cliffs, NJ: Educational Technology Publications.

Briggs, L. J., & others. (1992). *Instructional design principles and applications.* Englewood Cliffs, NJ: Educational Technology Publications.

Carlisle, K. (1987). *Analyzing jobs and tasks.* Englewood Cliffs, NJ: Educational Technology Publications.

Dewey, J. (1938). *Experience and education.* Old Tappan, NJ: Macmillan.

Downie, N., & Heath, R. (1965). *Basic statistical methods.* New York: HarperCollins.

Ferguson, G. (1966). *Statistical analysis in psychology and education.* New York: McGraw-Hill.

Gagné, R. (1985). *The conditions of learning* (4th ed.). Austin, TX: Holt, Rinehart and Winston.

Gilbert, T. F. (1974). *Behavior analysis in business and industry: The total performance system.* New York: Praxis.

Gilbert, T. F. (1978). *Human competence: Engineering worthy performance.* New York: McGraw-Hill.

Gilbert, T. F. (1996). *Human competence: Engineering worthy performance* (2nd ed.). Washington, DC: International Society for Performance Instruction.

Guest, M. (1989). *Official NCIDQ minutes, 1989.* New York: National Council for Interior Design Qualification. (Compiled and published for members by Loren Swick, executive director.)

Hale, J. (1993). The hierarchy of interventions. In R. Kaufman (Ed.), *Handbook of human performance systems.* New York: New York University Press.

Hale, J. (1998). *The performance consultant's fieldbook.* San Francisco: Jossey-Bass/Pfeiffer.

Hale, J., & Westgaard, O. (1984). *The competent manager's handbook for measuring unit productivity.* Chicago: Hale Associates.

Harless, J. (1983). *Behavior analysis and management.* Atlanta, GA: Stipes.

Harwood, B., & Westgaard, O. (1992). Certification in interior design: The NCIDQ examination. *Performance and Instruction.* Washington: NSPI.

International Facility Managers Association. (1993). *Facility managers certification.* Houston, TX: International Facility Managers Association.

Kaplan, A. (1963). *The conduct of inquiry: Methodology for behavioral science.* New York: Harper-Collins.

Kaufman, R. (1991). *Strategic planning plus.* New York: Scott Foresman.

Kirkpatrick, D. (1994). *Evaluating training programs: The four levels.* San Francisco: Berrett-Koehler.

Lewin, K. (1951). *Field theory in social science.* New York: HarperCollins.

Mager, R. F. (1963). *Preparing instructional objectives.* San Diego, CA: Pitman Learning.

Mager, R. F. (1973). *Measuring instructional intent.* San Diego, CA: Pitman Learning.

Mager, R. F. (1997). *Preparing instructional objectives.* 3rd Ed. Center for Effective Performance.

Mager, R. F., & Pipe, P. (1984). *Analyzing performance problems.* San Diego, CA: Pitman Learning.

Markle, S., & Tiemann, P. (1979). *Concept learning.* (A workshop conducted for Advanced Systems, Inc.). Chicago: Applied Learning.

McCampbell, J. (1983, July). *Measured results.* Unpublished lecture notes for a presentation made to the Chicago Chapter of the National Society for Performance and Training.

Ofiesch, G. (1972). *Programmed instruction.* Arlington, VA: Institute for Technological Solutions.

Partridge, E. (1968). *Educational planning service guidelines.* Greeley, CO: University of Northern Colorado, Educational Administration.

Roscoe, J. (1968). *The multiphasic polyphasic value inventory.* Greeley, CO: University of Northern Colorado Press.

Rummler, G. A. (1984). *Organizations as systems.* Paper presented at National Society for Performance Improvement National Conference, Detroit, MI.

Shrock, S., & Coscarelli, W. (1989). *Criterion-referenced test development.* Reading, MA: Addison-Wesley.

Swanson, R. (1994). *Analysis for improving performance.* San Francisco: Berrett-Koehler.

Taba, H. (1962). *Curriculum development: Theory and practice.* Orlando, FL: Harcourt Brace.

Thiagarajan, S., & Stolovitch, H. D. (1979). *Instructional simulation games.* Englewood Cliffs, NJ: Educational Technology Publications.

Twain, M. (Clemens, S.). (1938). *Letters from the earth.* New York: HarperCollins.

Webster, M. (1987). *Webster's ninth new collegiate dictionary.* Springfield, MA: Merriam-Webster.

Westgaard, O. (1985a, June). Describing performance. *Performance and Instruction, 24*(5).

Westgaard, O. (1985b, Oct.). Measurement versus evaluation. *Performance and Instruction, 24*(8).

Westgaard, O. (1985c, Nov.). In the teaching cycle. *Performance and Instruction, 24*(9).

Westgaard, O. (1985–1986). Measuring performance. *Performance and Instruction, 23*(6).

Westgaard, O. (1986a, May). How tests are biased. *Performance and Instruction, 25*(4).

Westgaard, O. (1986b, June). Statistical treatments. *Performance and Instruction, 25*(5).

Westgaard, O. (1987a). *The competent manager's handbook for selecting and evaluating training.* Chicago: Hale Associates.

Westgaard, O. (1987b, Oct.). Continua. *Performance and Instruction, 26*(8).

Westgaard, O. (1989). *Credo for performance technologists.* Chicago: International Board of Standards for Training, Performance, and Instruction.

Westgaard, O. (1993). *The competent manager's handbook for measuring unit productivity.* Chicago: Hale Associates.

Westgaard, O. (1997). The origins and critical attributes of human performance technology. In R. Kaufman, S. Thiagarajan, & P. MacGillis (Eds.), *The guidebook for performance improvement.* San Francisco: Jossey-Bass/Pfeiffer.

Westgaard, O., Silber, K., & Foshay, W. (1985). *Competencies for instructional design: The standards.* Chicago: International Board of Standards for Training, Performance, and Instruction.

Wheatley, M. (1992). *Leadership and the new science.* San Francisco: Berrett-Koehler.

Woods, D. (1960). *Test construction.* Columbus, OH: Charles Merrill.

INDEX

ABOUT THE AUTHOR

Odin Westgaard, Ed.D., is an acknowledged expert in strategic planning, assessment, evaluation, intervention design, development, and analysis. He is known for his ability to treat each new client and each new problem objectively and with insight.

Recent clients include Abbott, Walgreens, McDonald's, AT&T, ComEd, The American Cancer Society, Ameritech, Square D Company, National Council of Interior Design Qualification (NCIDQ), and International Facility Managers Association (IFMA). His recent work has been to design and implement programs for clients that are performance based and unchallenged (free of litigation); design and train clients to use evaluation techniques, including 360-degree evaluation; design and develop level four (Kirkpatrick) measurement and assessment; and provide a basic development program for "fast tracking" promising management candidates.

His publications include five books and more than three dozen articles on professional topics ranging from basic Instructional Systems Design procedures and psychological measurement to sophisticated analyses that take into consideration chaos and catastrophe formulae. His books include *Good Fair Tests* and *The Competent Manager's Handbook for Measuring Unit Productivity*. He has contributed chapters to two professional anthologies for the International Society for Performance Instruction (ISPI) and the American Society for Training and Development (ASTD). He also generated the *Credo*, an ethics statement for the profession adopted by ISPI and International Board of Standards for Training, Performance, and Instruction.

Dr. Westgaard frequently presents at international conferences. He has served as chapter president for Chicago ISPI and Phi Delta Kappa. He won an award for his process for identifying performance criteria and was a finalist for outstanding member of ISPI in 1984. He received a Presidential Citation for his work editing ISPI's professional journal, *Performance Improvement.*

Dr. Westgaard has a B.A. degree in mathematics from Western State of Colorado; master's degrees in secondary administration and statistics from the University of Northern Colorado; and a doctorate in curriculum development from the University of Northern Colorado.

He can be contacted at:

Heurists
4365 Lawn Avenue, Suite 9
Western Springs, IL 60558
(708) 246-7676, ext. 312
Fax: (708) 245-7689
E-mail: OewHale@aol.com

Printed in the United States
103339LV00005B/17/A

9 780787 945961